THE ESCAPIST

THE
ESCAPIST

CHEATING DEATH ON
THE WORLD'S HIGHEST MOUNTAINS

GABRIEL FILIPPI
WITH BRETT POPPLEWELL

HarperCollins*Publishers*Ltd

HarperCollins Publishers Ltd
2 Bloor Street East, 20th Floor
Toronto, Ontario, Canada
M4W 1A8

www.harpercollins.ca

Library and Archives Canada Cataloguing in Publication
information is available upon request

ISBN 978-1-44345-016-4

Printed and bound in the United States of America
RRD 9 8 7 6 5 4 3 2 1

To all those I hurt, involuntarily, with the start of every new climb.

Annie, Alexandra, Kelsey, Kim, Amy, and Rosie—you're always with me on the mountain, reminding me that the only thing that ever really matters is that I return home.

BASE CAMP

I wake to the crunching of boots in the snow outside my tent. It must be two in the morning; that's when the Sherpa start moving their clients for the day's ascent. I hear coughing and wheezing as they snake past the domed shelter I've erected on the icy ledge of Everest's Khumbu Glacier. One hundred or so climbers are playing follow-the-leader into the glacial expanse that rises to the east above my tent. They speak in all the languages of the world—Dutch, Korean, Russian, and English with a Texan's twang. Resting my head on a pillow, I try to fall back asleep. I roll over in my sleeping bag, turn my back on Everest's southern face and adjust the tuque on my head. I am just drifting away when the light from a straggler's headlamp filters through the snow-covered canvas. For a moment, I am illuminated. I glimpse my breath in the light, then it disappears. Soon all I hear is the sound of a dog breathing heavy in the snow. I sleep like the dead until the sun pokes over the mountains and warms the air in my tent. The first sounds of morning are the bells ringing on the necks of yaks shepherded in and out of this high-altitude campsite.

It's Saturday, April 25, 2015. I am an old man, relatively speaking. A fifty-four-year-old grandfather. Yet I rise in my sleeping bag feeling as if I were twenty-four. Like most climbers, I exist in a state of perpetual adolescence. People say I'm irresponsible, that I'm playing with death, that I'm a selfish bastard for leaving my wife, daughters, and granddaughter to be here. They scoff at my belief that I'll be safe where others die. I greet the day with a yawn and a cough. I bang the snow from my tent, then I light up my camp stove and begin heating water. I may be young in mind and soul, but my body needs these rituals of comfort. Everest Base Camp sprawls out before me as I unzip the canvas door behind my pillow and peer out over the snow-covered boulders. Eight hundred tents, maybe more, spread over a kilometre of rock and ice on the mountain's Nepalese flank. My water boils. I sip my espresso and watch as my fellow climbers crawl out into the snow.

The caffeine works quickly. I check my blood, note my oxygen saturation level for the day—91 percent, not bad for a man who just slept five and a half kilometres above the sea. Anyone but a Sherpa would be satisfied with 80. I pull on my jeans, put on my boots, grab my jacket, and head out into the snow. The stray dog greets me by the door of my tent. I call him Khumbu.

He sniffs my boots and runs circles around me as I head for the tent with the plastic barrel and the toilet seat on top. Then over to the dining tent, where I down another coffee and a bowl of porridge. My friend Sylvie, an anesthesiologist from the Laurentians, is paying me to get her safely up the mountain. We sit and review her plan for the day. We are stuck at base camp—the first of five camps that line the slope of Everest's southern face. I tell her how much confidence I've already lost in this climb. Some 150 climbers, maybe more, are lined up for hours waiting for their turn to cross the ladder bridges that mark the only "safe" passage through the icefall, a glacial expanse of deep crevasses and shifting ice walls. To make matters worse, it feels like the monsoon, which doesn't usually arrive until late May, has already rolled into the valley; there is too much snow on this mountain. It is late in the season to be waiting for a window to push upwards for Camp 1. "We'll stay here at least another night," I say. "Then we'll make a break for Camp 1. Hopefully there's a clear window without so many climbers. The trick will be to avoid a bottleneck higher up, especially in the Death Zone."

Everest is no longer our goal this season. I have decided that Sylvie and I will follow the crowd up to Camp 4, then veer east, away from the crowd, and tackle the world's fourth-highest mountain, Lhotse, instead.

Thick flakes fall from the sky as I exit the dining tent. Khumbu is waiting for me. I bend down and pat him on the head. He knows I have a boiled egg and chapati bread in my pocket. I lay the bread out in the snow beneath his nose and watch as he eats it. When he's done, we make our way across base camp, pausing briefly, so that I might catch my breath and take in the scenery. A woman sits in the snow by her tent, scrubbing at her underwear in a bucket of hot water while over her shoulder, smoke rises from a stone altar. A team of Sherpa and climbers feed juniper branches to the fire and lay offerings to the mountain. I hear the trickle of water running through base camp and down the mountain. It's the glacier melting beneath my feet. Khumbu turns and looks at me, and for a moment it is unclear where either of us is going. We are just two strays who've navigated the rocky footpaths and rope bridges that lead up from the valley, acclimatized to the perils of life in the shadow of the mountain.

The dog has been following me for days, eating what I eat, stepping where I step, seeing what I see. I've begun to wonder if perhaps he might soon try to follow me up toward the summit. There are always dogs on the mountain; they dig their claws into the ice and snow, panting as they pull themselves upwards. They turn back well shy of the summit. Without benefit of supplementary oxygen or Gore-Tex clothing, their survival senses eventually kick in. I've never seen a dog kill itself on the mountain, which is more than I can say for some of the men and women I've met in my travels. I pat Khumbu's head and continue on, through the camp, past prayer flags and tents filled with coughing climbers as I make for a friend and veritable brother.

His name is Elia Saikaly; he's a Canadian filmmaker with the same high-altitude addiction/passion as me. He tells me he's worried about this season on Everest too. He was up in the night, watching as his expedition leader sent his team's Sherpa up the mountain, carrying gear to Camps 1 and 2, noting, as they disappeared into the darkness that sending the Sherpa through the icefall is like sending your boys off to war. You never know if they're going to come back. I sneak into Elia's tent with a single-minded mission: to steal his Wi-Fi and fire an email home.

"We are four weeks into the expedition," I write, "and all teams haven't set upper camps yet. Weather is unstable. Forecast remains the same for next six days, which will take us into the month of May. At that point, there will be only four weeks to finish/start acclimatization and go for summit. If only one window, I will probably go for a single push from base camp with stop only once at each upper camp.

"As for my fellow Nanga survivors: I have met two climbers who were at Camp 2 the night of the killings. I wanted to talk to the Chinese survivor, the one who ran from the bullets and who knows more about Ernie's death, but he is no longer here. He has flown back to Kathmandu with edema."

Edema—the simple accumulation of water in the brain or lungs—is as dangerous on the mountainside as any flying rock or misplaced step into a five-hundred-metre crevasse. I'd nearly died of it myself fifteen years earlier. My emails complete, I mark the hour—10:58 a.m. Two hours to lunch. Plenty of time to walk back across base camp, crawl into my tent, and wait for a cook to bang a wooden spoon against a pan, announcing that a pot of broth has boiled.

Back in my tent, I look out through the open door at the cloudy, warm weather. The midday heat is melting the icefall, making it too dangerous to navigate. The climbers who left in the night should have reached Camp 1 by now, where some will be acclimatizing and resting, while others will be pushing for Camp 2, at 2,358 metres from Everest's peak. I'd have joined them if I'd thought it prudent, but there was no part of me willing to stand in line to climb into the Death Zone, only to get stuck in a traffic jam. I've been there, survived that. I've called home to a climber's family to explain she's succumbed while caught in a lineup 8,500 metres above the sea, and I have no intention of ever doing so again. So I stay at base camp, wait for my lunch, and play it safe. At 11:53 a.m., I record the day's weather report in my diary. I am still writing in my journal when the ground starts to shake beneath my tent. "Bizarre, it's moving," I write. It isn't until I find myself spelling the words "I'd say it's an earthquake," that I realize what's happening. I drop my pen.

I dart out into the snow in my socks. The dog is gone.

I hear the avalanche before I see it. A roaring wind that sounds like a freight train, followed by a dark cloud of flying rocks and sheets of ice. At first it seems to be travelling slowly. Then the roar grows louder and there is no other noise. I begin to run, putting my shoes on my feet mid-stride. A few people raise their cellphones to their faces to snap photos as the cloud envelops us. I scream, "RUN!" and point toward the icefall. The wind hits me in the back and, though I can barely breathe, I run faster. I glimpse Sylvie in the distance and I realize she is running in the same direction as me. Rocks and ice fly by my head. I lose a shoe. I spot a boulder. As fast as I see it, it disappears. Everything turns white. The wind lifts me from the ground and, for a moment, I feel as if I am about to take flight. I don't see the boulder again until I'm touching it. I wrap my arms around it, moor my body to its side, and pull myself behind it. I duck into the fetal position, closing my eyes as wind and snow pound against my eyelids, nostrils, and mouth. Rocks and ice smash into the boulder. I'm suffocating, drowning even. My lungs are full of air but I can't exhale. I feel as though my chest is about to explode, that I am about to pass out. Suddenly, the roaring stops. I open my eyes but I cannot see. I am blinded by the whiteness surrounding me. It is quiet. The earth is no longer shaking. I brush the snow from my face, check my hands for blood: I don't even have a scratch. I raise my body slowly out of the snow and pull myself up against the boulder.

I fear I'm the only one alive.

Again.

THE ESCAPIST

CHAPTER I

A LOST BOY

People ask me about the terrible things I've seen at the top of Everest. They ask about the bodies that litter the mountainside, about the friends I've lost trying to get to the summit, or about the avalanche that almost took my life. I tell them the truth: that up there, life is precious and sometimes terrifying, and I can't wait to get back. They look at me like I'm crazy, but that's because they don't understand where I come from. My perspective on life comes from the cage I was born in. I was the third child born to a French-Canadian mother and a French-Algerian father in Lac-Mégantic, Quebec, at the start of the 1960s. I had nine brothers and sisters, and I learned at an early age that life is both fragile and sometimes frightening.

One of my earliest memories is from when I was seven years old and home from school one Friday with measles. We were living then in a small house in the little town of Cowansville, Quebec, where my father had taken a job as a prison guard. I was sitting up in my bed, reading *Tintin in Tibet*, the story of the boy reporter who ventures to the Himalaya in search of a friend whose plane had crashed on the Tibetan plateau. My mother came to my door. She held my two-year-old brother Claude in her arms. He had a fever. "Gabriel," she said, "I need you to help me look after your brother." She placed Claude on a cot in my room while she returned to the kitchen to prepare another meal. I crawled onto the cot with Claude, opened my book, and began reading him the story of my friend Tintin and his dog, Snowy.

By Saturday, Claude was worse. I finished one Tintin book and moved on to the next. On Sunday, my mother asked me how Claude was doing. I told her I didn't know. She took his temperature and gave him Aspirin. On Monday, she called the doctor. He arrived at my bedroom door with a leather medical bag, took one look at my brother and called an ambulance. When my mother arrived at the hospital in Cowansville, she held my brother's hand, changed his diaper, placed the pin from that diaper in the pocket of her dress, and listened as the doctors told her to go home for the night. Claude was stable and they promised to call her if there was any change in his condition. I was awake when she returned home. I watched from my bedroom as she got out of a taxi and cried in the driveway before coming inside. My father told her to sleep; he'd stay awake in case the hospital called. The phone rang at one a.m. I overheard my father repeat the conversation to my mother. Claude was being transferred to a hospital in Montreal. We had no money and no car to get to Montreal in the middle of the night. My mother made plans to take a taxi first thing in the morning, but the phone rang again just before dawn. Claude was dead. My mother collapsed.

It was October 25, my sister's birthday. My mother dried

her tears, tucked the pin from Claude's diaper into her jewellery box, took Claude's cot away, and headed back into the kitchen to bake a cake.

The day I learned how to live with fear came a few years later.

I stood on a diving board overhanging the pool next to our house. My father was in the water, urging me to jump, saying he'd catch me. I was scared, but I followed his command. I reached for him but found nothing as I crashed into the pool and sank to the bottom. I couldn't swim. I panicked as water forced its way into my lungs. I screamed but it made no difference. I could feel the bottom of the pool against my feet as I reached for the air above my head, but there was nothing to grab on to. I thrashed about, knowing that my father was out there, watching me struggle. I don't know how long I was down there—five seconds, maybe more. Time always stops when you feel you're about to die. I searched madly for my father's leg. The only way for me to save myself was to find him and to climb him—scale his body like a mountain until I was on his shoulders, lunging for the pool wall, grabbing the ledge with one hand and then another. But I couldn't find him. I was still struggling when I felt his hands wrap around my body and lift me out of the pool. I crawled along the cement, coughing up so much water that I nearly puked. I gasped for breath as tears began mixing with the water on my face. I could hear my father laughing in the pool. I looked at him but said nothing. He shook his head at me as though he was talking to a baby and told me I had no reason to cry.

My father was a tough man, hardened by something I hoped never to understand. I didn't listen when he tried to coax me back into the water. Because of him, I'm afraid of the water. And

I certainly didn't listen when he spoke of the wars in which he'd fought, reliving them in graphic details that he seemed unable to forget.

Another memory: The telephone rang in the middle of the night, and I heard my father grumbling into the receiver down the hall. He put on his prison guard's uniform and stood in the darkness by the front window of the house. A prisoner had escaped and my father was going to help the police seek him out. He was still gone in the morning when I got up. I was usually the first at the breakfast table, joined quickly by a chorus line of siblings. My mother slipped me a piece of paper on which she'd written the score of the previous night's Montreal Canadiens game. At eleven years old, I was too young to stay up until the end of a hockey game, so I relied on her to chronicle every goal.

We finished our breakfast, then went outside to play make-believe in the forest across the street. After that, we sat on the stoop and listened to the radio, wondering if maybe our uncle Michel might come around to give us a ride in his old Chevy. When it became apparent that no one was coming, we picked up our road hockey sticks and began a game of shinny. I took control of the ball and shouted to my brothers, *"Faites attention! Moi, je suis Guy Lafleur!"*

I was always Guy Lafleur.

I darted down the driveway, stickhandling past one brother en route to the next. Then I wound up and fired the ball toward the net. The ball lifted off the ground and flew high, too high. My brothers and I watched as it sailed over the net and straight through the garage window. I dropped my stick. I was completely frozen with fear. One by one, my brothers gathered by my side.

"Maybe he won't notice," one of them piped up.

"He'll notice," I said.

"Maybe it won't be so bad."

There were six of us brothers and we had a pact. None of us would ever rat on another to our father because we knew what that would mean.

We were playing quietly beside the house when my father came home. He said nothing as he passed by. He didn't seem to realize the window was broken and, for a moment, it appeared as though we were safe. Several minutes passed before my father's voice beckoned us inside. He summoned all of us to the dining room and asked, "Who broke the window?"

Silence.

He repeated the question. "Who broke the window?"

Again, no one answered.

If he was frustrated, he didn't show it. He told us to leave the dining room, and then, one by one, he began calling us back. He interrogated the youngest to the oldest. By the time he got to me, I couldn't believe that no one had ratted me out.

He leaned back in his seat while I squirmed in mine. "So, Gabriel. Was it you who broke the window?"

I shook my head.

"And do you know who did?"

I shook my head again.

He squinted his eyes at me and nodded.

Then he let me go.

Time passed and I began to believe that maybe I was safe. Maybe all of us were. Then my father came out to join us.

"Everyone, come over here," he said. He stood next to a pile of garden stones at one end of the yard. We approached him, cautiously. "I have a job for all of you," he said. "Each stone must be carried to the other end of the yard. Once all the stones have been moved, they must then be carried back to their original pile. You're going to carry stones until one of you tells me who broke the window. Now get to work."

I looked at my siblings out of the corner of my eye. Not one of them was looking back at me. We were a united front. I don't know how many stones there were or how many times we went back and forth across the yard, but I know that the stones were heavy and that my arms ached as we carried them. I watched as my youngest siblings dropped their stones. My father watched too, never allowing them to pause for more than a few seconds before ordering them back to work. Minutes turned into hours. Back and forth we went.

I don't know exactly how that story ends. The memory of it often blurs with another from around the same time, when my father, enraged over something I can't remember anymore, ordered my brothers and me to kneel by the stairs just inside the front door of our house and stare at the wall. I knew the punishment well enough to know that I had to hurry into position if I was to avoid getting smacked across the back of the head.

For some reason, my younger brother Luc was taking his time. I didn't see the punch that sent him flying sideways down the stairwell, and I don't know that Luc did either. I expected to hear him screaming from down the stairs, but I heard nothing. Luc wasn't making any noise at all. We were terrified, all of us looking down at Luc, who appeared, in that moment, to be dead.

"LUC!" my father screamed. "LUC!"

There was no response. Suddenly my father was rushing down to the base of the stairs, where he got down on his hands and knees and cradled his son's head. *"Luc! Wake up! Wake up, wake up!"* It took a while for my brother to open his eyes—long enough to give my father time to pause. There would be no more punishments today.

Later, after my brother had been brought back upstairs and my mother had cleaned his scrapes, we gathered in his bedroom and asked him if he was okay. He smiled, told us to lean in closer, and revealed that he'd faked his injury because he knew it would scare our father. We covered our mouths, scandalized by his audacity. He was our hero.

My childhood wasn't all bad. I have fond memories of riding my bike down the street by our house, of playing tag in the nearby forest with my brothers, of skating on the small rink my father made on the grass next to the woodpile. And there was the time my father took me and my four brothers and three sisters on a trip to the south of France. My mother wasn't with us; she was back home, pregnant for the tenth time. My father helped my brothers and me play a trick on the French, who believed we *Canadiens* had come straight from the Wild West. We constructed a tipi on a beach on the Côte d'Azur to keep the ruse going. We laughed at our own ridiculousness as we sat inside that tipi.

For the most part, though, my father was angry and unpredictable, haunted by his past. My father had been a paratrooper, a commando, and an explosives expert who served in two of the more disastrous wars in France's long military history. He was nineteen years old when he deployed to Indochina, fighting the Viet Minh in the jungles and rice fields south of Hanoi in what became the last stand of French colonial rule in the Far East. All the while, he sent letters from around the world to the French-Canadian pen pal who eventually became his wife. My father never wrote to my mother about the war in Indochina, nor did he detail how different Algeria was when he returned in 1954, only to find himself deployed in what would soon become one of the most brutal urban guerrilla wars of the twentieth century. My mother would later recall that before meeting him in Algeria, her future mother-in-law took her aside to explain that my father was not the same as he was before he'd gone off to war. He had seen and done terrible things, things I couldn't even imagine, and he carried them with him every day.

My father always wore a moustache. When he met my mother, it was a Clark Gable moustache, short and trimmed. When I was born, it was much thicker—as was he. People who know my family say I have his eyes. They're cold, deep, and distant. There wasn't much I ever did well as far as he was concerned. Coming home from school carrying a test or a report card, I knew it didn't matter what grade I had gotten. His response was always the same. "You got 80 percent? That's not enough. Why didn't you get 85?" I'd go back to school and work harder and harder. Next time, I'd come home with 90 percent, but it was always the same. "You got 90 percent? That's not enough. Why didn't you get 95?"

I was seventeen when my relationship with my father broke down. It was the summer of 1978 and my older brother, Jean, had just done what he had always been told he'd have to do: he shipped off to France to join the army. My father looked at me across the dinner table and told me I was next. He said it went beyond duty, that it was the law. That at any given time, the French government could come to our door and drag me off to war. He said that if I didn't enlist, he and I would be through. I'd be out on my own, working at the local fruit stand just to be able to afford my wasted, directionless life.

One day, my father came to my room carrying what he said was a letter from the French military. He said it was time I went to the doctor to do my preliminary testing before enlisting. I told him I wasn't going. He said if I didn't go, he'd kick me out. I conceded to my father's will. While I was being examined, the doctor asked me what I planned to do once school was finished. I told him I didn't know, that my father insisted I had to join the French military or I'd risk going to jail. The doctor looked at me strangely and said, "You know that's not true, right?" I told him my older brother had already enlisted and that I didn't really know what to believe. He told me there was no law that would force me, a Canadian citizen living in Quebec, to go to France and enlist. "If your father insists, just come back here and I'll declare you unfit for service."

I left the doctor's office feeling as if I had control over my life for the very first time. I no longer feared my father.

Then came Thanksgiving weekend 1978. The weekend I turned eighteen. I sat down to supper, and my father asked me if I was going to be a man and join the army or if I was going to be a coward. It was one or the other. There was an irony to our dispute, but it was lost on me. I dreamt about escaping my existence and travelling the world. That trip to the south of

France had opened my eyes to a world beyond my little house on a wooded street in suburban Quebec. From that moment on, I was always reading and dreaming about a world filled with travel and adventure. I idolized men like Neil Armstrong, Ernest Shackleton, and Edmund Hillary.

My brother Jean was living that life, as if on some adventure, serving in Africa and the Middle East. But I disliked my father so much, there was no way I'd give him the satisfaction of sending me off to fight. I didn't ever want to fight. Not after what I'd seen and gone through in his house.

My parents didn't have enough money to send me to college after high school, so I began working as a chef and bartender at a big hotel on Lac Selby, Quebec. I lived for a while at the hotel, where I also DJed at parties. For once in my life, I felt like my own man. Then winter came and I was unemployed and forced back into my parents' home. I landed a job as a sales clerk at a local fruit store and began saving up money.

Then I met a girl. A beautiful girl. It all happened by chance. I was out delivering fruits and vegetables to a local restaurant when I spotted a red Fiat X1/9 for sale next to a garage. It was the sports car, so impractical yet fast, that lured me into the dealership. I bought it a few days later. And as I was making the purchase, I spotted a girl outside the garage. She was the daughter of the Fiat dealer. We caught each other's eye, and before long, she was in the passenger seat and we were heading out to the movies. Back home, my father took one look at my new car and told me I was immature and selfish, that in buying a two-seater sports car, I was thinking of no one but myself. He kicked me out of the house. I had nowhere to go, so I slept on my boss's sofa. After a few nights, my new girlfriend's parents let me stay with them, and before I knew it, I was engaged.

I was just twenty-two years old, and as I walked down the aisle of a Catholic church, I could see my mother smiling. I didn't particularly want my father there, but I had invited him on the off chance that someday our relationship might change and I would regret his not being there. We spent our honeymoon on a beach in Fort Lauderdale, Florida. Then we returned to Cowansville and, for five years, eked out a modest living. She worked as a hairdresser while I spent my days at the fruit store. We lived a simple life. I still had dreams of seeing the world, of becoming an explorer like the ones who'd inspired me as a child. But my mind kept putting up barriers between me and any sort of adventure. And so I spent five years delivering fruit and saving money to go back to school so that I could get a job that would afford me the chance to actually travel.

I decided to sell my little Fiat and enroll in a vocational school in Montreal. In my downtime as a student, I took a job as a flight attendant with a now defunct airline called Wardair. The perks of the job provided just enough adventure to keep me satisfied through my late twenties. We began spending weekends and holidays in London, Paris, Cuba, and Jamaica. I was finally beginning to see the world. Back at school, I was wrapping up my studies in finance when Transport Canada came to recruit people to work in airport towers across the country. I filled out the papers on a whim. Two tests plus two interviews later, my acceptance came in the mail, and suddenly it felt like my life was truly about to begin. I would learn the delicate art and science of navigating airplanes, helping them land safely in the darkness, through gales and snowstorms.

I completed my training as a flight service specialist and deployed to Sept-Îles, a small town on the northeast shore of the St. Lawrence River that was, until the mid-nineteenth century, known primarily as a destination port for European whalers. Reborn as a mining outpost in the 1950s, Sept-Îles was a small but bustling town when I arrived to take my place in the airport tower next to the tarmac. I stayed there for three years. I was good at my job, and I grew to love what I did. My wife took on clerical work in town and, for a while, we were happy.

We were seven years into our marriage when I learned we were going to have a child. I was both excited and scared to become a father. We were celebrating a belated Valentine's Day dinner when we cut our meal short to rush to the hospital. Twelve hours later, I was pacing alone in a waiting room when a nurse came in with my daughter. She was crying as I reached out for her. I looked into her face as she lay nestled in my arms, and already she seemed to be growing. I'd tried to forget all the bad things that my father had done during my own childhood, but there was no erasing the past. So instead, I vowed never to hurt her. I wanted to be there for my daughter every day of her life. I wanted her to grow up knowing that I loved her unconditionally. We named her Alexandra because we liked the way it sounded.

I took to her immediately, rushing home from work to spend as much time as possible crawling around on the floor beside her before bedtime. She seemed happiest when we were playing together with her toys. The feeling was mutual.

Alexandra was just a few months old when I got transferred

to another airport. We would be on the move again, heading north on what I mistook for a family adventure, this time to Radisson, a town of 250 people located in Quebec's far north, on the coast of James Bay, a town that would not exist were it not for the 162-metre hydroelectric dam that generated enough power to keep the lights on across Quebec.

It was late April 1991. I hadn't seen or spoken to my father in nearly a decade. But I wanted my mother to meet my daughter before I headed north to Radisson. I pulled up to my parents' home, unbuckled Alexandra from her car seat, carried her up to my parents' door, and rang the bell. I stood there, unsure what would happen next. A haggard old man met me at the door. He looked confused and asked me what I wanted.

"Is Mom here?"

He shook his head, still looking confused. Then my mother came hollering from behind me. I'd never been so happy to see her. She reached for my face, kissed me, then turned her attention to my daughter before ushering me inside. I tried not to look at my father, tried to pretend he wasn't even there, but he was impossible to ignore. Especially when he leaned into my mother's ear and asked, "Who is this?"

* * *

I settled into my new life quickly, working twelve-hour days, seven days a week. The airstrip was the busiest place in town. Planes filled with hydro workers arrived and departed at any given hour on any given day. The weather patterns were erratic; Radisson was susceptible to Arctic storms nine months of the year. I'd never lived in such desolate surroundings, but I was making good money and enjoying the experience, completely oblivious that my wife was moving quickly into the arms of another man. At first glance, he was far more adventurous than me. He rode a motorcycle and wooed her with promises of trips around the continent on the back of it. I was the last person in town to learn of their affair.

I called home to my mother. She listened as I poured my heart out into the receiver and then said, "Just one second, your dad wants to talk to you." There was no part of me that wanted to speak with him, but she put him on the telephone anyway, and suddenly I was having the only positive conversation I would remember having with my father. He told me he was sorry for what had happened to me, but that I mustn't let it break me.

I'd dreamt of having this type of father-son relationship for years, but I never believed I could rely on him for advice or comfort. We never spoke again.

I was still reeling from the collapse of my marriage when the phone rang in the airport tower. It was four days after Christmas 1992. My mother was on the line. She was calling to let me know that my father had died. She said he'd been fighting cancer and he'd lost that fight. I didn't know how to respond. I put down the receiver, gathered my thoughts, and looked out at the snow over Radisson. I realized I couldn't get out of the town for the funeral even if I wanted to.

I rarely speak of my father. I never think of him on the mountain. And I've certainly never allowed myself to believe that his style of parenting had any impact whatsoever on why I do what I do. Yet there are those in this world, my wife included, who will tell you that the reason I push myself to the edge of death and back just to climb some "stupid mountain" is, in some weird subconscious way, a means of accomplishing something greater than what my father ever expected of me. It all comes across a bit sad when my life is deconstructed by others in this way. A great many climbers I've known have shared a communal resentment for our fathers. I don't pretend to know what any of it means, other than to say that it might very well mean something substantial. Just as it's also possible that it means absolutely nothing at all. This much I know: my mother tells me that my father would be proud of what I've done with my life. I may have my father's eyes, but I have my mother's smile and I reveal it to her when she speaks of my father's pride. It's in those moments, with my mother and me both just sitting there smiling at each other, that I tell her, "You know he could never say that to me."

CHAPTER 2

A LOST SOUL

The light on the top of my answering machine was flashing red when I returned home. I knew the gist of the message without even listening to it. It was late September 1993. I was thirty-two years old. I came home from the airport day after day to messages on my voice mail from friends and siblings asking how I was holding up on my own. Some days, I didn't even check the messages. I'd just go to bed, sleep my usual dreamless sleep, then wake up, make myself a smoothie, look out at the grey sky through my window, and wonder if I'd become the loneliest man in Radisson. Then I'd put on my work clothes, pack my lunch, and go to the airport once more.

One day, shortly before my birthday, I took Alexandra away for a brief vacation to Montreal. We stopped by the apartment of my youngest sister, and I noticed that her boyfriend, Louis, was plotting out a great adventure to Colombia on a map on their coffee table. He was young and had an adventurer's heart. He told me I should join him. My sister agreed. She told me she thought I needed a vacation, that I should go somewhere to clear my head, have a good time. Live for the now and find new dreams for the future. She was young but knew what she was talking about.

A few months later, it was minus twenty-three degrees Celsius and I was driving to the airport. I checked my bags at the counter, grabbed a drink, and boarded my plane. The next time I stepped outside, it was thirty-two degrees and I was confronted by the bustling street sounds of Cartagena, a port city on Colombia's Atlantic coast. I'd never kept a diary before, but for some reason, I decided to take a journal with me. This was as much a soul-searching mission as it was an adventure. For eight days, Louis and I took in the sights and sounds of Cartagena, wandered the sandy beaches, and frequented the many pubs and clubs that lined the city's streets before venturing deeper into the countryside, snaking through jungle valleys and the Andean foothills of central Colombia as we made our way to Bogotá. We did as the tourists did back then and paid a visit to the grave of Pablo Escobar, the famed Colombian drug lord who'd been dead barely a month. And we dropped many pesos on *refajos* and *coco locos*—local drinks that helped you forget the midday heat. The trip was shaping up to be little more than just a head-clearing adventure until, by complete accident, I discovered hidden within myself the one true passion that would alter the trajectory of the rest of my life.

It was Monday, January 17, 1994. I woke up on a cot in a cheap hotel in Manizales, a coffee town that rests at the foot of Nevado del Ruiz, a snow-capped volcano. I rolled out of bed, put on my jeans and my hiking boots, and prepared for what I believed would be a simple stroll up the side of a volcano. I sat down for breakfast, completely oblivious to the fact that a 6.7 magnitude earthquake in the San Fernando Valley was bending freeways in Los Angeles, killing more than sixty people and injuring nine thousand more. It wasn't long before news of the quake had everyone pondering whether "The Big One" was just an aftershock away. If I had been paying more attention to the news, I might have asked myself whether it was a good day to take a long walk up the side of an active volcano. Louis and I finished up our Andean breakfast and headed out with four other trekkers and a couple of guides. We travelled by bone-shaking bus over the lava-scarred moraines of an ancient glacier, stopping along the way to let a herd of cows meander across the rocky road that snakes up to the base of the volcano. One of the guides informed us that this volcano was one of the deadliest peaks in the world. He said the summit was always covered in snow but sometimes the snow began to smoke, and that's when you knew the mountain was getting angry. He said that in the lead-up to the last big eruption, smoke poured out of the top of the mountain for nearly a year. Then, shortly after three on a Wednesday afternoon in November 1985, the peak of Nevado del Ruiz exploded. Thirty-five million tonnes of magma, sulphur dioxide, and other materials shot out from the summit, melting the glacier and sending thick landslides of wet volcanic debris—water, ice, and molten rock—down the flanks of the mountain and into the valley below, wiping out an entire village and killing 25,000 people. "It was the fourth-deadliest eruption in recorded history," he said.

I looked up at the peak. It rose more than five kilometres into the sky and appeared to be steaming. "Don't worry," the guide said. "Nevado del Ruiz always steams." Then he offered an assurance to calm my nerves. "The volcano always screams out a warning well before it explodes, and right now, it isn't screaming."

We stepped out of the bus and into the snow. We were already 4,200 metres above the sea and it was another 1,121 metres to the top. The guides and the four other trekkers with us didn't want to climb to the summit, but Louis and I were determined. We weren't properly equipped for anything more than a hike, and we weren't more than a few steps from the bus when we began slip-sliding on the ice. One of the guides opted to stay with us—in case, he said, we stumbled upon one of the speckle-faced Andean bears that lived on the mountainside. "The summit," he said, "presents a different kind of danger. It's an open volcanic crater." It all sounded so exhilaratingly dangerous. "The real danger," our guide explained, "is not in the mountain, but in you." Then he told the story of a kid who'd died up there a week earlier after suffering a pulmonary embolism when one of the arteries in the boy's lungs began to clot as he made his way up the volcano. "People often get sick up here," he said. "And they don't know why until it's too late."

I looked at Louis. He was still raring to go. So we took off, trekking and scrambling for hours over ice, snow, and molten rock, seeing no sign of animals or other humans. We were venturing where others had gone before, but it felt as though we were on a journey of exploration. I felt driven to reach the top, though it soon became apparent that Louis and our guide did not possess the same drive. While waiting for them to catch up,

I took a few moments to pause and look out at the surrounding peaks and valleys. Louis and our guide looked so small and vulnerable in the distance, stopping every few steps to catch their breath. The clouds were coming in, rolling over the distant peaks on the horizon. I knew those peaks were tall, but I stood taller. And beyond them, I could see nothing, no sign of any other human whatsoever. I knew that somewhere down in the valley below, there was a bustling city with nearly a million inhabitants. But from my newfound vantage, none of them seemed to matter. It took a while for Louis and the guide to reach my side.

"Gabriel," Louis said, gasping for breath. "I'm done."

"But we're barely a hundred metres from the top," I told him. "We've got to keep going, no?"

"I don't care about this volcano." He said his head hurt, that he'd been struggling to breathe, and that all he really wanted was a cigarette.

"Okay, okay," I said. "We'll go down." I let him take the first few steps, then I looked out at the world at my feet and reflected for a moment on just how great it felt to be standing up here, completely detached from all the clutter. The last thing I wanted to do was leave this mountain and return to the mess that was my life.

CHAPTER 3

CHIMBORAZO

Radisson was cold, dark, and desolate when my plane touched down on the tarmac. It was early February and twenty-five degrees below zero. I dropped my bags and said *salut* to the men and women in the tower. They asked me about my Colombian adventure; what did I think of the beaches, and the people, and the food? I told them it had been an eye-opening experience, that Cartagena was a hell of a town, but that the most enjoyable part had been the long trek up the side of a frozen volcano that had killed a great many people. None of them seemed to understand why anyone who was forced to spend nine months of the year hiking through snow at home would choose to do so on a vacation. "You should have stayed on the beach," they said.

"There's not much to explore on a beach with two thousand other people," I replied. I didn't bother explaining that I was terrified of the water. Then I asked them how the last month of their lives had been. They said the days had been slowly getting longer and the planes had just kept coming and going.

I was planning my next adventure before I even turned my key in my front door. Alexandra was still living with her mother and her mother's new boyfriend in a house across town, and my life was dull and unfulfilling.

I slipped back into my twelve-hour shifts in the tower. I spent as much time with Alexandra as possible, but it never felt like enough. Then summer came and the evenings grew long. Some days, I'd get out of the tower before dusk and head over to pick up my daughter. I'd pack her into my truck and we'd head up to a lookout on the outskirts of town. I'd lift her onto the hood of my truck and unpack a picnic dinner of ham sandwiches, cheese and crackers, juice boxes, and nuts for dessert. We'd rest there with our backs against the windshield for hours, talking about everything and nothing at all while the northern lights rippled through the sky. She was just four years old, and her most pressing concern was losing sight of her favourite stars. I helped her find them again. In these moments, I was happy. Then I'd drop her off at home and go back to my lonely life.

The days passed and the seasons changed, but I never stopped dreaming of South America. I felt as though I'd fallen in love with some distant beauty, though I wasn't yet wise enough to recognize her face. There was something pulling me back to South America. Something inside me was telling me I needed to go back to the Andes. I thought it was the Andean culture. I requested a month's leave from work and opted to spend it in Quito, the highest capital city in the world, where I'd live with a family and learn to speak Spanish. When I told my family and friends about my plans, they looked at me as if Quito was a town from which I'd never return. Their fear was contagious.

As much as I tried to keep it out of my mind, I confided in my baby sister that I was uneasy about this trip. I told her that if I didn't come back, to please care for Alexandra, make sure she knew who I was and how much I loved her. I'd given Alexandra a telescope so she could find her stars without me, but part of me worried that she would stop admiring the world above without me to guide her. I boarded the plane, feeling as though I was setting off on the greatest adventure of my life, writing in my journal, "We cannot live our lives in fear of death. Death is our destiny." Then I closed my journal and drifted off to sleep.

I adapted to my new home quickly. For three weeks, I lived in a closet-sized room in a small house with a family of three in the centre of Quito. I spent my mornings with my adopted mother, Anna-Maria, peeling potatoes and learning the intricacies of Andean cuisine and the Spanish terminology for everything from a guinea pig to a kettle. Every afternoon, I'd grab my textbook and my notebook and go to a little schoolhouse to study verb conjugation. In the evenings, I'd head out on the town with my fellow adult students. We were a small yet eclectic mix of lost souls from around the world. Many nights, I didn't get to sleep until five a.m. I was enjoying my Ecuadorean sojourn, though I began to suspect that it was not some burgeoning love for the Andean culture that had lured me down here, but rather the urge to climb another mountain. I spent hours staring out over the cityscape at Cotopaxi, the volcano that rises high above Quito. One day, I told Anna-Maria that I thought I might head out to climb it. She raised her hand and waved her finger at me. "*No, no!*" she said. "*Tienes que escalar el Chimborazo!*"

"Chimborazo?"

She told me to forget about Cotopaxi and go instead to the infinitely greater volcano called Chimborazo. She said Chimborazo was not just the highest mountain in Ecuador, but that because of its proximity to the equator, anyone fortunate enough to reach the top of Chimborazo is standing farther from the Earth's core than any other human on the planet. This all sounded very romantic, and soon I was on a bus twisting through Andean valleys toward the foot of Chimborazo. We snaked our way 220 kilometres down the Pan-American Highway. I was the lone gringo on the bus, seated with my knapsack on my lap next to a man with a live chicken. Locals jumped on and off every few kilometres. The bus ride was a gut-wrenching journey of switchbacks and sudden stops. We'd barely left Quito when the first passenger leaned into the aisle to vomit. I cringed and gagged as the puke slid down the aisle with the pitch of the bus. When we reached the bottom of the valley and began ascending the next mountain, I covered my mouth, lifted my feet, and closed my eyes as the puke slid back in my direction. It was the longest four-hour bus ride of my life. We rolled into the town of Riobamba. I was still thirty kilometres away from Chimborazo, but already it dominated the skyline. Immediately, I understood why up until the early-nineteenth century, this dormant old volcano was believed to be the highest peak on Earth. The mountain is enormous, larger than any in North America. It is so big, in fact, that an airplane once disappeared into its side and wasn't found for twenty-seven years.

I wandered into a local tourist hut and met a mountain guide who outfitted me with a snowsuit, harness, climbing boots, helmet, mitts, rope, ice axe, and spiked crampons to attach to my boots. My guide's name was Marcello. He was forty-two years old and had spent the last twenty-five climbing up and down the slopes of Chimborazo. I needed his help putting on most of my gear. He handed me a waiver. I was still relatively new to Spanish, but I understood that I was signing my life away. Marcello gave me a basic understanding of the route we would take to the top of the mountain. We'd be travelling in the footsteps of Edward Whymper, a nineteenth-century English mountaineer responsible for first ascents on three continents, including that of Mount Whymper in British Columbia, which was named in his honour after he stood on its summit back in 1901.

We took a taxi up a winding road, passing llamas and alpacas as we cut across the lunar landscape at the base of the mountain. Our destination was a small hut 4,850 metres above the sea. It was six p.m. when we arrived, and Marcello told me that we'd sleep a few hours, then push off up the mountain at midnight. I lay down on a cot and watched the sunset through the holes in the wall of my room. I barely slept. Marcello rapped on my door, told me it was a beautiful night for a climb, then offered me some eggs and cheese. We suited up, tossed our packs over our shoulders and headed into the night, passing a couple of old women as we went. They looked at us, their hands clasped in front of their faces, and I realized they were saying prayers for our souls. We hiked up the mountain, guided primarily by the moonlight, but after barely an hour, the moon disappeared behind the mountain, leaving us with just the light from our headlamps to find our way.

We passed crosses bearing the names of the climbers who'd disappeared on the mountainside. I was still far too naive to understand that this was going to be a real climb with real risk. Up and up we went into the darkening night. We were at around 5,700 metres—560 shy of the summit—when we put on our crampons. I took my first few steps onto the glacier, dug the spikes of my crampons into the crust of the mountain, and got a beginner's feel for how the things worked. Marcello stopped me. "You step where I step. Nowhere else." He tied us together with a twenty-three-metre rope and told me that we were surrounded by *grietas*—deep crevasses that could kill us both if one of us took the wrong step. I watched as he navigated the glacier as if it were a minefield. For hours, we proceeded up the glacier at a gingerly pace. By noon, we were standing at 6,100 metres, just 168 vertical metres from the summit. There was no one above us, and I wondered if we'd already climbed high enough to be, in that moment, the humans farthest from Earth's core. I scraped the spikes on my feet against the glacier's crust, then looked out at the lush green pastures of the Ecuadorean countryside. It was as marvellous a view as any I'd seen out the window of an airplane. I breathed in the tropical air. This mountain was high, but soon, I'd be higher. The anticipation of successfully scaling this massive volcanic protrusion on the Earth's belly had a strange way of making me feel both significant and extremely insignificant at the same time. I felt like I'd come all the way up here in order to find myself, and now that I'd done so, I was being reminded for the first time since Nevado del Ruiz just how small I really was.

Whatever euphoria I was feeling disappeared when Marcello told me that we were in a tricky situation. The sun would soon start melting the snow on the mountaintop, triggering avalanches in our wake, creating snow bridges that would mask the *grietas* and increase the chance of a fatal misstep. "If you put your weight on an ice bridge, good night," he said. "You're gone. A Japanese man did that last month and he died." He'd barely finished his warning when I heard the sound of something cracking. It sounded like Tostitos crunching in my ear. Marcello held up his hand calmly and said, "Don't move. Sit there. Stay still." Then he pointed twenty metres in front of us where a slope of snow broke away from the mountain and disappeared from our sight. My heart jumped as the snow fell away; I feared that the ground beneath us was unstable. I watched, helpless, as the fault line in the snow inched closer. I gripped my ice axe in my hands, but I had little understanding of how I might use it to brace my fall. Closer and closer, the ground disappeared. Then the snow stopped falling away.

Marcello looked at me. "We should head back down now."

Back at the hut at the base of the mountain, the women who'd prayed for us were waiting to cross themselves upon our return. I looked at them, wondering why it was they cared so much for our souls. Inside the hut, Marcello handed me a souvenir book and told me I should keep it, even though we technically didn't summit. In it, I wrote my first thoughts on mountain climbing: "There's nothing I've ever felt before like standing on this mountain." It was impossible for me to properly describe the sensation I had had standing 6,100 metres in the air. I didn't care that I hadn't reached the top; I would climb other mountains. I'd seen the world from a different angle, and the sheer beauty of it had engraved itself on my mind. So had Marcello's explanation for why we'd turned around.

"You must never fight with the mountain," he'd said. "You must simply admire it."

CHAPTER 4

ACONCAGUA

The plane ride home from Quito was punctuated by moments of anxiety and fear. As soon as I touched down in Radisson, I knew I was returning to a life I no longer wanted. I'd been trying to figure out how I might become a climber like Marcello. I searched my mind for the names of people I knew who climbed. The only one I could think of was Patrice Beaudet, an acquaintance from my days in Sept-Îles. I wrote down his name in my journal. I circled it. Patrice was a flight service specialist like me. I had vague memories of him coming into the airport communications centre with stories of weekends spent dangling from the side of a frozen waterfall north of Quebec City. I'd thought he was insane the first time I met him. I drew another circle around his name.

I was midway through my first shift back in the tower when I found a number for Patrice. I picked up the phone and called him. I told him about the experiences I'd had atop two different Andean volcanoes. "I think I understand the bug you've got for the mountains," I said. It felt as though I'd found my calling.

I wondered if this was how pilots felt when they got their first glimpse of an airplane. Or what Wayne Gretzky or Michael Jordan felt when someone first handed them a hockey stick or a basketball. I knew almost nothing about climbing, other than the simple fact that it was all I actually wanted to do. "I'm looking to go to climbing school," I said. "What's the best one in Quebec?" Patrice laughed at my naïveté and asked me when my next vacation was. Before the call was over, we had made plans for a rock-climbing expedition to the Shawangunk Ridge, a ninety-metre cliff wall of quartz conglomerate with one thousand different climbing routes, located about a two hours' drive north of New York City. He told me to buy a helmet, some proper climbing shoes, and to meet him in Montreal and we'd drive down together. Then I subscribed to every rock-climbing magazine I could find, in order to better understand what I was getting myself into.

I headed across town to see Alexandra. I'd barely said hello when my ex-wife told me that she would soon be leaving Radisson. She said she'd found a house on the outskirts of Quebec City. She said she'd be moving at the end of that summer, and she'd be taking our daughter with her. I was so upset, I could barely put my feelings into words. I worried that this meant I'd be losing my daughter, and I tried to find a way to follow her. I requested a transfer to Quebec City, but I didn't have the seniority to get there. There was nothing I could do to keep from losing her. Once they were gone, I'd be completely alone, living in a stationary motorhome and wandering this small town. I put in my request to Transport Canada for a transfer. I didn't care where they wanted to send me; I just wanted out of here.

I pored through the pages of the magazines that started

arriving at my door. They were filled with stories and photographs of spectacular climbs by a who's who of contemporary mountaineers—Rob Hall, Alex Lowe, Scott Fischer, Ed Viesturs, and Reinhold Messner. I began to understand that there is a fraternity among climbers that is amplified by the literal bond that comes from being tied together. I learned that for every master climber there is an apprentice, and that whenever you tie two climbers together, one's going to learn something he didn't know before. I studied these magazines as best I could before heading down to Montreal to meet Patrice.

Just before dawn on August 19, 1995, I woke up at my kid sister's apartment in Montreal, grabbed what gear I had— untested rock-climbing shoes, a helmet, a harness, and a bag of chalk—and headed out to the street corner to wait for Patrice. We weren't yet on the road to the "Gunks" when he handed me a shoelace, showed me how to tie a figure-eight knot, and then told me to repeat that knot until I could tie it with my eyes closed. "This is your first lesson," he said. "You learn how to tie this knot and it will save your life."

As we drove through the Appalachian Mountains, we compared stories of our respective adventures on Chimborazo. He told me about his most recent high-altitude attempt on Aconcagua, the highest mountain outside of Asia, located in the Argentinian Andes, fifteen kilometres from the Chilean border. He said he'd been forced to turn back just shy of the summit a year earlier. He was already planning his next attempt on the mountain. He asked me how much I knew about the Seven Summits and explained that his life's goal was to stand at the highest point of each of the seven continents.

"They say climbing is a vertical dance," Patrice continued. "A mixture of power and grace." I didn't quite understand what he was talking about until we arrived at the Gunks and made our way to the base of our first cliff wall. Patrice walked me through the basics, showing me how to safely belay rope to my partner and use my own body weight as a potential anchor should my partner fall off the cliff face. "Your life is in my hands, and my life is in yours," he said. "You save me, and I'll save you."

We pitched our tents in a campground five minutes away from the cliffs. All through the night, I tied and retied my figure-eight knots. Dawn came, and Patrice told me to leave my chalk bag at our camp. He said chalk is cheating. It gives you added grip, but it ruins the climb for all who follow, because they'll just put their hands where you put yours and they won't have to think out their own route up the wall. Patrice double-checked every knot I tied, then he taught me the science and art of the climb. As I made my way up the cliff, heeding each instruction carefully, I learned that Patrice was not so crazy after all. In fact, he was extremely prudent. He calculated his every move, approaching the climb as if it were a mathematical challenge. He moved slowly up the wall, wasting no extra energy. I admired the grace of his form immediately. I, on the other hand, exhausted my energy by dangling from the cliff like a stranded spider. I forced myself to fail over and over and over again, refusing to back down from challenges I was not yet ready to take on. Patrice pointed out that my determination was my greatest asset as a climber, but that it was also my most dangerous trait. "Knowing when to quit is the most difficult part of the climb," he said. It's great to push yourself to the limit. But if you go beyond that limit, you're dead.

On our drive back to Montreal, my body ached from head to toe. My feet were blistered, and my toenails were nearly gone, like the skin on my elbows. Pulling myself up a vertical wall had left me pained in ways I'd never felt before, and I decided I liked the pain in some weird masochistic way. According to Patrice, I was a naturally gifted climber, and what I lacked in grace, I made up for in raw power. I liked the way he talked. We set the date for our next adventure: an ice climb up the side of an eight-metre frozen waterfall just south of the St. Lawrence River.

That was the trip where Patrice gave me a crash course in driving metallic screws into ice and scaling a waterfall with crampons on your feet. We moved on to climbing vertical walls with ice axes and ropes. We'd barely made our way back to his Honda when he asked me if I'd like to join him for his attempt on Aconcagua. He thought I could handle all the technical difficulties except one. "Altitude will be the great unknown for you when we get there," he said. "There's no telling how your body will react after a sleepless night at 6,000 metres."

I told him I was in. He said good, but I was already behind on my training. Then he handed me a list of equipment to buy and dropped me at the curb.

The days were short and cold back in Radisson. I set myself on a six-week mission to whip my body into the best shape possible. In the tower at night, when the airport was dead, I turned the PA system on extra loud so I could hear it in the stairwell. Then, with a backpack weighted down with books and four-litre bottles of water, I sprinted up and down the stairs until I could not climb one more step. Away from the tower, I borrowed a co-worker's retriever, named Jaymze, and headed out on long runs through the snow, jogging my way up and down the hydro-electric dam. Jaymze was a natural deterrent to wolf packs that prowled the forests along the outskirts of town.

One day, my mother called and asked if I'd be coming home for Christmas. She was worried about me spending the holidays alone. When she learned of my plan, she said, "I don't understand. You've never climbed anything." Then she reminded me that I had a daughter and should perhaps think of her before heading off on some absurd climb. There was nothing she could say to make me change my mind.

I left Radisson for Montreal a few days before we were to fly to Argentina. I headed into the climbing store called Blacks. The walls were lined with rough-cut lumber, and Tibetan Zen meditation music greeted me from the speakers. I felt as though I'd just walked into a hut at the base of a mountain. Postcards and framed posters of Himalayan peaks were hung around and between backpacks, harnesses, and other gear. The store was empty but for the man behind the cash: a Polish émigré and retired mountaineer named Jacques Olek. He wanted to know everything about my climbs, where I'd been and where I was going. I told him I was about to depart for Aconcagua. He told me it was a great mountain, then he shared with me the details of some of the adventures he'd had around the world. Was I aware that his countrymen were among the finest mountaineers on the planet? It turns out that the Polish are specialists in winter ascents. He pointed to a photograph on the wall of K2, the world's second-highest mountain, and told me about the time he and a team of his countrymen tried to become the first men to scale its sides in the dead of winter. "How much do you know about K2?" he asked. I didn't know much, but I knew it had killed a lot of people. He talked to me for hours about K2. He seemed obsessed; he fixated on it as if it were the great white whale. He said you have to be careful which mountains you let into your soul, because once they're in there, you can't get them out of your mind.

"The trouble with climbing," he said, "is that once you reach the top of one mountain, you're already thinking about the next one. It's like a beautiful sickness." He said he was too old to contemplate another high-altitude attempt on K2, but it was all he ever thought about. It was ten years since he had last seen it, and he wanted to get back, even if just to gaze up at its glory from the low slopes of some neighbouring peak. He struck me as an aging mountain sage, one whose true love was a massive protrusion along the China-Pakistan border. He fascinated me like few people I'd ever met. I bought hundreds of dollars' worth of gear and headed for the door, but not before he told me, "You're going to be a great climber someday. You have the body for it. Now you just need to feed the passion." It was dark by the time I exited his shop.

On Christmas Day, my mother went to the church where I was baptized, the one with the red brick steeple that towers over the centre of Lac-Mégantic. There, she shared her fears for my soul with a priest, who raised a chalice above the tabernacle and gave mass in my name.

In Montreal, I woke up early and headed out to my former in-laws' house so that I could spend Christmas morning with Alexandra. I slipped a gift under the tree and then waited for her to wake. She was four years old and still obsessed with the sky and the stars. I had created a little French verse for her, and I repeated it to her as we sat on the floor by the tree and chatted. Here is the translation: "I love you more than the clouds, the sky, the stars, the moon, the sun, the universe, the planet, and the mountains. I love you so much." She laughed and asked me to repeat it. She didn't understand where or why I was going. I didn't bother trying to explain because I knew I couldn't. Instead, I told her I'd write to her from the other side of the world. Then I kissed her forehead and left her in the arms of her grandparents. I was still repeating the verse as Patrice and I jumped in a car and made for the airport. I boarded the plane with Alexandra's picture in my pocket.

* * *

The road from Santiago, Chile, to the base of Aconcagua is a long and vomitous journey marked by Incan ruins and locals with mythological tales of ancient human sacrificial offerings to the mountain gods. We crossed into Argentina by bus, then proceeded on foot up the Vacas Valley. I was farther from home than I had ever been, but I felt as if I belonged here. We were three days into our travels when we got our first glimpse of Aconcagua. We gasped in awe. It rose into the clouds above us, which shielded the peak from view.

Patrice reminded our team to keep hydrated; even at the base, we would need to drink four litres per day just to keep from getting sick. We had come with three weeks' worth of rations and were prepared for a long and eventful siege on the mountainside. We made our final approach up toward what the locals call Plaza de Mulas but which climbers have come to refer to as base camp. The ground was cold, rocky, and riddled with tents. This was one of the largest base camps in the world, second only to Everest. We staked out a corner of the camp to set up our tents in by dropping our packs in the dirt and gravel. There were five men in our group, and I was the runt of the litter. As the last man to sign on for this expedition, with scarcely a few weekends' worth of actual climbing experience, I took the lead in setting up our camp because I didn't want anyone to question whether I belonged there or not.

We hadn't even made our dinner before other climbers began visiting our camp, telling us of their difficulties up on the mountain. There was a lot of talk of El Niño and the freak weather patterns that had rendered Aconcagua too inhospitable to climb. Recently, three people had died on their attempt to summit. As we ate our first supper at base camp, we did so without knowing that in just a few days, another life would be lost on the mountain.

I awoke early the next morning, feeling like someone had been hitting me on the head all night with a hammer. It was my first experience with altitude sickness. My brain felt like it was swelling to the point that it would explode outside my skull. My throat was dry and aching, and I'd developed a violent cough overnight. We were only at 4,300 metres. I drank six litres of water and recovered a little.

We'd decided to attack Aconcagua from the northeast, traversing the Polish Glacier, which was so named because it had first been crossed by a team of Polish climbers in 1934. For the next two days, we set off from base camp and trekked our way up the mountain, gradually increasing our comfort by acclimatizing. The climber's maxim is "climb high and sleep low." By day, we'd push our bodies upwards until the decreased pressure in the atmosphere at higher elevations began to make our stomachs turn and our heads ache. Then we'd descend to rest, allowing our bodies to adapt, before pushing farther up, repeating the process. We'd come prepared for a long, cold, and tortuous siege, setting up three camps higher up on the mountain. By the afternoon of New Year's Eve, we were back in base camp, sipping tea on the gravel rocks outside our tents and trying to warm our hands and feet, when we were interrupted by the approaching sounds of a mule hoofing it into camp.

A young girl dismounted near our tents, and we wondered what on earth a nine-year-old was doing up here. She said her name was Natasha and that her mother and father were not far behind her. It was several minutes before we saw her parents trekking into camp from the valley below. Her father commanded our attention. He carried his gear in a backpack that was more valuable than our entire camp. Patrice recognized him immediately. "That's Laurie Skreslet."

I looked at Patrice blankly. The name meant nothing to me. "He was the first Canadian to climb Everest."

My mind doubled back on itself, searching for distant memories of newspaper articles or broadcasts about the 1982 Canadian Mount Everest Expedition. I had absolutely no memory of Laurie's climb; my love affair with the mountains was barely two years old, and climbing hadn't made much of an impression on me before that. Laurie was the first man I'd ever met who had been to the top of Everest. He was cordial and kind, but took one look at our camp, and told us he thought we had brought too much stuff.

"You don't plan to bring any of this with you up the mountain, do you? You guys are going to burn yourselves out if you carry that much weight with you."

We'd provisioned ourselves with three weeks' worth of food and camp fuel, even though we knew that the climb took eleven days on average. We looked at one another and knew that he was right. Laurie set up camp nearby. Over dinner, we told ourselves that perhaps his presence here would bring us a change of fortune on the mountain. It was as if we believed this great climber would somehow help us find a way to beat El Niño.

As it turned out, we were wrong.

For eight days, we pushed up and down the flanks of Aconcagua, lugging backpacks full of gear, camping fuel, tents, clothes, food, and water as we manoeuvred over an ever-steepening rocky trail until, suddenly, the rocks beneath our feet turned to ice, forcing us to zigzag our way up the mountainside in order not to burn ourselves out or lose our footing on the pitch. All the while, we were battered by fierce winds and incessant snowfall. On the third day, I pushed myself so hard that I puked on the side of the trail down from Camp 1. Then I crawled into my tent, drank two litres of water, and shivered into my sleeping bag. The minus-twenty-degree wind had chilled my body to the core. Time and time again, we encountered men and women descending, all of them abandoning their climbs because of the conditions at the top.

On the eighth day, we woke up to sunshine at Camp 1 and were determined to push on for Camp 2 on the Ameghino Col,

a high-altitude pass that connects Aconcagua to the neighbouring peak of Ameghino. We departed at noon, marching up the
mountain with the wind at our backs until the weather changed.
The sun disappeared behind a wall of clouds and mist. I squinted
upwards, trying to catch a glimpse of Patrice and Rene, the two
most experienced climbers in our group, through the thicken-
ing fog. I couldn't see them. I could barely see my feet, or the
tracks of the men climbing just a few metres beyond my shrink-
ing field of view. The snow was falling hard now, pelting us in
the face from every angle. It felt like we were wandering into a
tempest as we blindly made our way into Camp 2.

We crawled straight into our tents and tried not to shiver. I
was weather beaten, sleep-deprived, and suffering from the altitude by the time I pulled my body into the tent. I knew I should
shut down for the day and just rest, but my head was pounding
and it was clear that one of us was going to have to head back
out into the cold to gather snow to melt on the stove. I scurried
about outside the tent, gathering chunks of snow and blocks of
ice. Once back inside, I sat by the stove for hours, fiddling with
the flames and preparing brews of water and juice. Patrice came
into our tent, looked at my face, and told me I was turning a
purplish shade of blue. He pointed out that I'd been coughing
for days and said that he and the others were starting to worry
about me. He took over the stove and urged me to settle down.
He told me that I'd already proved my worth on this climb and
that I needed to take better care of myself if I was to have any
hope of making it to the top.

Misery had befallen our tent, and over our drinks, we
questioned how it was that we had had such bad luck as to climb

this mountain during a freak storm season. I lay down in my sleeping bag and tried to sleep, but I couldn't stop coughing. Patrice and the others prepared a meal and encouraged me to eat, but I couldn't. I didn't know what was wrong with me. Patrice told me we were going to head back down at first light. I lay awake in my corner of the tent, thinking only of Alexandra and wondering for the first time since I left her whether I'd ever see her again. It was a terrible feeling, one that kept me awake when really all I wanted to do was rest. I didn't let on to the others just how troubled I felt. Instead, I concentrated on lying still in the night to avoid waking them with my coughing.

We rose after dawn to the sound of a violent wind rattling our tents. I was feeling better and wanted to push on. Patrice warned me that we were heading into avalanche territory from here on up and, though I might be feeling strong, I still looked weak. I insisted on continuing.

For the next two days, we journeyed back and forth between Camp 2, at 5,330 metres, and Camp 3, at 5,900. We were still 1,000 vertical metres from the top when our climb was halted by a series of snowstorms that left us unable to move from Camp 3. There, we learned that Laurie Skreslet had abandoned his climb. We dug ourselves in for a long and frigid night, barely comprehending the conditions that had forced the most accomplished man on the mountain to turn around.

On Sunday, January 14, 1996—ninety-nine years from the very day a Swiss alpinist named Matthias Zurbriggen made the first successful ascent of Aconcagua—we left our tents and pushed on up the mountain, irrationally focused in the face of increased odds. It wasn't long before we found ourselves split up, trying to traverse the mountain to position ourselves for an easier ascent *away* from the Polish Glacier, which had become too dangerous due to the weather. One man in our group of five, Sylvain Boudreault, an experienced ice climber from Sept-Îles, ended the day two-and-a-half hours off our pace. He was confused, babbling about how he needed to buy bread and butter from a grocery store before finally crawling into his tent, exhausted and dehydrated. His senses returned to him in the night. The next morning, he told us his climb was finished, that we should go on without him and collect him upon our return from the summit. I envied him for giving up this close to the top. I knew he'd be warm and safe while we struggled through another day's climb in the freezing wind and blowing snow.

Our summit day began early. It was still dark when I reached out into the vestibule beyond my tent and lit my stove to begin boiling water. My body was broken by exhaustion, but I was more determined than ever to get to the top. I put on my gear. The snow crunched under my feet as I stepped out into the cold. Patrice and the others were ready to go. We decided not to tie ourselves together. We were so tired, we agreed, it was safer to climb every-man-for-himself style rather than risk one man pulling the other three over a cliff.

We looked at the rising sun over Aconcagua's summit and trudged through the snow into the Canaleta pass, a three-hundred-metre slope known for its pitched ice and the sun-bleached bones of a human skeleton. I was feeling slow and weak, but I kept step with Patrice. Then I heard screaming. Incoherent shouts began echoing down the mountain from above. The words were foreign, but the context was universal.

It was the sound of sheer horror. I looked toward the noise and saw a man bouncing down the mountain. He gained speed as he fell, his body twisting and turning as he ricocheted off rocks. He looked as limp as a rag doll. I don't know if he was conscious when he passed me, but he was no longer the one screaming. He fell out of sight very fast, and I heard a sickening crack as his body smashed to the ground below. I felt weak in my legs and head as I looked down. I couldn't see him, but that didn't stop my mind from creating its own image. For a moment, everything was quiet. None of us knew what to say. We were in shock. Then came the sound of more screaming, again from above, as the dead man's friends scampered down the slope, until they caught a view of his mangled body.

I was distressed. Terrified, even. I didn't know whether to keep going or to give up. I'd never seen a man die. None of us had any idea what we were supposed to do next. My pulse raced faster as I checked my feet to make sure they were firmly planted on the side of the slope. Unattached to any ropes, I reached into my pocket and felt the photo of Alexandra. I didn't need to be reminded that I had a reason to get home safely; I just wanted to feel close to her. Patrice looked at me and I at him. We couldn't see the fallen man, but we agreed that there was nothing we could do; he must be dead. We triple-checked our gear, made sure our crampons were securely fastened, and tried to measure our distance to the top.

Patrice looked to the summit. "Should we keep moving?"

It was a human question demanding an inhuman answer. We nodded and continued on, climbing into a cloud, our pace slow, our minds attentive to our every step. None of us wished to make the same mistake as the man we'd just watched slip and fall to his death. For two hours, maybe more, we pushed on blindly toward the summit. Then Rene looked at me and I could tell he'd had enough. He was gasping for breath in the cold. He turned himself around and took a few steps back down the mountain.

I called out to him, "Stay with us, Rene. We're so close; we'll do this together." He took another few steps in my direction.

Then I looked upwards at Patrice, who'd stopped for a drink of water. We paused there, thirty minutes from the top, rallied our energy for a moment, then carried on up the mountain until, suddenly, the clouds broke and we could see the peak just before us. I checked my watch: it was five p.m., far too late to be just getting to the top. I knew we'd be forced to climb down in the dark, but I didn't care. I was standing higher on Earth than I'd ever stood. The sky was blue, the sun hovering out over the horizon beneath our feet. I looked around the summit. We were still on Earth, but in that moment, it felt like we were higher than the sun. There was an ice axe planted in the crust, an American flag attached to its grip. It felt as if Neil Armstrong had just been here. Then I pulled the mitts from my hands, reached inside my pocket for Alexandra's photo, and cried at the thought that she'd have to come here herself if she was ever going to fully understand why I'd left her on Christmas Day.

As I looked at the clouds beneath my feet, Alexandra's verse came to mind: "I love you more than the clouds, the sky, the stars, the moon, the sun, the universe, the planet, and the mountains."

I was still crying when Patrice reminded us that it would soon be dark and we had to get down.

CHAPTER 5

TROPICAL HIGH

It was cold and it was grey. The October wind ripped leaves from the trees while the rain beat down against the windshield of my car. I sat behind the wheel, staring out at a line of gravestones. A year and a half had passed since I'd summitted Aconcagua, and I was back in Cowansville again. It was the thirtieth anniversary of my little brother's death. I hadn't asked anyone to join me. I never wanted my mother to know how often I still thought of Claude. How I wondered where he was and whether, in some distant reality, he'd survived that trip to the hospital all those years ago and grown to be a man. I wondered if I'd recognize him if I saw him today and if he'd recognize me and what we might talk about. I'd long since lost my faith in God and the afterlife, so there wasn't much spiritual purpose in my visit. And yet I felt drawn to his grave, year after year, even if, deep down, I really felt like I was only ever speaking to myself.

My windshield wipers barely kept up with the falling rain. I parked my car and looked out over the field of crosses and headstones. Claude was resting by the riverbank beyond the trees at the far end of the cemetery. I got out of the car, extended an umbrella over my head, and walked toward the place where I'd spoken to my brother a year earlier. I don't know what I wanted to tell him, perhaps just that I'd been thinking of him. Or that, after all these years, I thought I'd found a purpose to my life. Or that, every so often when I thought of my daughter, I realized that she'd already lived a longer life than he'd been granted. I'd never felt guilty over what happened to Claude, although I'd also never understood why it was him who died that day when it could just as well have been me. I'd been sick too, after all. He'd spent his last waking hours on this earth listening to me reading to him in his cot about some romantic adventure in the Himalaya. Maybe it was the thought that my voice had been the last he heard that troubled me.

I walked to his grave. I stood near the place where I'd stood countless times and looked to the spot where his cross had been hammered into the ground. I found myself staring at a different gravestone altogether. It took a while for the shock and disbelief to convert itself into pain. I feared that someone had removed my brother's grave.

I discovered later that the church hadn't removed his bones, just his cross. Because of that, though, none of us really knows exactly where he lies. The whole experience left me with the understanding that, in time, all of us are forgotten. I tried to tell myself that I shouldn't be so easily bothered by such things, that a grave is little more than a hole in the ground marked by a rock, that a life unmarked by a gravestone is no less significant than a life marked by one. But it bothers me still. On the rare occasion when I have told this story to friends or psychologists, they question whether this has shaped my own view that to vanish on a mountainside would be no great tragedy, even though it would haunt those who love me. It would leave them in a seven-year legal purgatory before anyone would officially declare me dead and grant them the closure required to move on.

I thought of Claude often on my climbs. And I wonder if, on some subconscious level, it was my own fear of being forgotten that drove me, especially in those early years. It seems ridiculously vain, of course, to risk one's very existence on a mountainside just to step where no one else has. It's what consumed George Mallory and led him to inadvertently kill himself while trying to become the first man to summit Everest. But it's also what drove a lanky beekeeper from New Zealand named Edmund Hillary to do what Mallory could not: reach the summit and come back to tell the tale. It was Mallory's failure that left an empire in mourning, but it was Hillary's success that inspired generations of climbers to dream of doing things that had previously seemed impossible.

Doctors and scientists will tell you that the Death Zone begins eight kilometres above the sea, where the atmospheric pressure is so low that all life begins to die. Think of that the next time you peer out the window of an airplane and find yourself looking down on a field of clouds. There's a chance you may be no higher than I've been when I've stood atop Everest. Only fourteen mountains peak into the Death Zone. We call these mountains "the eight-thousanders" because they rise eight thousand metres into the sky. Many climbers determine their worth by their ability to survive at such altitude and climb these mountains. There was a time when I believed it too, when I described the Death Zone as a place that was confined high up in the atmosphere. I know better than that now.

In the days and weeks that followed my return from Aconcagua, I found myself back in my motorhome on the edge of Radisson, with a stack of mountaineering books piling up by my bedside. I immersed myself in the first-hand accounts of Sir Edmund Hillary and Tenzing Norgay's 1953 ascent of Everest's southern face. As a child, I'd never really had a hero; as an adult, I latched on to Hillary. I felt a kinship with the self-proclaimed "shy boy with a deep sense of inferiority" who'd grown up fearing his father until he reached the age when he feared nothing at all. I soon started dreaming of climbing Everest just as Hillary had. It was not yet the spring of 1996—the spring when Everest revealed itself for what it had become: overrun by tourist-climbers, all of whom seemed, in some way or another, to have been seduced by the romance of following in Hillary and Norgay's footsteps up the mountain. When I finished reading Hillary, I moved on to the more harrowing and inspirational account of Maurice Herzog's 1950 ascent of Annapurna, the first of the eight-thousanders to be successfully climbed. There was something in this early account of hardship in the Himalaya that I found as seductive as any adventure book I'd ever read. Herzog was the great French alpinist who lost every single one of his toes and the majority of his fingers to frostbite suffered on the mountain. He and his French climbing companion, Louis Lachenal, mapped and climbed Annapurna, the tenth-highest mountain in the world, all in a single season. I was gripped by every word in his book *Annapurna*, which came out one year after the climb and which spoke to me and millions of other people around the world.

But it was the book I read after that, the account of Dick Bass, the Oklahoma millionaire who in 1985, at the age of fifty-five, became the first man to scale the highest peaks on seven continents, that truly broadened my view of what was humanly possible. Bass had made his fortune running ski resorts in Utah and Colorado and was already in his fifties when he and his friend Frank Wells, one-time president of Walt Disney, began their quest. Bass's descriptions of adventures on seven continents captivated me—those, and the fact that he'd gravitated toward climbing at an advanced age. His pursuits would lead countless millionaires to the flanks of Everest with a disagreeable and not entirely accurate belief that for the right price, a Sherpa and a guide would carry them to the summit. He made me want to do something greater.

Inspired by Herzog's ordeal on Annapurna, I began to wonder what chance I might have in joining the more elite group of climbers led by Tyrolean Reinhold Messner, who, at that time, was one of only five mountaineers to have summitted each of the fourteen peaks that reach above eight thousand metres. I was curious if I might ever get so adept on the mountain that I could repeat any of Messner's more memorable climbs. But that question didn't linger for long. I may have been a gifted climber, but I was no Reinhold Messner. He was the Michael Jordan of mountain climbing, and I was more of a gifted amateur who liked to play pickup when he wasn't stuck in an office.

So, sitting alone in my trailer, I set myself what I believed was a more obtainable goal for a climber of my ability. I wanted to be the first human to summit both the highest- and second-highest peaks on each of the seven continents. Mine would be a historic first. And though I knew it sounded somewhat strange to say I wanted to climb the second-highest of something, I knew full well that my goal was actually substantially more dangerous than the one Bass had set himself. I would have to climb not just Everest but also K2, which had a much higher death rate. In fact, with the exception of Denali (the highest peak in North America, which is a more technical climb than its number two, Mount Logan), the second-highest peak on every other continent was considered more difficult than the highest. I had no idea how I might finance and survive the thirteen climbs I'd have to complete if I were to accomplish the goal that had now lodged itself in my head. All I knew was that I needed to carry on climbing and training if I had any chance of actually becoming a climber of any significance.

In late August 1996, I returned home to Radisson after a successful summit up the north face of Mount Assiniboine, a 3,618-metre shard-shaped peak along the Alberta–British Columbia border. That climb, a technical ordeal of vertical rock and ice on which I employed and honed my skills under the watchful eye of Patrice, was a warm-up for our next great adventure in the Peruvian Andes.

The September issue of *Outside* magazine was waiting for me upon my arrival home. Like all climbing enthusiasts of the time, I can still recall sitting upright in my bed, completely gripped by Jon Krakauer's account of that year's Everest disaster. The introduction to the magazine story caught my attention immediately: "Everest deals with trespassers harshly: the dead vanish beneath

the snows. While the living struggle to explain what happened."
I read every word. A year later, when he turned that magazine
story into a book, I read that too. I'd already become acquainted
with many of the names in the book because of the magazines
that had been coming to my door for months: Rob Hall, Ed
Viesturs, Scott Fischer, Anatoli Boukreev. Though I hadn't
met any of them, I was familiar enough with their exploits to
know that these men were the ultimate mountain adventurers.
The deaths of two of their lot on Everest served as a humbling
reminder to my nascent climbing mind of the message Marcello
had given me at the base of Chimborazo: "You must never fight
with the mountain. You must simply admire it."

By the time *Into Thin Air* came out, every one of my family
and friends were familiar with the story. For them, the accounts
of hubris, confusion, and death at the top of the world sucked all
romance and purpose out of climbing. They questioned me at
every opportunity, wanting to know, now more than ever, how
I, a father with a good job and a long future in front of me, had
become so infatuated with climbing that I was now exhausting
nearly all my vacation days scaling cliffs in the Rockies, spending my lunch hours reading about obscure Himalayan peaks,
and planning my next big trip to the Andes.

I'd known from the moment I left Aconcagua that I would
attempt Everest one day. And though that day still seemed
far away, the sun never set on a day in which I didn't devote
at least some time and energy toward that feat. By early June
1997, I was back in Jacques Olek's shop in Montreal, listening
to his Tibetan prayer chants and replenishing my gear for a trip
to Peru, where Patrice and I planned to climb four of South

America's highest and more technically demanding peaks. Over tea at a little restaurant next to his store, I told Jacques of our plans to acclimatize on Alpamayo, a conspicuously perfect Peruvian pyramid-shaped peak of ice and snow that rises 5,947 metres above the Cordillera Blanca. Featuring two sharp summits separated by a narrow corniced ridge, Alpamayo is considered the most beautiful mountain in the world. From Alpamayo, we would move on to the much more formidable and treacherous Huascarán, the highest point in all of the Earth's tropics. Then, time and energy permitting, we would rocket up two more Andean peaks before concluding our climbing season back on the cliff walls of the Shawangunks in New York, where we had started together.

"It's going to be a hell of a trip," I told Jacques, who was only half-listening as I detailed my plans. The parts of his mind that weren't focused on my words seemed consumed by the paper placemat in front of him, on which he'd begun to draw the silhouette of a mountain covered in snow. At the foot of the mountain, he drew a trail that seemed to cut up over a hill and lead toward what he labelled as "base camp." I stopped talking and began looking at his little sketch. He pencilled in clouds above the little mountain he'd drawn and wrote one word: Nanga. Then he flipped the placemat around, put it in front of me, and asked, "Are you interested?"

The mountain he was talking about was Nanga Parbat, the ninth-highest in the world. If Huascarán and Alpamayo were to be warm-ups for my first Himalayan adventure, then Nanga Parbat would serve as a great testing ground for a future attempt on Everest and K2. The western anchor of the Himalayan Range,

Nanga Parbat is located in northern Pakistan. It has earned its nickname "the Man-eater" because it rarely gives up the bodies of the dead. The 8,126-metre mountain had been left undisturbed until 1895, when Albert F. Mummery became the first man to set out for its summit. He's still up there somewhere. Born in England in 1855, Mummery was one of the best-known mountaineers of the nineteenth century. He inspired a generation of climbers (including George Mallory) with his exploits and his writings from the Alps. He and two Gurkhas vanished from Nanga without a trace, as did twenty-eight others before the mountain was finally conquered in July 1953.

Jacques was far too old to make an attempt on Nanga himself, but the Polish team from his 1985 attempt at a winter ascent of K2 was reconvening and planning to take a run at Nanga, which was another eight-thousander that had never granted a human being a winter summit.

"My plan," Jacques explained, "is to lead the first team ever to break a winter trail through the Mazeno Pass." I didn't know what the Mazeno Pass was. From the drawing on Jacques's placemat, it just looked like a long walk over some rolling hills leading to the Polish base camp. He described it as a week-long trek through waist-high snows with minimal technical difficulty. I didn't yet realize that in addition to being all of those things, it was going to be a treacherous journey up a path stapled to the side of a cliff in minus thirty degrees with jet stream winds topping 280 kilometres per hour. Or that a group of Germans had once tried to break the same trail, only to all die in an avalanche. Had I known, it probably wouldn't have changed a thing. Jacques was offering me my first glimpse of the Himalaya, and though I knew I wasn't likely to get higher than base camp on this journey, I was feeling crazy enough, on some level, to dream that maybe when we got there, one thing would lead to another, and I'd find myself completing a first winter ascent with the Poles, announcing my arrival to the mountaineering world and earning my own little place in history.

"I'm in."

Jacques raised his cup of tea. "Just make sure you get back from Peru first."

* * *

Patrice had already disappeared behind a rise in the ridge to do another day's reconnaissance on our planned route to the top of Alpamayo when I crawled out of my tent, lay down in the grass, and vomited another cup of coffee out through my nose. We'd been trapped at base camp for days as I struggled with diarrhea and an upset stomach. Though I'd initially believed myself to be the victim of a case of altitude sickness, I eventually concluded that when we set up our base camp in a meadow surrounded by cows, I'd inadvertently made myself sick by drinking from a slew contaminated with cow shit. I was still sitting outside the tent when Patrice returned. "How are you feeling?" he asked.

"Slightly better," I lied.

"Maybe tomorrow, we give it a go?"

"Sure, I hope to have some energy back by then."

I retired to my tent for another evening's rest.

I'd arrived in Peru feeling both more focused and more confused about my place in this world and on these mountains than ever before. Though Patrice and I hadn't yet talked about it, I suspected that this journey would be the last of his foreign high-altitude forays. He met me at the airport in Lima with his wife. They had been touring Peru for weeks, and though I didn't like to think about it, I could tell by the way Patrice kissed his wife goodbye that he and I were destined to go on separate journeys once this trip was completed.

Though I'd said goodbye to Alexandra days earlier in Quebec, she was the first thing on my mind when I crawled back into my tent and opened up my journal. My turmoil at having left her revealed itself in the words I put down on paper: "There are many things in life that will catch your eye. But only a few will catch your heart (like climbing). Pursue those." I turned off my headlamp and tried to sleep. Moments later, I was awake again, writing: "A hundred years from now, it will not matter what my bank account was, the sort of house I lived in, or the kind of car I drove, but the world may be different because I was important in the life of my child, Alexandra."

I don't know how many days I spent crawling around my tent at base camp, or when I realized the water was poisoning me. But I was still weak and emaciated, having lost four and a half kilos in less than a week, when we started our way up the side of Alpamayo, chopping away at the crust of snow that covered its southwest flank, digging steps into the mountainside. I don't remember much about the early stages of that climb, except that I was exhausted the entire way. It seemed like forever before we set up our next camp. Waiting in our tents within reach of the summit, I lay in silence, secretly hoping that bad weather would stall our ascent, while Patrice poked his head outside, searching for the stars and banking on a clear midnight sky.

"If it's cloudy, we'll stay here," Patrice said. I passed out cold in my sleeping bag, only to be awoken by Patrice what felt like seconds later. The stars were out and it was time to go.

The mere thought of putting on my gear nearly paralyzed me. "Pat," I said, "I haven't eaten in four days. I'm too weak."

For forty-eight more hours, it was more of the same. I don't know what it was that got me out of that tent and pulled me up the rest of that mountain. It may have been guilt that Patrice was just wasting his time and money, waiting for me to build up strength. Or it may have been fear that I wasn't going to make the most out of this climb. (Perhaps it was the hot chocolate I drank for breakfast, the most substantial thing I could stomach.) Regardless, at first light, we took off for the top. We had our crampons on before we left camp, and my first steps were timid and slow. It didn't take long before we reached the Ferrari Route, a steep impasse that would require my full concentration in order to scale it. Ice axes in my hands, I swung at the frozen cliff face. My axes stuck, then I pulled my body up and reminded myself that this was what I had come here for. Soon, we were both clinging to the side of the steep ice face, our every step driven into the side of a vertical wall that towered high above Peru. On some strange subconscious level, I was aware that down in the valley, other climbers and trekkers were monitoring our progress up the side of this most beautiful of mountains. I imagined how we might appear in their photos: like dark-suited insects blighting an otherwise picture-perfect postcard. Digging fresh footsteps into the snow and ice as we made our way up, we climbed, unhooked from anything but each other, both of us knowing that if one slipped off, the other would follow. Then, after four hours of hand over hand advances against the mountain, Patrice reached the summit and called down to me that the view was as beautiful as any he'd ever seen.

The sky was clear and blue when I got to his feet. I collapsed into the snow as Patrice breathed in the mountain air and looked out at the jagged peaks on the horizon. The rugged snow cliffs of the Cordillera Blanca rose and fell in and out of the sky like perfect triangles of white plastered against a dark blue canvas. Then I looked toward a turquoise lake down in the valley from where we'd begun our ascent. I'd never imagined the summit could be so pointed. There wasn't really enough room for Patrice and me to stand at the peak at the same time, so we straddled the summit awkwardly, shuffling carefully around as we caught our breath and snapped a few photos. I took out the picture I carried of Alexandra and held her in front of my face as I spun 360 degrees on the mountaintop. And then we were gone, rapelling with the use of old anchors left on the mountainside and down-climbing the rest of the way.

It was nearly dusk by the time we reached our camp. I slept well that night, exhausted yet strangely primed for the next big peak. We were just a few hours removed from Alpamayo's summit, but already my mind was on Huascarán.

* * *

We arrived at the base of Huascarán, energized by our success in the face of my unexpected illness on Alpamayo. We'd journeyed the distance between the two mountains by bus, gripping our gear in our arms and looking as out of place as two mountaineers on a public bus possibly could. After a couple days' break in the climbing village of Huaraz, we carried on for Huascarán, travelling quickly from the base of the mountain through a couloir, a steep and narrow gully between two imposing cliff walls prone to avalanches, until we were three-quarters of our way to the summit. The weather was perfect, the skies clear, the days warm. We were already acclimatized to the altitude, having just come off Alpamayo, but Patrice was completely devoid of energy. We set up our final camp just an eleven-hour round trip from the summit. As I boiled water for him shortly before dinner and a nighttime snowstorm, I watched as he struggled to lift his head to sip a cup of grape punch. I averted my eyes as he leaned over and vomited it up just outside our tent. We were perched at 5,900 metres, and we watched while teams of other climbers came and went on their way to the summit. All the while, Patrice was sweating, suffering from an illness neither of us could understand. At one point, he told me to leave him, climb through the night to the top with a team of Dutch climbers, and then return to him in the afternoon. But I couldn't leave him. Not in his state. That night, as Patrice lay crippled from dehydration, altitude sickness, and possibly a bug picked up from some of the food he'd bought in the valley below, I wondered how I would get him off the mountain if he was still sick come morning. All around us, we could hear the mountain letting go of pieces of itself, and though we were relatively safe from avalanches, there was an inherent risk in staying in our camp for too long. I awoke in the middle of the night to the sound of Patrice's heaving, wrenching cough.

I was boiling him a fresh coffee by the time he woke up. He told me he wasn't yet feeling well enough to ascend. I told him that was okay, that I thought we should go down together instead. We gathered up our gear. I let him lead the way down the mountain with fifty metres of rope between us, just enough for me to brace his fall should he stumble.

But for a Peruvian guide and a French climber we passed along the way, we seemed to have the mountain all to ourselves. They asked us how our summit had been. We shook our heads and told them we hadn't made it. Then we wished them luck and watched as they carried on for the high camp we'd just abandoned.

It was nightfall again by the time we stopped. I was satisfied with our decision to abandon the climb. Patrice was lethargic, absent even. Sitting on a rock outside our tent after dinner, at 5,400 metres, we watched as an electrical storm lit up the sky in the Amazon valley below. Never before had I watched such a scene from above. It was a starry night, illuminated even more by the southern lights rippling through the sky like neon waves.

"Patrice," I said, "aren't we lucky? Peruvians who have lived here for so many years, how many of them get to see what we're seeing right now?"

I don't know what he said after that. I don't even know if he was truly well enough to appreciate the beauty of what was in front of us. But I got a sense that he was somewhat saddened by our failure on the mountain.

There was nothing I could say—he'd been my mentor, after all. He'd taught me everything I knew about climbing and mountaineering. He'd opened up my eyes to the possibility that I might climb Everest and other Himalayan peaks, but in doing so, he'd really just been sharing his dream with me, passing it down along with his expertise.

I told him, "Wherever I go from here, wherever I climb, I'm always going to make sure there's a spot for you with me."

He smiled and, after a few moments, told me what I already knew. "Gabriel, this was my last high-altitude climb. I've got a family now, and I've got to stop."

We sat looking at the stars, saying nothing, and just enjoying this last moment together in the high altitude. I felt nostalgic for our earlier climbs and wondered if Pat felt the same way. I knew him well enough to appreciate how difficult it was for him to say those words, to let go of a dream that had consumed him for years. I didn't say anything more. I knew, as did he, that I'd been sucked in by the mountains, and that I wasn't strong enough, complete enough in my life, to make the same decision.

Instead, I crawled into my sleeping bag and began questioning whether I'd become addicted to the climb. It seemed an insidious disease. I was no longer scaling these mountains without consequence. When I wasn't climbing, I was dreaming about climbing. I was becoming so accustomed to the mountains that I was beginning to feel dependent on them for my own happiness. They'd become a drug. The prospect of spending a weekend at sea level felt unbearable. I craved the precipice. My relationships were suffering, work was becoming a distraction, and my money was tight. All my energy was consumed by the planning for the next big peak. I lay awake listening to Patrice breathing heavily in his sleep, and I asked myself, *Has the climb taken over my life?*

It wasn't until two days later, in the safety of a bus station down in the valley, that I found myself staring at a headline in the local newspaper telling of two deaths near the top of Huascarán. An avalanche had taken out our former camp, killing the Frenchman and the Peruvian guide we'd passed along the way. It was the first time I'd dodged death by what seemed like a sheer fluke. I bought the newspaper and tucked it into my pack. Then I wandered around town, searching for a pay phone so that I could call home to say I was alive. And that I was coming back home.

CHAPTER 6

THE MAN-EATER IN WINTER

I stared out the cockpit window, searching for a peak I might recognize from my studies of the Karakoram range. We were somewhere over northern Pakistan. A layer of clouds was spread out beneath our wings, shielding the mountains from view. It was January 9, 1998, and I stood behind the pilots in the cockpit during a turbulent flight from Karachi to Islamabad. From our cruising perch, the engines humming in both my ears, I fixed my eyes on the crystals of frost on the window, a gentle reminder of the extreme cold outside. The altimeter read 10,000 metres. We were in the Death Zone, cruising just above the mountains, when the pilot pointed at an elevated swirl in the clouds and said, "That's K2." I looked to Jacques, who was next to me. He said nothing. Instead, he simply stared at the black shard on the horizon that had occupied so many of his thoughts over the last decade. The pilot pointed out the other window at another jagged peak.

"Nanga Parbat," I said.

Its southern face was magnificent, the highest cliff wall in the world. Known as the Rupal Face, it had been the site of one of the most harrowing and controversial summits in mountaineering history. At the base of that massive face, which was almost completely covered in snow, the Tyrolean alpinist Reinhold Messner and his younger brother Günther set out from their camp, determined to become the first men to tackle the peak from its most formidable side. They reached the top on June 27, 1970. Six days later, a severely frostbitten and emaciated Reinhold collapsed into the care of some local shepherds on the other side of the mountain. It would be thirty-five years until Nanga Parbat revealed the location of Günther's remains.

I stared out the window, in awe of the mountain, until it disappeared from sight.

Our journey had already been eventful. We'd departed Montreal in the middle of what would become known as the "Great Ice Storm of 1998," one of the largest natural disasters in Canadian history—a cyclone of freezing rain that left thirty-five people dead and four million without power in the dead of winter—and arrived in Karachi airport, which was full of security. They suggested we remove our baseball caps and try to disguise ourselves as anything but North Americans; four tourists from the United States had just been killed, and the airport was in a state of emergency.

Our arrival in Islamabad was equally unnerving. The city was an endless and hectic mess of organized chaos, and for four days, we tried to stay out of sight while our baggage slowly caught up to us. By the time it arrived, we were eager to break out of Islamabad and go barrelling up the Karakoram Highway—the highest roadway on Earth, built upon the ancient Silk Road—in a convoy of jeeps. Winding over snow, mud, and rock, we were getting close to the valley beneath Nanga when we passed an ominous road sign that read, "Killer Mountain."

Heavy snowfall in the valley beneath Nanga had rendered the Karakoram Highway completely unnavigable. I was eager to get out of the jeep and make my way on foot, which would be infinitely safer than to continue slip-sliding up a highway that felt like an unmaintained roller coaster track carved into the side of a five-hundred-metre cliff face.

We were still a few thousand metres below the Mazeno Pass when we set off on foot from the highway. As we trudged through the snow, our group seemed to collect porters and mules, who lined up behind Jacques and the others in our group while I broke a trail through waist-deep snow en route to the pass. Each day seemed the same. We'd trek thirty minutes out of camp, and already I was out of sight, alone and twenty minutes ahead of the rest of my team, including the Hunza, the local tribesmen who'd joined our expedition as porters. I'd spent the previous six months focused on my goal of being the first human to complete this trek in the winter. I'd been transferred out of Radisson shortly after my return from Peru, and though I'd hoped to be placed somewhere nearer to Montreal, I'd ended up in Iqaluit, where I quickly befriended members of the RCMP and began an intense training regimen in their garage.

I'd spent hours hoisting tires, dragging weights across the floor, leaping up and down from makeshift platforms before stepping outside into minus-thirty-five-degree weather for a run. The Arctic cold had hardened me and given me the opportunity to test my winter camping gear out on the tundra, where I'd spend days and nights dogsledding along the frozen shores and inlets of Baffin Island. By the time I arrived in Pakistan, I was in the best shape of my life. And though Jacques and the others had done their own training for this trek, none seemed to have obsessed over their preparations quite as much as I had—which explained why, in addition to breaking the trail to the Mazeno Pass, I often found myself alone, looking backwards at my own footsteps and wondering how long it would be before the others in my group caught up.

I slowed my pace to keep us together. We reached the base of the Mazeno Pass several days behind schedule. It was cold— the dead-of-winter-in-a-high-mountain-range kind of cold. We slept two men to a tent to keep warm as the nights dropped well below minus thirty degrees. Every night seemed to bring more snow. We'd awaken to hoarfrost from our breath on the inside of our tents. The slightest movement would cause the frost to dislodge from the canvas and fall in our faces. A bigger problem was the amount of snow accumulating *on* our tents in the night. Too much snow on the outside of the tent might trap our own carbon dioxide inside and suffocate us while we slept. (This is one of the lesser-known risks associated with a winter climb.) Regardless of the intense cold, I felt strong enough to break the trail all the way through the Mazeno Pass, but members of the group were arguing about whether we should proceed at all. Over our radio, we heard of the troubles the Polish expedition was having up at Nanga Parbat Base Camp, trying to secure their climbing ropes to the mountainside and build their camps.

Our spirits wavered even more after we passed a cemetery

full of climbers killed while attempting to summit the Man-eater's many faces.

Twelve days into our trek and just two hundred metres from the crux of the pass, our porters were suffering. Ill-equipped and coping with frostbite, they didn't share my passion for trudging through snowdrifts above our waists. For them, this trip was becoming excruciatingly difficult and ultimately purposeless. Soon, even Jacques gave up on our attempt to complete the first winter traverse of the pass, deciding instead to retreat to the highway and take the traditional footpath up from the valley to the base of Nanga's western face. I got the sense that it was more important for him to witness his Polish friends complete the first winter ascent of the actual mountain than for us to conquer the pass.

On the trek to the Polish base camp, I found myself alone again, more than an hour ahead of Jacques. It was the twenty-ninth day of January, a day I noted every year because it was my brother's birthday. I thought of Claude as I trudged alone through the snow, wondering where he was and if there would ever come a year when I wouldn't think of him on his birthday. He stayed in my thoughts while I sat down in the snow to wait for Jacques to catch up to me. We were barely twenty minutes from base camp, and I thought it right to grant him a grand entrance as he reconnected with his countrymen and former climbing partners.

The Polish base camp was abuzz with excitement as we made our final approach. It was midday and snowing again. Andrzej Zawada, the Polish expedition leader and Jacques's long-time friend, stood outside the main dining tent, conversing with his climbers. At sixty-nine, Zawada was a legend among the Polish climbing community, which meant that he was a legend among the Polish people in general. The Polish climbers were a proud group; their winter exploits on the world's greatest peaks were well documented by their national press, who sent journalists to the mountains every time a Polish team set out. Zawada had led several such missions. He'd been the first man to step above eight thousand metres on Lhotse in the dead of winter, which he did in 1974. He'd followed it up by leading the first team to summit Everest in the winter in 1980. He'd repeated that success five years later on Cho Oyu, the sixth-highest mountain in the world, and again on Lhotse in 1988.

Jacques shouted out a greeting to Zawada, who in turn gave a cheerful welcome to his old friend. I felt such deference to him that I referred to him afterwards as "Mr. Zawada." Before long we were all seated inside the dining tent, downing hot tea, cold cheese, and warm biscuits and discussing the situation up on the mountain.

A reporter from the main Polish newspaper had been resting at base camp for days. The camp had been bombarded by heavy snowfall for weeks. As a result, the Polish team had barely made any progress up the mountain whatsoever. The reporter, Monika Rogozinska, took notes as Mr. Zawada explained that the journey from base camp to Camp 1 required their team members to scale a glacier full of crevasses covered by snow bridges. Stepping on one of these would result in a long and painful, or more likely deadly, fall. The constant snow had made the route to Camp 1 extremely dangerous. Worse still was the fact that there was no Camp 1.

"We keep getting hit by avalanches," Mr. Zawada explained.

We sat in the dining tent for hours as the snow fell outside, learning about the perils on the mountain. Every member of the group knew this climb was already over, but no one was yet willing to abandon the mission. Among the climbers was Ryszard Pawlowski, a famous Polish alpinist who'd summitted Nanga five years earlier in the summer. He spoke of his adventures in the mountains, of his exploits on Annapurna, Everest, and K2. He had summitted nine of the fourteen eight-thousanders. He fascinated us with stories of how he got to the top of Gasherbrum I and Gasherbrum II (the eleventh- and thirteenth-highest mountains in the world, respectively) just a few days apart. He'd spent ten months of the previous year climbing around the world. He said it would be more of the same this year. I told him I thought he was living the dream. Then he informed me that he was really just missing his thirteen-year-old son. He spoke often of the boy and said that he hoped the two of them might climb together around the world one day.

I thought of Alexandra and wondered what she was doing. She'd crossed my mind often on this trip, just as she did on all of them, but I'd had no way of communicating with her; we didn't have a satellite phone. We'd said our goodbyes at the airport, as had become our custom. I'd hugged her there and tucked her photo into my backpack. I looked at it every night before bed, and now, as I listened to Ryszard talk of his plans for adventures with his son, I wondered if I would ever be able to bring Alexandra to a place like this—assuming she'd even want to come.

The thought lasted but a few moments. The Polish reporter was telling us how she had made Ryszard a household name in Poland after she published an account of his harrowing survival of two avalanches on the slopes of Pumori. The first had pushed him three hundred metres down the mountainside, and the second had launched him fifty metres into the air. Somehow, he'd managed to land back on the mountain and stop himself from sliding just shy of a steep gorge that would surely have killed him.

Later, as we exited the dining tent and made for our own tents to sleep, I walked with Mr. Zawada. Our headlamps illuminated the snow, which showed our tracks intermingling with the paw prints of what I assumed were wolves. Mr. Zawada said the prints were big enough to be from a yeti.

Mr. Zawada explained, with brutal honesty, just how much this climb had tormented his team. The winds from the jet stream had pummelled his team for days. It had taken them two weeks to fix the lines between Camp 1 and Camp 2, a job that would take no more than a day in the summer. It had taken them seven hours to trek across. In good weather, this would have taken no more than an hour.

I had no business joining his climb, and I didn't have a permit to go any higher than the advanced base camp at the base of the glacier. But I felt both strong and bold, a result of my success in breaking the trail over the Mazeno Pass and Mr. Zawada's depiction of his team's troubles on the mountain.

"Do you think it would be okay for me to join your team? Just up to Camp 1?"

Mr. Zawada put his hand on my shoulder and said that if he could legally get me on his permit, he'd let me go with his men all the way to the top. "You're a strong climber, Gabriel," he said. "I wish I had you on my team."

The next morning, I departed with a radio and some gear to replenish the stock of the climbers who'd spent the previous day rebuilding Camp 1. For three hours, I climbed over the glacier, lugging a pack filled with provisions, watching each step while monitoring the sky, which had turned foggy and was now masking the trail. I was only up there a few hours before bad weather forced us to head back down to base camp and out of the avalanche zone. I'd spent less than a day above base camp, but it was time enough for everyone to draw the same conclusion: I belonged up there. I could barely communicate with the men I was climbing with, but that didn't matter. We were all just listening to the mountain anyway.

By nightfall, we were back at base camp, listening as Mr. Zawada recounted stories of the hardships his team had faced during that first winter ascent of Everest in 1980. After dinner, he took me aside and invited me to join one of his future expeditions. He was already organizing a winter attempt at Makalu, the only eight-thousander in Nepal that hadn't yet been climbed in that season. His confidence in my abilities left me feeling, for the moment, as if anything was possible.

The next day, as I packed my gear and prepared for the long trek back down to the Karakoram Highway, Ryszard came by my tent, offered me a handshake and his business card, and told me that if ever I found myself back in the Himalaya, to get in touch. He expected he would soon return again to Everest and said it would be fun to climb together. I thanked him for the offer, then made my way down the valley and onward to Islamabad, where I was forced again to shield myself from view, thanks to the heightened tensions between the United States and Iraq. As

I waited in my hotel room for my flight home, I turned on the television and watched coverage of an earthquake in Afghanistan that the reporters said had left four thousand dead.

Days later, back in Montreal, I was lying on a couch next to Alexandra, wondering how the Poles were doing back at Nanga Parbat, when my phone rang. It was Jacques bearing news from Pakistan. The climb was over. Camp 1 had been destroyed again by an avalanche that had nearly killed Ryszard. It had taken five days for the weather to clear enough for a helicopter to evacuate him and the rest of his team to Islamabad. Jacques said Ryszard had a broken fibula.

"He's lucky he got out of there alive," I said.

Then I held Alexandra close and counted the hours on the clock on the wall, knowing that soon I'd have to leave her again and return to my lonely life in Iqaluit.

CHAPTER 7

EVEREST: THE FIRST ATTEMPT

I was delirious and could barely breathe. I collapsed, unconscious, in a mushroom-shaped tent at Everest's Southern Base Camp. To my Sherpa companions, I'd gotten what was coming to me. I was a cursed man, a hubristic fool who'd taken the mountain for granted. Deep down, I didn't feel I was any of those things. But that didn't matter. My actions had angered Sagarmatha, "Goddess of the Sky." The doctor took one look at me and told the reporter at my side, "This man will either recover in the night or he'll be dead by morning."

It was Wednesday, April 12, 2000. My strength had left me in the night. I was shivering uncontrollably, my body having gone hypothermic. My blood was dangerously low on oxygen. Fluid was filling my lungs and possibly my brain. For fourteen hours, I lay unconscious while a journalist sat by my side, doubling as a nurse. If I succumbed, I'd be the 171st human to die on this mountain.

I'd mortgaged my life to get here. I'd spent the previous six months criss-crossing Canada, trying to sell T-shirts to raise money for cystic fibrosis and for this climb, so that I might have the chance of becoming the first Canadian, if not the first person, to climb Everest in the new millennium.

I'd been daydreaming of coming here ever since I'd stood, purple-faced and exhausted, on the top of Aconcagua four years earlier. But I hadn't believed myself ready for Everest until that winter's day in Pakistan when Mr. Zawada told me I had what it took to make it to the top of the world without being carried by a team of Sherpa. I'd left Nanga Parbat, hoping that Mr. Zawada might one day call me to join one of his expeditions, but he was sick on that trip without even knowing it. Soon after, he was diagnosed with brain cancer.

I'd returned to my life in Iqaluit, filled with confidence but with no prospects for future climbs. I had stopped asking myself whether my urge to climb had crossed the line between passion and obsession, and I began the long and difficult process of reinventing myself as a professional alpinist. It wasn't a very lucrative profession. Many of the full-time climbers I'd come to know and respect were borderline vagrants who could fit their worldly goods into a tent. There was a romance to it all that I admired, but I was still a long way from getting paid to climb a mountain. I had never guided and I had no sponsors. All I had was my gear and my experience, which didn't open many doors.

I spent long winter nights trying to think of ways to finance an expedition to Everest. The permit alone cost fifteen thousand dollars; the total cost of a trip with proper guides and support would run me at least eighty thousand dollars.

On September 1, 1999, I sat in an auditorium in downtown Montreal, along with Jacques Olek and dozens of other would-be Himalayan mountaineers, listening as the most famous Sherpa since Tenzing Norgay spoke of the nine times he'd stood atop Everest. Short and somewhat fat for a mountaineer, his name was Babu Chiri Sherpa. I'd read about him months earlier after he'd spent a record twenty-one hours on the summit of Everest without supplementary oxygen. He was travelling the world on a mission, speaking on behalf of his people, trying to advance the global view of the Sherpa as more than just silent porters who dutifully carry the gear for Western climbers. Now here he was, describing how he'd led a team of Westerners to the top of the world and then waved to them as they went back down to safety, while he pitched a tiny tent and hunkered down for a cold yet memorable night.

Babu was the most accomplished member of the most impressive group of climbers in the world. His family had lived in the high Himalaya for five hundred years, and their genes had adapted to the elevation. Scientific studies show that the Sherpa have a "super athlete gene" and tend to have larger lungs than the average human, as well as blood vessels that constrict in thin air. According to research studies, this gene helps the Sherpa to efficiently use smaller amounts of oxygen, allowing them to power their movements at altitude without suffering the same exhaustion as the rest of us. It also serves to regulate the body's production of hemoglobin, the molecules in red blood cells that carry oxygen through the body, giving the Sherpa a built-in resistance to pulmonary edema, the fluid accumulation in the lungs that affects almost every climber at high altitude.

I stuck around after his talk, waiting until there were no more admirers left, to shake his hand and tell him what an inspiration he was. I told him of my ascents of Aconcagua and Alpamayo and of the trust and confidence that Mr. Zawada had instilled in me during my winter journey to Nanga Parbat. And I told him how I'd been struggling ever since to try to find a way to get to Everest. He listened intently. Then he told me of his plans for the new year, how he was putting together a small expedition of Western clients. He said he was picky about who could join his expedition. He wasn't looking to make a fortune on the mountain, but he would help me get to the top, if in return I would pay him a generous sum that he would then use to establish a school for his village in the mountains.

"I want to advance my people's cause," he said.

I left the auditorium that night feeling inspired and determined to join him on Everest in the coming season.

Back in Iqaluit, I asked for a leave from work. Soon, I was exchanging emails with Babu, who'd returned to Nepal, and by Christmas, I'd officially joined his expedition. Days later, as the world prepared to enter into the new millennium, I sat at my computer and designed both a website for my climb and a T-shirt that I would sell in an attempt to fund it.

By January 2000, I'd found what I believed to be an altruistic purpose to my climb. I chose to raise money to combat cystic fibrosis, a disease that attacks the lungs—fitting, I thought, because the thin air atop Everest would assault my own lungs were I to succeed in my campaign. So, I set out on a mission across Canada, raising money for the Canadian Cystic Fibrosis Foundation. For every dollar I raised selling T-shirts, NAV

Canada agreed to contribute one dollar toward my climb. Until then, I'd never known anyone who suffered from cystic fibrosis, and I knew I'd made the right choice. For two weeks, I toured the country, appearing on TV and in newspapers from New Brunswick to British Columbia and hawking T-shirts for a good cause.

On March 11, I was the guest of honour at a gala in Montreal and was surrounded by my closest friends and family, all of whom had gathered to wish me luck. I don't remember much from that night except that I was humbled to have everyone in my life gathered in a restaurant to support me and my next great adventure. I know there were speeches said in my honour. And I know that my mother and Alexandra and Patrice were there, and each of them approached me individually that night to tell me how much I meant to them. It was the type of send-off I expected from my mother, but I was surprised when I saw, even within Patrice, a hint of fear. By the way he wished me luck after dinner, I could feel that he thought maybe I was taking on more than I could handle. In some ways, it felt as though I were attending my own funeral. I took the guest book from that night with me to Everest. Flipping through the book on my way to Kathmandu, I felt as if I were heading off on some adventure from which I might never return. "Remember to hold on to the strength you need to bring yourself back safely to your family and friends. See you soon, I trust. Patrice." Patrice had always been the more gifted climber of the two of us, and yet even he thought Everest was beyond him. I tried, as best I could, not to question myself or my abilities. Now was not the time to give in to self-doubt. I closed the book, but not before pausing once more to admire the drawing on its first page. Sketched in pencil, it showed a man climbing to the top of a mountain. It was by Alexandra. She was nine years old. Next to the sketch, she'd scribbled a message that I looked at again and again over the next six weeks. "To Papa," she wrote, "I will miss you so very much. I love you. Alex."

I wasn't the only Canadian trying to reach the summit that spring, nor was I the most accomplished. And I certainly wasn't the best-equipped for the task. I'd arrived in Nepal with no expectation of glory or fanfare. There were hundreds of other climbers hoping to summit that spring. Seven of them were also from Canada, but none had made the journey on such a shoe-string budget as I. Unlike the other Canadians who'd come with porters and reporters in tow, I'd travelled solo to Kathmandu, where I'd slipped into the expedition with Babu, another Sherpa, an Israeli, and a Mexican. Among the other Canadians hoping to be the first of the new century to summit the mountain was a foursome from Quebec who'd opted to attempt the North Col, a sharp-edged pass on the other side of the mountain that cuts between two glaciers and leads to the Northeast Ridge. It was the first route used by the British during the early expeditions of the 1920s. The Quebecers had travelled to Tibet instead of Nepal and were preparing to dig their crampons into the same ice walls that had claimed the lives of George Mallory and dozens of others. The rest of us had chosen to approach the mountain via the South Col—the narrow ridge that runs along the eastern edge of Everest's southern face, the route Sir Edmund Hillary took up the mountain from its Nepalese side. The climb from base camp to the South Col is more than 2.6

vertical kilometres in elevation and is reached only after climbers have scaled the Lhotse Face (a 1,125-metre wall of glacial blue ice), which is itself only reached by way of the Western Cwm (a bowl-shaped ice valley named by Mallory when he first saw it in 1921 and which is sometimes called the "Valley of Silence") and the Khumbu Icefall. A treacherous glacial landscape in a constant state of movement, the Khumbu Icefall has claimed roughly three dozen lives, including that of the first Canadian, Blair Griffiths, a cameraman who was crushed to death when a six-storey glacial column of ice, known as a serac, came loose and pinned him to the floor of the icefall during Laurie Skreslet's 1982 expedition.

The majority of the deaths on Everest had occurred on this route. Nevertheless, it had a reputation for being the easiest way to the top; it was called "the yak route" by those who mistook it to be a veritable yellow brick road.

With my gear, some Bob Dylan CDs, and an audio recorder to chronicle my adventure, I boarded a small prop plane that took me from Kathmandu to Lukla, a small town in the Khumbu Valley some 2,800 metres above the sea. The gravel tarmac had an 11.7 percent gradient, which contributed to its reputation as the most dangerous airport in the world. I sat quietly in my seat with my eyes fixed to the ground below, judging, in my head, the speed of our descent. I knew full well that even the slightest error on the part of the pilot or the tower would cause us to run straight into the stone wall at the end of the runway.

We landed with a jolt, the pilot braking hard. I grabbed my stomach, then got off the plane and started the long and winding trail up to base camp. From Lukla, I journeyed over a well-worn trail that cut through dirt and rock, snow and mud, into and over the Dudh Kosi Gorge, the deep river valley filled with fast-flowing glacial runoff from Everest, which created a natural trail toward the mountain. Blossoming cherry trees and massive prayer rocks etched with scripture lined the early part of the trail. The local Sherpa always walk to the left of the prayer rocks for good karma, and I quickly followed suit. The trek was beautiful until I got caught in a long lineup of wealthy wannabe climbers, attended by their well-equipped guides and quiet sandal-footed porters, trying to keep pace with the zopkios (hybrid yak bulls) carrying loads of gear through the valley en route to the Sherpa village of Namche Bazaar. My body was wet from the sweat of the midday heat as the sun poked up over snow-capped peaks in the distance and beat down on the valley with tropical force. I crossed the last rickety suspension bridges over the gorge.

I was already exhausted by the time I got my first glimpse of Namche Bazaar, having lugged my own gear and pushed myself too fast to properly acclimatize. And I was disgusted by the pop cans, candy wrappers, and other garbage left along the trail by my fellow climbers. Just outside Namche, I set about searching for Lhakpa Dorje, the retired Sherpa guide who'd helped Skreslet to the top of the world back in 1982. I'd come to know Skreslet in the years since our first encounter on Aconcagua. Patrice and I had even stayed with him in Calgary during our climbing expedition to Mount Assiniboine. I'd called Skreslet from Vancouver airport shortly before departing for Everest, in the hope that he'd give me some last-minute advice. During the conversation, he'd asked me to check in on the old Sherpa.

When I couldn't find him, I carried on for base camp, trekking behind a long line of yaks through the rhododendron forests near Tengboche, stopping to acclimatize and snap a few photos of the Buddhist monastery there before carrying on through increasingly cooling temperatures toward Dughla, a small rest spot with two lodges and a helicopter pad, where the moraine of the ever-shrinking Khumbu Glacier has left the well-trodden landscape looking dusty and lunar. Here, I came upon the first chorten—a sort of bodiless gravestone built by the Buddhist Sherpa out of stone and rock to pay tribute to those who have perished on the mountain. Soon, I found myself among a group of tourists snapping photos of the chorten commemorating the life and death of Scott Fischer, the Seattle-based guide who'd raced into the Death Zone on May 10, 1996, and died up there during the disaster that would later become the subject of *Into Thin Air*. It had taken me the better part of seven days, trekking with twenty kilos of gear on my back, to get here. I'd gained more than two thousand metres in altitude, and I was feeling the effects in both my breath (which was short) and my head (which was aching), but I wanted to keep going up, to put a bit of distance between myself and the tourist climbers who were sidling up to Fischer's chorten to pose for a souvenir photo.

I continued, trekking upwards over a dry riverbed and the moraine until, less than an hour's hike from base camp, I crested one last ridge and came face to face with the one thing I'd come to see.

"Sagarmatha," I said, staring at the massive wall of ice and rock before me.

The sky was clear and bright, and there she was: a perfect

triangle, the mountain I'd thought about nearly every day for the previous four years. She was unobstructed by clouds, neighbouring peaks, or dust kicked up by the hooves of yaks or the boots of my fellow climbers. I stopped and stared until my neck ached. Then I sat down on a rock and stared some more. I'd had a tough trek in. I was tired and discouraged by the hordes of tourist climbers in my wake. But at that moment, I knew why I'd come. Rising more than three vertical kilometres above me, the southern face of Everest spread out over the horizon like nothing I'd ever seen. It was absolutely mammoth. From this angle, it dwarfed everything else around, even the sky itself. And yet, in some strange way, its presence made me feel even bigger than I was. I felt, for the moment, as if I would be alone on this mountainside, as if our climb would be more like the ones undertaken by Skreslet, Hillary, Mallory, and all the others who'd journeyed here during a more romantic time, escaping society to come to this mountainside and push themselves to the limit of what was humanly possible.

I continued up the moraine toward the icefall, craning my neck to watch the South Col disappear behind the West Ridge and the lowly peak of Lho La, which rests at the foot of Everest like a big toe pointing upwards and rises some seven hundred metres above base camp, obstructing the view of the summit.

My first glimpse of Everest Base Camp dispelled the aura of romance. There, in the highest tent city on Earth, I walked through what seemed like a burlesque circus show. I'd come expecting to see a smattering of tents surrounded by the Buddhist prayer flags I'd seen strung from all the chortens down in the valley. Instead, five hundred tents, maybe more, flew the flags of corporate sponsors: Michelin, Starbucks, Jazzbolt.com, and others. I was no Buddhist, I had not come here to worship the mountain, but even to my godless eyes, the sight bordered on sacrilege. I found my way through the circus to a place near the uppermost edge of the camp. Babu had staked out our site nearest to the icefall. He said it was his favourite section of camp because it offered easy access to the cleanest water running straight off the glacier; we could let it run into our bottles without having to worry about contamination from the rest of the camp. But more important, being in the last tents before the glacier meant we'd get the most up-to-date information from the climbers coming down from the icefall. I dropped my bags, pitched my North Face tent, and thought myself deserving of a nap, until I looked out my tent. Babu and the other Sherpa were busy moving rocks to make a flat space for our dining tent. Guilt trumped exhaustion, so I wandered over and began grabbing rocks.

"No, no, you no need help," said an energetic young cook boy named Dawa Gyelding as soon as he understood what I was doing.

"Please. I know how to move rocks. I grew up moving rocks."

That evening, as I sat outside the dining tent, admiring the glowing sky and looking out at the camp, I thought of how lucky I was. It had taken nearly all of my financial, emotional, and physical resources to get here, but it was worth it. I thought about the next few weeks and of my prospects on the mountain.

I was proud of what I'd already accomplished just to get here, but I was put off by the circus show. I'd come here to be among some of the world-class mountaineers I'd grown to respect over the years. Peter Habeler, the great Austrian alpinist who'd summitted Everest without oxygen alongside Reinhold Messner back in 1978, was in base camp, and I really wanted to meet him. There were other climbers here whose exploits on the mountains had inspired me. But for every one of the greats, there were countless others who'd come in the hopes of "conquering" the mountain just so they could go home with a photo for their office and a story for their friends and admirers.

On my first morning at base camp, I awoke around four thirty a.m. to the sound of hushed conversations mixed with clinking carabiners, the metal spring-loaded clips that climbers use to secure themselves to ropes, outside my tent. I unzipped my sleeping bag, put on my jacket, stepped out into the moonlight, and saw, for the first time, the full human pageantry of Everest just before dawn. Charlie Gillis, then a reporter with the *National Post*, described it in a dispatch back to his newspaper just a few days later. It ran with the headline "Because it's there: The annual convention at the base of Everest is quickly becoming one of those derby-style events that synthesizes sport, business and media."

The spectacle reaches its apex between 4:30 and 7 a.m. each day, when dozens of oxygen-deprived climbers trudge across the rocks to the foot of the Khumbu Icefall, wheezing out oaths in German or English or Spanish before falling into single file at the base of the mountain. A look through binoculars at this point recalls famous photos of prospectors headed to the Yukon: A phalanx of pack-laden, slow-moving figures hunched over in the steady, frozen march to their own personal Klondikes.

By the second week of April, there were an estimated five hundred climbers, guides, cooks, porters, doctors, photographers, and other hangers-on at camp. And though I was under the watchful care of the most accomplished man on the mountain, Babu, I couldn't help myself from getting caught up in the carnival of my fellow Western climbers.

I'd always been a quiet man, more comfortable washing dishes after a dinner party than engaging in post-meal banter. I'd done what I could to come out of my shell, to woo interest in my cause. After all my efforts at finding sponsors and raising capital for the climb, my main supporter was an Oregon-based energy supplement company that few people other than myself had ever heard of. So I wasn't surprised when I learned that, to the journalists on the mountain, I had become known as "the indie climber."

I wasn't the only indie climber on the mountain. In fact, I wasn't even the only Canadian who could have been branded as such. Camped somewhere at the base was Jeffrey Warden, a search and rescue sergeant from Winnipeg who'd been hoping to climb Everest completely solo. I didn't get to know him on the mountain because he didn't stay for long; his climb was foiled by the flu. Among the other Canadians was a group of three Québécois who were climbing under the guidance of a Toronto-based documentary filmmaker and high-altitude adventurer named Ben Webster. That team had the corporate backing of Quebecor, who'd not only sponsored their climb but had sent two writers and a photographer to chronicle it for their newspapers. I liked the team a lot and grew to enjoy our daily interactions at base camp.

I found it less fun, however, being around the leader of the other main team from Canada: Byron Smith, a car salesman from Alberta who'd arrived at base camp with a reported million dollars in sponsorship deals and an agreement to provide live daily updates on CBC *Newsworld*. Smith, whose camp flew the flags of several corporate sponsors, was even more gifted than Everest herself at making those around him feel small. I chose, instead, to spend more time with his teammates, Virginia Robinson and Tim Rippel, who became my good friends, and in the company of Babu and the rest of my team.

Of all the Canadians on the mountain that spring, the two who left the greatest impact on me weren't even climbers. The first was Charlie Gillis. Newly married and just a few years younger than I, Charlie never boasted about who he was or what he was doing, even though he was clearly one of the more important print journalists in the country. He'd been sent to base camp on a hunch of his editor that the new millennium would bring more climbers to Everest than ever before, and that with all the foot traffic trying to get to the top, their man would be well positioned to report on a disaster of epic proportions. He told me this, and I nodded, thinking it made complete sense. This place was quite crowded, after all, and it wasn't hard to spot the people who'd likely have problems higher up on the mountain. Charlie was a kind and interesting man who I came to think of as a friend, even if he did scribble most of our conversations into a notebook and then head back to his tent to type them up for publication.

And then there was Sean Egan, a professor of human kinetics from the University of Ottawa. Sean was a fifty-eight-year-old

Irishman who'd come to the mountain as part of an academic study. He wanted to catalogue the type of characters willing to come up here and push themselves to the brink of death. He had a name for mountaineers, which seemed less academic than honest.

"You guys are the fucked-up bunch," he liked to say.

Egan had a way of opening people up with a mix of foul language and Irish charm. I liked him immediately because he was honest and interesting. He was an academic, but he was also a hopeless romantic, easily seduced by adventure. Trekking to base camp had been just one of the many adventures of his life. He'd grown up above the cliffs of County Clare in Ireland, where he'd trained and competed as a boxer and kick-boxer before relocating to Canada. He'd been a long-distance cyclist, having once ridden from suburban Ottawa all the way to Oregon just to see a friend. He was proud of the fact that his bicycle was worth more than his car. He'd wrecked his knee as a kick-boxer but still fancied himself a bit of an athlete and liked to regale mountaineers with stories of day-long hikes he'd taken up the side of Jay Peak in northern Vermont. He'd come looking to have deep and meaningful conversations with the climbers on the mountainside, but he couldn't stand talking to some of the egotists who'd arrived searching for nothing but their own glory. He was fascinated by the spiritual connection between man and mountain. I took him for a closeted Buddhist, but he assured all that he was an atheist who just liked to wake up at four a.m. and meditate for at least three hours before dawn, preferably in a sauna. Sean had hunkered down alongside Ben Webster's team, which seemed to have joined forces with that year's Mountain Madness expedition, the Seattle-based outfitter that was founded by Scott Fischer in 1984. Christine Boskoff, a kind-hearted adventurer who'd made her mark on the mountains after becoming the first American woman to reach the summits of six of the eight-thousanders, had purchased the company from Fischer's estate after Fischer sat down near the Southeast Ridge balcony (a small, flat spot on the mountain 8,400 metres above the sea) during the freak storm of May 10, 1996, and died there. It was Sean who, shortly after befriending me at base camp, introduced me to both Boskoff and Peter Habeler. I was awed by both climbers, but especially by Habeler, who, at fifty-seven, was so well known within the climbing community that I felt inspired just to be around him. That was the case, at least until he was forced to head home after he started spitting up blood on the mountainside. His struggles, though reasonable and understandable given that this was Everest and he was fifty-seven years old, should have served as a reminder to me and everyone that even the most accomplished of climbers are not immune to the perils of the mountain. But I wasn't yet ready for that lesson.

For three days, I wandered around base camp with a pounding headache, sore throat, and nagging cough as my body slowly acclimatized to life at 5,364 metres above the sea. When I wasn't lying in my tent with my hands gripped to my forehead, I could generally be found exploring the moraine up to the edge of the glacier, a camera in one hand and my voice recorder in the other. In my mind, the mini cassette tapes I was recording were to serve as a journal that I could listen to years in the future. However, there were times when, for one reason or another, I started my entries by addressing Alexandra, making me wonder now if, on some subconscious level, I was actually making these recordings so that *she'd* have something to listen to should I not return from the mountain. During those early days at base camp, I spent hours hanging out in our team's dining tent, where Babu and I enjoyed many conversations over a steady diet of french fries while the other Sherpa played card games.

During one such meal, Babu explained that of all the things to worry about on the mountain, the biggest was the state of the soul. "Many from the West, they don't understand," he said. "They take the mountain for granted, and so they die."

I listened as he explained the importance of the puja, a Buddhist ceremony generally performed in front of an altar at the base of the mountain. To Babu, the puja, performed by a lama (or high priest of the Buddhist faith), was a sacred and essential precursor to any climb and more important than any physical preparations. No Sherpa ever dared go higher than base camp without first taking part in a puja. Each expedition was responsible for its own puja. I had missed ours by taking an extra day on the trek in to base camp. While Babu and the other Sherpa built a chorten and an altar on which offerings of cake, yak milk, fried dough, chocolates, and whiskey were given to the mountain, I was down in Gorak Shep, still trying to work my way up to base camp. More alarming to Babu, however, was the fact that I'd not been present at the moment when the monks waved wands of burning juniper around the members of our expedition and blessed our bodies and our gear, praying for their good fortune. He told me how each ceremony ended with the climbers smearing grey flour on their faces, a symbol that they intend to one day grow old and grey.

"No puja, no fortune," he said. "Bad idea to climb no puja."

He got up from his seat, reached into his jacket, and pulled out a Buddhist prayer scarf known as a *khata*. He told me to stand up and placed it around my neck. He said the scarf was a symbol of purity before the mountain, to show that I was here for the right reasons. I thanked him for the scarf, and I assured him that I would partake in another expedition's puja before venturing any farther up the mountain. He was happy about that, put his hands on my shoulders, smiled and said, "Good. You take expedition spiritually. I pray for our group."

I never followed through on my word to Babu. I don't know if it was laziness or if I simply forgot. But it didn't take long before I realized that the Sherpa had noticed I was the only climber wandering around base camp without having actually participated in the ceremony. Days later, when one of the Sherpa porters attached to our group had to be evacuated from base camp after he became so sick that he couldn't even stand, I was completely unaware that I was being blamed for having brought bad luck to our expedition.

* * *

The headaches didn't disappear and neither did the cough or the sore throat that had plagued me from my first day at base camp. Nevertheless, after five days spent acclimatizing at the foot of the Khumbu, I was desperate to begin my climb. I'd watched as the others in my expedition went into the icefall, and I'd listened in our dining tent to the crackle of radio noise coming out of Camp 1 to learn of their progress. They were already more acclimatized than I was, and I knew that if everything progressed at this rate, they would reach the summit without me. Babu didn't need any acclimatization; he had gone all the way up to Camp 2 before I'd even strapped on a crampon to take my first few steps on the glacier. But now, he was back at base camp and eager to get me started on my climb.

On the morning of April 6, I awoke at five a.m., boiled some water, and poured myself a hot chocolate. I loaded up my gear, put a photo of Alex into my pack, kissed a necklace she'd made for me and tucked it into my jacket, then exited my tent and found Babu so that I could follow his lead into the icefall.

Babu and others preferred to climb this stage of the mountain during the cold of the early morning. The Khumbu Icefall is a living thing that expands and contracts as if it were breathing. I climbed through the dark until dawn came and revealed the true power of the glacier. I found myself staring at a deep and seemingly bottomless crevasse that could only be crossed by way of eight stepladders roped together and leaning haphazardly against a distant ledge. The ladders, which seemed to wobble under their own weight as the glacier shifted of its own accord, creaked and cracked under our steps. I was scared but tried not to show it. When I stopped to take a photo of the natural beauty of the icefall, Babu turned to me and said that if I wanted to hang out here, I should take a seat next to the frozen backpack near the crevasse, a dark reminder of a climber who had disappeared into the glacier below, and wait for it to swallow me whole.

"At any moment, the Khumbu can decide to kill you," Babu said.

Humbled, I remembered something Skreslet had told me: "The Khumbu is no place for a picnic."

I quickened my pace to match Babu's, and upwards we went until, four hours and forty-five minutes after departing base camp, we reached Camp 1. It was just before noon, and though I was eager to push on for Camp 2, Babu shook his head and decreed that we would head back through the Khumbu to base camp. We had to visit the doctor and make sure our bodies had responded well to the six-hundred-metre change in elevation. And so we headed back into the icefall, retracing our footsteps as quickly as possible with the goal of getting down before the glacier started to melt in the midday heat.

It would be two more days before I set off again up the mountain, this time without Babu. I still didn't feel well; my headache had returned and my cough and sore throat had got-ten worse. I said nothing to anyone but set out alongside the Mexican and Israeli climbers from our group. For the next four hours, I struggled to keep up with their pace. I'd barely climbed halfway to Camp 1 when I crossed paths with Babu on his way down, having just gone to Camp 2, a third of the way up Everest, for a morning's worth of acclimatization. He took one look at me and said, "You go too slow. Must go faster or not go at all." I nodded at him but then shrugged off his suggestion. "I think I'm going to keep going. I want to reach Camp 2 today." He shook his head and told me it was my choice so long as I understood that I had to double my pace.

I heeded his warning but struggled to move any faster up

the mountain without breaking into a fit of coughing. By two p.m., as the sun beat down upon the glacier, causing it to melt and crack all around me, I was cursing myself for not being able to move any faster. I hoped that the blocks of ice beneath my feet and towering over my head would hold together until I could safely cross the last crevasse and collapse into a tent at Camp 1. When I finally reached the camp, I was alarmingly exhausted. I crawled into a broken tent, put my hands on my forehead, and fell asleep.

I awoke shortly after dawn, feeling substantially better than when I'd closed my eyes. Soon, I was back on my feet, energized, trekking into the Valley of Silence and gaining another 450 metres of elevation on my way to Camp 2. There, I quickly prepared for a cold and windy night camped out in minus-twenty-five-degree weather.

The stars, so beautiful in the Himalayan night, spangled the sky like bright snowflakes trapped forever above our heads. On a clear night, perched halfway up the Valley of Silence, Camp 2 offers a privileged moonlit view of the icefall below and the towering facades of the West Ridge of Everest on one side of camp, and the eastern face of the Lhotse-Nuptse massif on the other. I stood outside my tent in the wind and the cold, admiring the view longer than anyone else before unzipping my tent, unraveling my sleeping bag, and crawling inside.

The wind funnelled through the valley as if being pushed through a turbine, shaking our tents and buffeting us with freezing blasts. I leaned forward in my bag, grabbed hold of the zipper, and pulled it all the way to the top. Then I rolled over, stretched out my legs, and relaxed as my body heat rose inside the bag. It was a snug fit, as it was meant to be. I thought nothing of the pressure on the bag until I heard the zipper buckle, followed by a *POP!* My feet shot out the bottom of the bag, releasing all my body heat into the tent. Fingers of extremely cold air found their way inside my underwear and left me shivering inside my bag.

In minus-thirty-degree weather, a sleeping bag is no damn good unless it's completely sealed, encasing your body heat inside a down cocoon that insulates you from the cold. I sat up in the bag and began examining the prongs of the zipper. They were all screwed up. I fidgeted with the zipper, but there was no way to get the bag to close again. For nearly ten hours, I lay freezing on the floor of the tent, my body writhing in the cold while my mind downplayed the severity of my situation.

Morning came and I was completely exhausted. I hadn't slept, not even for a moment. My strength had left me, and my cough, which had been an uncontrollable hack before the sleepless night, was now deep and filled with phlegm. Though I should have descended the mountain right then and there, I thought it wiser to stay put, radio down to our base camp, and request that one of the two Sherpa about to journey up through the Khumbu bring with him the spare sleeping bag from my tent at the base of the icefall. I had every intention of remaining at Camp 2 for two more nights to maintain my acclimatization.

The Sherpa arrived in mid-afternoon. I was disturbed to see the group travelling so light. That feeling turned to utter fear when they told me that they'd departed base camp before being asked to collect my replacement sleeping bag. It was, by this point, far too late in the day to descend even to Camp 1, let alone to base camp via the icefall. As the sun set, I prepared, more mentally than physically, for another sleepless night in the cold.

What followed remains hazy. All I know is that by the time I crawled out of my tent on the morning of April 12, I made barely any sense to the other climbers. My core temperature had dipped into hypothermic territory and I had no strength.

Over hot tea that morning, Pema Sherpa, a cook attached to our Camp 2, took one look at me and said, "Gabriel, you go down. You go down now."

I'd barely finished my tea before my bag was packed and I was on my feet, wandering down the mountain alone, like a drunk man. Deprived of oxygenated blood and weary from two nights spent shivering in the cold, I struggled to focus on the footprints in front of me. Completely weakened, my legs folded inward and outward beneath me. By the time I reached Camp 1, I was barely able to describe what had happened to me. A Spanish doctor put me in a tent, examined me, and determined that I was suffering from high-altitude pulmonary edema. My lungs were filling with fluid, and if I did not get off the mountain quickly, I would soon begin to drown. She pulled down my pants, stuck a needle in my thigh, and filled me with dexamethasone, a steroid to slow the accumulation of fluid in my lungs and postpone the onset of high-altitude cerebral edema (HACE), which, if present and unchecked, would put me in a coma. (My oxygen-deprived brain would begin to draw more and more blood to itself, causing inflammation and swelling that would eventually kill me.) My pants were barely buckled when Babu, who'd just arrived from base camp, ordered me back on my feet and set about guiding me down through the icefall.

How he ever managed to get me down all the ladders and across the makeshift bridges that straddled the crevasses, I'll never know.

What I do know is that by the time I reached base camp, I was completely incoherent. The level of blood oxygen in climbers who are adequately prepared to make an attempt at Everest from base camp is over 80 percent. My blood oxygen level had dropped to 33 percent. Babu placed my body in an orange tent, where I lay for fourteen hours, fading in and out of consciousness while Virginia Robinson, the base camp doctor attached to Byron Smith's team, monitored my vitals and pointed out to Babu and others that were we anywhere near a hospital, I would have been incubated in order to increase my chance of survival. Charlie Gillis of the *National Post* stood watch all night, ensuring that an oxygen mask remained pressed to my face, while Virginia popped in and out to monitor my progress.

When at last I awoke, I crawled outside the tent and lay in the sun. I knew I had no right to be alive, that the mountain owed me nothing. I was still lying there, my hand clutching the necklace Alexandra had given me, when Babu came by to ask how I felt. I coughed into my hands, punched my chest to help myself breathe, and told the Sherpa that I would like to recuperate and try again for the summit.

"Gabriel, your expedition over," he said. "You lucky to be alive."

His words hung between us in the cold.

I told him I was sorry for having let him and the rest of our team down, that I was sorry for not having done the puja, and that I was sorry, most of all, for having caused so much worry to the man responsible for my well-being.

He smiled, leaned down to my level, and pulled a small Ziploc bag of multicoloured rice from his jacket and placed it in my hand.

"Take rice," Babu said. "It blessed by the Dalai Lama."

I looked at the bag. He said the rice was sacred in the Sherpas' eyes. Babu had carried it everywhere he'd climbed. He said that at times when he was scared and felt as if he might die on the mountainside, he had always reached for the rice, held it in his hand, and remembered how the Dalai Lama had blessed it and given it to him. When he was *really* scared, he'd remove some of the rice from the bag and sprinkle it on the mountain as an offering. Now Babu wanted to share it.

"You take the rice," he said. "Take the rice and remember what I tell you: you take the climb spiritually. Very important."

I thanked Babu, placed the rice in my backpack next to the photo of Alexandra, and told him I'd keep it with me, always.

"Now all be okay," he said, and got up and walked away.

CHAPTER 8

EVEREST: SECOND ATTEMPT

I emerged from my fourteen-hour sleep as if resurrected. I was hungry, groggy, and not entirely sure just how close I'd come to death on the mountain. My memories of the ordeal were so vague that even as I lay outside my tent, staring at Babu's rice, I struggled to remember exactly how I'd gotten down from Camp 2. I had vague memories of our escape through the icefall, of seracs falling and crashing into the crevasses beneath us, and of ice melting all around us. I had been far too out of it to be terrified. I remember Babu looking into my eyes, examining them, and asking if I needed to take a break. I remember shaking him off, telling him, "I just want to get out of here." The fastest man on the mountain had stuck with me—the slowest. What I remember most of all was the panic in the eyes of those who saw me when I arrived at base camp.

Virginia, the doctor who'd saved my life, pleaded with me to head down into the valley to renew my energy and get rid of the liquid in my lungs. I didn't listen. I didn't want to hear that. It wasn't until Sean Egan, the professor from Ottawa, came by my tent to parrot the doctor's words that I finally conceded.

"You nearly died last night," he said. "You're lucky to be alive. If you're really serious about going back up, you have to head down into the valley to get stronger."

He was right. I knew all of them were right. But I was terrified of going home a failure. I'd failed at my goals on mountains before, but they had never stung me like this. My failures had never been newsworthy; this one would be. I'd spent a lot of money, told everyone in my life that I was going to climb this mountain, and had even gone so far as to tell a whole bunch of sick children across Canada that I was going to climb it on their behalf. I looked around the camp at the crowd of clients, with a fraction of my experience, still primed and ready to take on the mountain. How could I be the weakest man at this base camp? I was depressed, and I pitied myself for my own stupidity at remaining at Camp 2 that second night instead of retreating immediately. It took a while, but finally I nodded at Sean, then got up and prepared to head down to Dingboche, a small Sherpa village in the Khumbu Valley roughly nine hundred metres below base camp. I refused, however, to pack up my tent. I wanted everyone to know that I would be back. I grabbed a cereal box, cut it up, and wrote on the inside with a marker, "Back in five minutes." I crossed out "minutes," replaced it with "days," and tied the sign to the slip of my tent. Then I retreated, quietly, down into the valley. My descent from base camp was a lonely, miserable, and metaphoric affair.

I'd never felt blinded by summit fever before, but as I trekked back over the moraine, losing a thousand metres in elevation on the day's walk to Dingboche, I thought about what had driven me to nearly kill myself above. I don't know if it was the sight of chortens commemorating the dead, or the loneliness of the trek, but soon my self-pity dissolved and I remembered Babu's words: a climber must have a greater purpose than himself if he is to succeed on the mountain. For two days, I rested in a small hut in Dingboche, recounting some of my most memorable conversations with Babu into my recorder. He'd explained to me that a climber must never fight with the mountain. "You must respect the mountain. Respect the mountain, and the mountain respect you."

Babu may have been the most accomplished man I knew to utter those words, but he was far from the first. I thought of my previous climbs, of the moment five years earlier when Marcello, my Ecuadorean guide on Chimborazo, had turned us around within striking distance of the summit, explaining that we were not there to conquer the mountain but to admire it. I had learned so much since then. How had I not learned the most important lesson of all?

I'd paid little more than lip service to the mountain. Back in my hut, I rummaged through my bag in search of three sheets of hotel stationery on which I'd jotted notes during my last-minute phone call to Laurie Skreslet before this trip. He'd given me instructions for how I might show respect to the mountain with a private, personal ceremony. He had explained that before climbing Everest in 1982, he stood alone and prayed. He said he faced east "to call on the energy of the new day, the new beginning, the new life." He dropped tobacco by his feet as an offering before turning south, toward the midday sun, the heart of the day. The south represents the fullness of emotion, he said, the core of your relationships, who you are thankful for, the most important people in your life. Again, he said, he dropped tobacco as an offering. Then he looked west, to the place where the day goes to die. "Remember the people who have died in your life. Confronting death will help you to let go of yourself, so that if you die, you will be at peace." Again he told me how he offered some tobacco to the mountain before finally facing north. "The north represents the way of the warrior," he said. "Your goal lies to the north. It's what's clearly on your mind. You must fight with what is to the north if you are to realize your goal. Acknowledge that, then offer the tobacco."

I'd performed the ceremony with little feeling during my initial trek into base camp, but now I was reviewing, dissecting, and memorizing the particulars of the ritual as I lay in bed. On my third day in Dingboche, I awoke with a fit of energy, went out for a full-day's hike to keep my legs strong, then returned to my room, feeling completely renewed and focused on a return back to base camp and the camps above.

On my last night in Dingboche, I wandered the dirt foot-paths of the village and called home to Alexandra. She told me about school and all the things she'd done in the month since I'd last seen her. I told her about the snow and the stars and the interesting people I'd met. I didn't worry her with the dangers of the climb or my brush with death.

The next morning, I gathered my gear and headed back for base camp, meeting, by sheer chance, Virginia along the way.

She asked me how I felt, and I asked her what would happen if I went back up the mountain.

"Well," the attending physician began, "if you still have traces of HACE in your brain, then you'll start getting headaches before you reach Camp 2. You'll run the risk of slipping into a coma if you don't quickly come back down."

"Okay," I said. "And if I don't have HACE?"

"Then you should have no symptoms and should be able to continue on to the Death Zone."

It was a risk I was prepared to take.

She said, "I'll give you some dexamethasone. Keep it in your pack, and if the problem comes back, shoot yourself and come back down. At that point, your expedition will be over." She handed me a syringe with the needle capped and taped to part of an old box to make sure I didn't bend it or accidentally stab myself.

I'd barely removed the "Back in Five Days" sign from my tent before Charlie Gillis noticed my arrival and asked me a question: "What are you doing back here?"

The next day's newspaper arrived at my mother's door, quoting me as saying that only the mountain knows whether my climb here is over. That in order for me to find out, I'd have to go back up, spend a night at Camp 1 and, if all went well, sleep at Camp 2 before climbing the Lhotse Face up to Camp 3 at 7,300 metres. Then I'd head down to base camp to rest.

"I'm no longer obsessed by the summit," I told the journalists quoting me that day. "If the symptoms come back, I will simply leave and it will be finished. I have a nine-year-old daughter who is waiting for me, and I don't intend on leaving my life on the mountain."

Satisfied, the reporters left me alone—except for Gillis, who stuck around my tent to make sure that I was, in fact, in as good a shape as I'd claimed. I assured him that he wouldn't have to write my obituary, and that if the headaches returned, there would be no question about it: I would be coming straight back down to pack up my gear and head home.

Babu came by my tent next. He welcomed me back and informed me that he'd paid a monk to have a puja for me in my absence. "Your soul now ready to climb mountain," he said.

Reintegrating into my group proved more difficult than I'd hoped. In order to prepare our expedition for a possible summit push in early May, Babu had planned three rotations on the mountain to ensure we'd all be acclimatized by the end of the first week of May. On our first rotation, our team had made it to Camp 2 before returning to base camp to recover. Because of my near-death experience, I had missed out on the second rotation, during which my teammates had climbed as high as Camp 3 before returning to base. While Babu was satisfied with how everyone else's bodies would react, neither he nor I had any idea if I'd start to die when I reached Camp 2.

For weeks, bad weather and lineups of climbers kept our team from heading up through the glacier on what would be our one and only attempt at the summit. Babu paced the dining tent, speaking to every single member of our team, ensuring we all felt primed and ready. Though he'd been to the summit nine times before, Babu was more amped up than any of us. He was planning his speed ascent. He would see us off from base camp and direct us up the mountain via radio to Camp 4 in the Death Zone. Then, with our team more than a three days' climb up the mountain, Babu would take off in the night from the base and meet us just below the summit shortly after dawn on the morning of our summit push.

"Big picture. Everyone on summit," he liked to remind us, then he'd sit back and eat another plate of dal bhat, a traditional Nepalese dish of steamed rice, vegetable curry, and hot lentil soup.

Shortly before lunch on May 17, Babu declared that the weather looked clear enough to begin our final ascent up the mountain. He would see us off from base camp at dawn.

At five a.m. the next morning, with the sacred rice secure in my backpack, I crawled out of my tent and joined my team, and we began snaking our way through the glacier. Some six and a half hours later, we emerged at Camp 1. I checked my pulse, listened to my lungs, and shook my head to see if it hurt.

"I feel good," I said to Lhakpa Nuru, the Sherpa next to me who would become my trusted companion on future expeditions. "I feel like I can climb this mountain." Lhakpa couldn't really speak English, but he could read the nervous enthusiasm on my face, and he nodded as I continued to build myself up for the climb. Two hours later, we reached Camp 2. There, I ate some soup, drank a cup of tea, and slept in the very tent in which I'd nearly died just a few weeks earlier. The next day was a big one. To carry on to Camp 3 would mean venturing higher than I'd ever ventured on any mountain anywhere. The rest of my team had already been to Camp 3. They planned to stay there one night before moving on into the Death Zone and making a midnight push for the summit. I was destined to lag behind them at some point because I wasn't as acclimatized, but I wanted to stay with them as long as I could. On our second day out of base camp, we climbed for several hours, passing the elevation of Aconcagua and rising some 823 metres to Camp 3. I fell asleep feeling strong, albeit cold, a little short of breath, and devoid of any appetite whatsoever. By two p.m. on our third day, we stumbled into Camp 4, just below the South Col. It was windy when we arrived; monsoon storm clouds were brewing off in the distance over Nepal. Kicking past years' worth of discarded oxygen tanks and shredded tents that had been left on the mountainside out of necessity but had accumulated into piles of garbage, we walked toward a waving Sherpa who was directing us into a tent for shelter. There, just a few feet away from a bootless body lying face down on a rock next to our tent, we lay down and tried to drink hot tea and stay focused on the task before us. Huddled next to the Israeli, the Mexican, and the Sherpa who made up my team, I didn't speak of the body outside our tent, and neither did anyone else, though I did wonder where his boots had gone. We began communicating with Babu down at base camp. We warned him that a storm seemed to be hitting us at the top of the mountain, but he didn't seem to care. At five p.m., we received a notice over the radio that Babu had left base camp and was on his way up.

Sometime after dinner, I set out in search of a meteorologist who I believed was up on the col with another team. The storm seemed to be getting worse, and I wanted to be as informed as possible before heading any higher up the mountain. I wandered around camp, poking my head in and out of tents. It was dark and frigid, and exhausting to be on my feet. Feeling somewhat disoriented, I began tugging at the zipper of a tattered tent, thinking it might contain the meteorologist. I unzipped it and was half inside when I saw a climber dressed in aging clothes on the ground. It took a few seconds for me to realize that it was the body of a climber who'd fallen asleep long ago and never woken up. I yelped in fear as I crouched there. I'd read about the bodies on Everest and thought I'd be able to steel my mind to their presence. But there was no way I could have prepared myself for accidentally poking my head inside someone's canvas tomb. I backed out of the tent slowly, so as not to disturb the dead. But I paused before zipping the door back up. I didn't want to look at the corpse any longer, but I was unable to avert my eyes. I was breathing heavily now and feeling very vulnerable. If I wasn't careful, I might wind up as another frozen corpse forever trapped on the edge of the Death Zone. I closed my eyes and resealed the tomb. It was nearly nine thirty by the time I got back inside our tent. I was just in time to hear the crackle of the radio declaring that Babu was already above Camp 2.

For the next two hours, I tried to sleep, waiting for the wind to cease beating our tent. So long as the storm was raging, we didn't have the confidence to step outside and begin the long march up the South Col to the summit. The wind abated just before midnight and we took off. For nearly three hours, I climbed, lagging a great many paces behind my team, trying, as best as I could, to maintain some sort of rhythm and keep them in my sights. It was shortly after three in the morning when I reached the Balcony, a small plateau 8,400 metres above the sea. I gasped for breath in my oxygen mask—four breaths for every step. The snow was deep and the winds were blowing at 93 kilometres per hour. It had taken me four hours to gain some

450 metres in elevation, and as I struggled to calculate how long it would take me to complete the last four hundred, I felt a tap on my elbow. I turned around and there was Babu, purple-faced and breathing heavily. Fuelled by yak meat, tea, and dal bhat, he had taken just ten and a half hours, without supplemental oxygen, to reach my side. He looked like he'd just sprinted up the mountain, but it was clear he still had more to give. He stood with his chest out and his hand on my shoulder, exuding confidence (in himself) while, at the same time, making it clear that he was worried about me.

"Gabriel, okay?" he asked.

Unable to speak with my mask strapped to my face, I nodded and waved him through, but he could tell by the way I laboured over every step that I was struggling to keep up with the others. He pointed to the lightning bolts crashing down around us, paused his speed ascent for a moment, and told me I'd better turn back if I didn't want to die. He continued up the mountain.

My decision was already made. I'd been climbing alone for hours, and the storm was starting to scare me.

I watched for a few moments as Babu clambered into the storm, disappearing from sight ten metres in front of me. I wanted to follow, but I knew he was right. I looked up at the sky and, though I couldn't see any stars, I thought of Alexandra. I reminded myself that no matter what, I had to get home. I turned myself around and started back for the shelter of Camp 4.

Shortly after two that afternoon—precisely sixteen hours and fifty-six minutes after he had left base camp—Babu stood atop Everest. He had broken the previous record for the world's fastest ascent by more than three hours.

I learned of his success as I staggered into Camp 4 to rest. I was feeling groggy when I saw him in person a few hours later when he strolled into Camp 4. I clapped for him and wanted to keep up with him as he made his way back down, but just as he'd gone up at an inhuman speed, he was now descending too fast for me as well. He urged me not to try to keep up. I nodded and carried on at my own pace. Climbing completely alone down the Geneva Spur—a rock buttress just below the South Col—I was switching my carabiners on the rope when my crampon let loose, causing me to free-fall fifty metres, maybe more, until, by luck, I found myself dangling from the next anchor on the rope. Minus one crampon and slightly shaken, I continued slowly down the mountain to Camp 3, where I'd had no intention of stopping, but where I was forced to sleep, alone, in a desolate camp of abandoned tents devoid of oxygen, fuel, sleeping bags, and any other humans.

That's when the hallucinations started. As I lay shivering alone in the cold, my mind wandered on down the mountain, where it found two Sherpa coming up from Camp 2 with a Thermos full of hot tea to bring me back to life. I snapped awake in the dark, looked at my watch, and realized that though it felt like I'd slept for ten hours, I'd only actually been out for thirty minutes. I knew then that I was in trouble. I'd barely eaten the last two days. I was dehydrated, borderline hypoxic, and totally exhausted.

It was two a.m. and I was afraid to fall asleep. I crawled out of my tent in search of help. I knew I should clip onto the fixed line of rope that the Sherpa had attached to ice around the camp in order to safeguard against a potentially deadly fall down the Lhotse Face, but I was too frantic to take the requisite precaution. I stumbled, almost drunkenly, from tent to tent, looking for anything—a human, a sleeping bag, an inflatable mattress—that might help me stave off the cold. Every tent I tried was empty. I could feel myself going mad with fear. I was crying, screaming, and cursing at myself as I struggled to open a tent, when I heard the sound of another human. There was snoring inside the tent. Snoring! *Thank god*, I thought. *I'm not alone!* Then my incoherent madness took over. "Shhhh! Shhhh! Shhhh!" I shushed myself and backed away so as not to wake my fellow climber.

I continued my search for help. But I found no other humans. Then I opened one last tent, placed my hands inside, and felt a mattress. At least it would shield me from the cold beneath the tent. I manoeuvred inside and collapsed on the mattress. Then my arm dropped to my side and fell upon a sleeping bag. I reached over, grabbed the bag, and pulled it closer. I was too exhausted to crawl inside, and I was strangely conscious that it belonged to someone else. I could feel my feet freezing in the wind outside, but I didn't even think to drag them inside. My crampon was still on and I didn't want to damage the tent I was now squatting in. Madness is a curious thing. I was in dire straits and yet still strangely preoccupied with maintaining my civility.

All through the rest of the night, I struggled with my own fear, trying to fight off sleep in the belief I might never wake up. But I couldn't fight it, and I faded in and out of consciousness to the sound of avalanches breaking off from the cornices of Everest, Lhotse, and Nuptse, which towered above my tent.

The third of ten kids born to a saintly woman and a troubled man. Here I am in 1961 with my mother, a few months old but already climbing her shoulders.

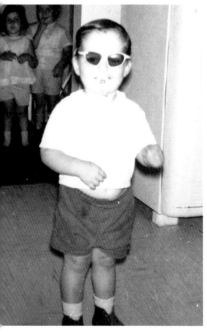

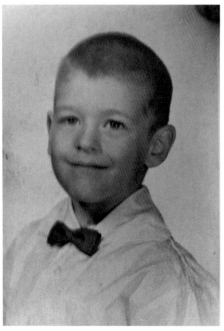

My brother Claude in 1967, aged two years and eight months. He died about a month after this photo was taken. His death taught me at an early age that life is fragile.

A school photo taken of me in 1967, the same year my brother Claude died.

Just another mid-century French-Canadian family (circa 1973). Posing with seven of my siblings and one cousin. I'm the one wearing the Montreal Expos cap, reclining on the picnic table.

My father in his French military fatigues. I never wanted to know the things he saw or did i the wars in which he fought.

My daughter, Alexandra, in 1995, aged four, drawing on the water bottle that I later took with me to Aconcagua.

Heading for the peak of Chimborazo on my first real climb, 1995. I rented every piece of my gear.

Carrying far too much gear on my first team expedition, Aconcagua, 1996.

Admiring the beauty of the Cordillera Blanca from the top of Alpamayo, 1997.

Patrice Beaudet and me at the top of Alpamayo in the Peruvian Andes, 1997. The stuffed bunny was a gift for Alexandra.

In the "meadow" at Nanga Parbat Base Camp, February 1998. Andrzej Zawada is the tall man on the right. Jacques Olek (in the green jacket) is on my left.

)n Mera Peak (6,476 metres) in Nepal after snowstorm in 2011. The view from the ıountain is one my favourites in all ıe Himalaya.

Crossing one of the many ladder bridges in the Khumbu Icefall, 2007.

Vednesday, April 12, 2000: I lay unconscious in medical tent at Everest Base Camp for urteen hours, on the brink of becoming the 71st person to die on the mountain.

My mother has always been one of my biggest supporters. Here she is posing in my gear for a photo after a talk in my hometown, Lac-Mégantic, 2000.

Rémi Tremblay/l'Écho de Frontenac

At Nelion peak on Mount Kenya, 2003.

My idea of a beach vacation—rock climbing over the Mediterranean in Penon de Ifach, Spain, 2001.

Rappelling from the peak of Mount Kenya, 2003.

Late night at the top of Denali on my solo ascent in June 2002. The Arctic sun cast long shadows over everything.

With Laurie Skreslet, the first Canadian to summit Everest, 2006.

Rock climbing with Annie's youngest daughter, Amy, when she was too little to climb on her own, 2002.

Guiding Sylvain Bédard in 2003 to the top of Mont Blanc was a highlight of my career. Befriending a man on his second heart gave me perspective on what's important in life.

Training my late friend Sean Egan for his pending journey through the icefall, 2005.

Sean Egan at Everest Base Camp on April 28, 2005, the night before he died. We said our goodbyes shortly after I took this photo. The man under his arm is Lhakpa Tsheri Sherpa, who was with him when he died.

Frank Ziebarth relaxing outside his tent at base camp on Everest's north side, just days before his final summit push, 2009.

Elia Saikaly

With Miss Elizabeth Hawley in Kathmandu, 2016.

Morning came, and I stepped outside with my one crampon into fifteen centimetres of fresh powdery snow. I looked around for the rope that would lead me down the mountain, but it was gone, covered up by the previous night's snowfall and avalanches. I had no other option but to climb down unattached to anything, triggering miniature yet disconcerting snowslides every few steps. I journeyed cautiously and slowly. When I reached a crevasse in my path, I took off my backpack, heaved it over the abyss, then ran and jumped over it myself. Then I saw it: a line of nylon rope just barely sticking out of the snow. I clipped in, took a quick look around, thought for a moment how nice it was to have Everest all to myself, and then carried on down to Camp 2. The weather was cold but calm when I arrived. It was getting dark again and I crawled into a random tent while another storm rolled in from a neighbouring peak and dumped snow on the camp while I tried to sleep. I rose early the next morning and continued to the base.

I was ecstatic by the time I made it back to base camp. Yet my throat was so sore I could barely even drink water. Sean was at my tent to greet me as soon as I got back. Ever the professor conducting his study, he asked me how I felt. I told him I was relieved to be back at base camp. He said he was happy to see me, then he asked, "Does it bother you that you didn't reach the summit?"

I told him, "Look, I'm happy because I never thought I would go that high."

Then he pulled out a bottle of whiskey from the pocket of his parka and poured me a shot.

CHAPTER 9

THE CALL OF THE MOUNTAINS

I don't know that I ever really took the time to thank Babu for saving my life on Everest. I like to think that I did, but my memory of that emergency descent is so hazy, I'll never know for sure.

The monsoon was wreaking havoc on Everest by the time we left base camp on May 26, 2000. Before leaving, I took some of the Buddhist prayer flags from the site of our expedition's puja. I packed them in my bag as a memento of how close I'd come to death on the mountain. Back in Kathmandu, I accompanied Babu to the office of Miss Elizabeth Hawley, the Chicago-born former Reuters reporter who journeyed to Nepal in 1960 and never went home. A sharp and spry seventy-six-year-old who darted around Kathmandu in a baby blue VW Beetle, Miss Hawley had, for forty years, kept statistical track of the successes and failures of every climbing expedition to venture onto Nepal's eight-thousanders. Her steely inquisitions were legendary among alpinists who feared and adored her for being the keeper of the mountains, the moral compass of the sport, and the Himalaya's only defence against the pretenders who would lie about summitting mountains like Everest, Makalu, or Annapurna. I listened as the amiable yet expressionless old archivist recorded the particulars of Babu's climb into the unofficial database that both she and the rest of the climbing community considered gospel. Of all those who'd tried for the top of Everest during our summit push, only Babu and his brother were entered into Miss Hawley's database as having reached the summit—a point that would later become the premise of a controversial lawsuit when Alberta's Byron Smith sued the archivist for insinuating that he had not made it to the top of the world on May 21. I had my own opinion about Byron's claim, but I kept it to myself. I said my goodbyes to Babu at the hotel, told him I hoped to climb with him again someday, then got on a plane and began the long flight home.

Alexandra and her grandparents were at the airport in Montreal to greet me when I arrived. I hadn't expected or earned a hero's welcome, but I was surprised by the looks on their faces when I exited the gate and saw them. I could tell by the way they just stood and stared that I'd come back looking like a fraction of the man who'd left ten weeks earlier. I was grizzly-faced and thirteen kilos lighter than I had been before the expedition, and Alex pointed out that I didn't really look like her father anymore. I kneeled down, showed her the necklace she'd made me as proof of my identity, then hugged her tightly. To her grandparents, my former in-laws, I said very little about my ordeal. They knew almost all of it anyway, having read the reports of my near-death experience in the newspaper.

There wasn't much time to celebrate or even acknowledge my return before I had to jump on another plane and depart Montreal for my job in Iqaluit.

I'd returned home feeling strangely satisfied despite not having summitted. Byron Smith was all over the media, branding himself as the most recent Canadian to step on top of the world. I'd done everything I could, and though I'd failed, I'd learned a lot about myself. Granted, I'd left a certain degree of confidence somewhere on Everest. I'd hoped to return from the mountain with enough experience to become a full-time climber. Being the first Canadian of the new millennium to summit would have positioned me well as a guide and public speaker. Instead, I'd come away as just another guy who hadn't quite cut it. But perhaps I had needed to be taken down a notch or two. I'd certainly learned humility.

Slipping back into my regular existence in Iqaluit was far more difficult than I'd thought it would be. I'd always loved my job, but my life up on Baffin Island was becoming increasingly lonely. I began spending less and less time in the government-sponsored hotel room I called home, and more time out rock climbing or visiting friends back in Montreal. On my days off, I'd wander out of the tower and onto a plane heading back to the mainland. I'd been honest with friends and family about what had happened to me up on Everest. Their responses were almost always the same. They'd listen to me tell of how I'd nearly died as a result of a broken zipper and then recovered enough to get within four hundred metres of the top. They'd nod, tell me my story sounded "harrowing," and then ask, "So have you gotten the mountain out of your system?"

I'd just smile. If anything, the entire experience had etched an image of the summit so deep in my soul that I could barely get through a day without thinking of the mountain.

Everest had a reputation for calling climbers back to it year after year. Not a day went by that I didn't wonder what might have been had I just followed Babu up, up, and away into history. I'd kept in contact with him by email after the climb and had even met him again in Montreal when he came back to talk about his speed ascent. He'd given me an open invitation to join him again, and I was eager to take him up on the offer. There was something about having borne witness to his record-setting speed ascent that made me feel connected to him in a special way, even if I had been little more than a pylon near the top of the mountain that he had to step around on his way into history.

One day, while sitting on a plane from Montreal to Iqaluit, I opened up a full-length feature article on Babu in *Outside* magazine. A year had passed since I'd left Everest, but my sense of connection to both Babu and the mountain remained constant. "There's nobody more qualified to drag you to the top of the world than Babu Chiri Sherpa," the article began. "And he'll gladly do it. But when he's through, he's got some business of his own to attend to. Namely, obliterating every last climbing record on Everest, shattering the myth of his people as high- altitude baggage handlers, and taking the Sherpa brand global." I read the article with great interest, noting just how lucky I'd been to climb with this man who, as the writer pointed out, seemed immune to all the dangers on the mountain.

The article was only a few weeks old when disturbing news filtered down from the mountainside.

Babu was dead.

The man who'd taught me the greatest lesson of all had fallen into a sixty-metre crevasse while taking a shortcut back to Camp 2 after snapping some photographs of the sunset.

I was shocked. Babu was the greatest climber I'd ever met. He'd spent time and energy ensuring everyone who climbed with him understood that there was no point in climbing just to impress others, that there was no one on the summit who was going to give you a medal. There was no one to congratulate you. He always said you have to climb the mountain for a greater purpose than yourself. But above all, he said, you must always respect the mountain.

I was too troubled by the news to fully appreciate that his death would serve as a final lesson for all those who knew him.

It was by chance that I found myself in Montreal in the days after Babu's death, learning that members of the local climbing community, many of whom had been inspired by Babu when he'd visited the city, were hosting a memorial in his honour. There, I met a young, blond woman who'd seen Babu at a talk a year earlier but had never climbed anything herself. She'd been compelled by the Sherpa's story and found herself drawn to pay tribute to this man who had done as much as, if not more than, any other to advance the cause of his people.

I'd brought Alexandra with me to the memorial but soon found myself standing alone on a stage, having been asked to talk about the Sherpa as both a man and a climber. I told the crowd how the most important thing to Babu wasn't the mountain, but rather the school he'd built in his village near Everest's base. I was barely off the stage when I got cornered by well-intentioned climbing enthusiasts who wanted to talk about my experiences on the mountain and how they might support Babu's school. I watched from the corner of my eye as the blond woman sat down next to Alex and began entertaining her, asking her questions about her life and how she'd found her way here. It wasn't long before Alex was pointing at me next to the stage, telling the stranger that I was her father. Soon, Alexandra was introducing me to her new friend.

Her name was Annie, and I was taken with her immediately because of the way she focused on my eyes when I spoke, and the way she seemed fascinated by my daughter. She struck me as special—kind, beautiful, and curious about the world. My stories about climbing behind Babu on Everest may have been interesting to the others, but this woman seemed more interesting to me than all of that. Our encounter lasted but a few minutes and then she was gone. After I dropped Alex back at her mother's, I found myself alone again in the Arctic, daydreaming about escaping the doldrums of my life.

Babu had taught me many lessons, not the least of which was to think differently about my relationship with the mountains. I'd never actually climbed anything solo, and I hadn't approached a climb with a true alpinist's mindset since Alpamayo and Huascarán with Patrice. I'd gone to Everest as if heading off to war, and I'd laid siege to its flanks in the tradition of men like George Mallory and Edmund Hillary. I'd employed "Himalayan style" climbing, using a fixed line put down by the Sherpa to the top of the mountain and establishing a series of camps all the way up to the summit. There are obvious merits to this siege-style approach, but it's not everyone's favourite. There's a whole block of climbers who obsess over the "purity of the climb," and I was soon to join them, understanding the urge to be self-sufficient; to carry all the food, shelter, and equipment necessary to summit on one's own back; to make one long and steady push from the base to the peak without any assistance from fixed ropes, porters, or supplemental oxygen. This is what's known as "alpine style" climbing.

There is a long list of alpinists who made their names on such climbs, beginning with Hermann Buhl, who'd carried out one of the most harrowing first-ascents and alpine climbs of all time. Buhl was an Austrian mountaineer whose legend was as tragic as it was triumphant. A week after becoming the first man to summit two of the world's eight-thousanders, he stepped through a cornice near the top of Chogolisa (the world's thirty-sixth-highest mountain) and fell eight hundred metres to his death in the Karakoram mountains of Pakistan. Much like his most famous acolyte, Reinhold Messner, Buhl loathed the expedition style because he thought it disrespect-ful to the mountain. Buhl was the first man to step on Nanga Parbat's summit, which he reached solo on July 3, 1953, only to get stuck on his way back down. Without enough gear on his back to perform an emergency bivouac, he was forced to spend an entire night in the Death Zone, untethered to anything and standing on a little ledge with his back pressed against a sixty-degree ice slope. He wrote of that night in his autobiography *Nanga Parbat Pilgrimage: The Lonely Challenge*, published a year before his epic ascent of Broad Peak (the world's twelfth-highest mountain) and his untimely death just a few weeks after that.

> *Utter weariness came over me. I could hardly stay upright, and my head kept falling forwards, my eyelids pressed on my eyes like lead, and I dozed off . . . I woke with a start, and straightened my head up. Where was I? I realized with a pang of fright that I was on a steep rock slope, high up on Nanga Parbat, exposed to the cold and the night, with a black abyss yawning below me. Yet I did not feel in the least as if I were 26,000 feet up and I had no difficulty with my breathing. I tried hard to keep awake but sleep kept on defeating me. I kept on dozing off, and it was a miracle that I didn't lose my balance.*

* * *

I had no interest in going through anything as harrowing as what Buhl had, but I felt that in order to fully appreciate the relationship that climbers like Buhl, Messner, and Babu had with the mountains, I would have to at least try to do as they did. And so, as I boarded a single-engine propeller plane bound for the small Alaskan town of Talkeetna, I did so with only as much gear as I could carry on my back or drag behind me on a sled.

The plane touched down gently on skis, which glided us to a halt on the Kahiltna Glacier, a smooth and relatively crevasse-free, flat bed of ancient ice that runs off the West Buttress of Denali and which doubles as a landing strip for incoming climbers. I grabbed my gear from the plane's cargo hold, strapped on a pair of cross-country skis and made my way toward Denali's base camp. Once there, I pulled my shovel from my pack, dug a floor into the snow, pitched my tent, and built a makeshift wall to protect my camp from blowing snow. Camp made, I buried the back ends of my skis on either side of my tent to serve as flagpoles. Then I pulled out the Buddhist prayer flags I'd taken from Everest and hung them over my tent in memory of Babu and all that he'd taught me. For the rest of the day, I hung out at base camp, allowing my body to re-acclimatize to life at 2,200 metres above the sea. Dining outside on a reheated bag of freeze-dried lasagna, I set about planning my solo ascent up Denali's West Buttress route, a classic route first traversed by Bradford Washburn, a Harvard-educated cartographer who became a pioneer in aerial photography, using the technique to help properly map out a large swath of the Himalaya. Washburn was forty-one years old in 1951, when he summitted Denali after having first mapped out the West Buttress and determined it to be infinitely more accessible than the mountain's southern face, the route first taken by Hudson Stuck and Harry Karstens in 1913. Washburn was responsible for helping to prove false the alleged summit of a New York–based physician named Frederick Cook, who claimed to have reached the peak of Denali in September 1906. (Cook made a similarly false claim two years later when he returned to New York from the Arctic and began lying to the American press about being the first man to reach the North Pole.) I liked the fact that Washburn had gone to lengths to protect the dignity of the mountain. Maybe the fact that I'd met disagreeable men like Cook up on Everest made me want to follow in Washburn's footsteps. Or maybe it was just that Washburn's route seemed the least insane way up the mountain.

I sat alone, admiring Denali's massive ice walls. I'd snapped a few photos of the mountain from the airplane during our approach. It dominated the Alaska Range when viewed from the sky. Now that I was seated at its base, it seemed to wrap around me like a snow-covered fortress. It was the largest thing I'd seen since Everest, and it sparkled and glistened now beneath the Arctic sun. But even as I sat there, I was already thinking of my next mountain, about how I would climb the Seven Summits and then the second-highest summits on every continent. I recognized on some level that it was a weird goal to set myself, but there was still an element within me that felt compelled to etch my name in history, to be forever known, like Stuck, Washburn, or Karstens, as the first to do *something* on the mountains.

I finished my lasagna, crawled into my tent, and fell asleep. In the morning, I packed up my camp and skied up a marginal incline toward the Advanced Base Camp. I snapped my toes out of my ski bindings at 3,352 metres, switched into my climbing boots, and proceeded on foot, refusing any assistance—even a cup of tea or an offer to clip on to one of the fixed ropes on the mountain—as I went. There were roughly 250 other climbers on the mountain, and I didn't really want to climb with any of them. I pushed on quickly, until I reached 4,350 metres. There, I pitched my tent and waited out a storm in a camp that was populated by three young men from Knoxville, Tennessee, who'd been struggling their way up the mountain in an attempt to raise money and awareness for a two-year-old boy named Connor who lived back in Knoxville. Connor had spinal muscular atrophy, a rare neuromuscular disease that was attacking every muscle in his body. I'd first met these three men nearer down the base of the mountain, when they'd told me of their climb and showed me a picture of the boy they were trying to help. When I saw their tent in the storm, I approached it to ask them how they were making out. The Tennesseans were pinned down in the storm at 4,267 metres, and one of them was suffering from acute mountain sickness. They said they were being forced to abandon their climb. I listened as two of them told me of the trio's third member's delirium in the cold. His hallucinations were starting to scare them, and they'd decided to head down as soon as the weather broke. I was sad to hear it, though it was the only thing to do. These men weren't going to make it much higher without courting disaster. I was on my way back to my tent in the storm when they began hollering out at me to ask if I'd carry Connor's photo up to the mountain on their behalf.

"It will really mean something to his parents," they said, "if you can get him to the top."

I took Connor's photo, placed it in my jacket pocket next to my heart, and agreed that I'd leave it at the summit when I got there. There was no "if" in my dialogue. My mind was steeled and determined to get to the top of this mountain. I'd never met Connor and knew nothing about him or his family other than the few facts the Tennesseans had given me. But in handing me a photo, they'd given me a sense of purpose that seemed infinitely more grand than the admittedly selfish motivations that had gotten me here thus far.

At the first lull in the storm, I took off again, travelling as light and fast as possible, using a technique championed by Mark Twight and other world-class climbers who'd made their names on speed ascents. I carried no tent, no sleeping bag, and just two days' supply of food and fuel, straight into another impassable blizzard at 5,250 metres. I staggered forward into the highest established camp on the mountain, known as "the Crow's Nest." My face and body were literally cracking from the beating of a howling minus-twenty-five-degree wind. There, I met a ranger who offered me shelter.

"You've got to get out of this storm," he screamed, his voice barely cutting through the wind.

I nodded, then held up my hands to shield my face from the wind as I screamed back at him, trying to explain my predicament. "I'm on a solo ascent," I shouted. "Alpine style. Can't take assistance from anyone."

He shook his head at me. He'd clearly dealt with people like me before. Then he continued screaming into the wind. "There's an old snow cave somewhere out there." He pointed off toward a cloud of billowing snow beyond the camp. "Some Russians dug it out a while back. Not sure if it's collapsed yet or not. Good luck finding it." Then he turned around and found his way back toward the shelter of his own tent. I looked toward the direction in which he had pointed. It seemed implausible that I would find anything out there, but I had to give it a try. I pushed forward, my hands outstretched in front of my face to break the wind as I went. For thirty minutes, maybe more, I wandered around searching for a small hole dug into the snow that would mark the entrance to the Russians' cave, employing a search and rescue technique I'd learned from a Royal Air Force pilot who'd once told me that if you're ever looking for a downed airplane in the middle of nowhere, you draw a large square on the ground and start closing in the edges of that perimeter until you're sure that you've searched every inch inside your original square. My search square had gone from large to small, and I was beginning to fear that all was lost, when my hand suddenly sunk into a hole the size of my torso. I dropped my pack next to the hole, got on my knees, and slid on my stomach through the hole. Once inside, I could see, despite having no headlamp, that I had found the cave that would become my home for the next four days. Chiselled by hand out of tightly packed snow, it was big enough to sleep three or four climbers. I unpacked a blue foam mat to serve as my bed and wedged my pack, along with some chunks of ice, into the hole to block out the wind. Then I fell asleep in my cave while the storm ravaged the mountain outside.

I had enough fuel and food to last two days only, but the storm lasted for four, so I began to ration both. Whenever I began asking myself why the hell I was there, I reminded myself of that little story about Hermann Buhl and the night he'd spent perched on a ledge the size of a footpeg near the top of Nanga Parbat. And when that didn't work, I thought of the little boy I'd never met but whose picture I'd said I'd leave at the top. No one would really care if I failed on this climb, except for me. And so I hardened my resolve and lay there in my dark, little snow cave like a man in solitary confinement. I began to view the storm for what it was: a temporary prison guard that would eventually take its leave. And when it did, I was ready.

The storm subsided, I repacked my gear, crawled out into the light, and carried on up the mountain. It was clear yet windy, with a 110-kilometre-per-hour crosswind cutting sideways over the ridge to the summit. By ten p.m. on my eleventh day on the mountain, I was standing on the highest peak in North America, gazing up at the Arctic sun, a field of clouds spreading out into the valley beneath my feet. I knelt in the snow, reached inside my jacket, and pulled out Connor's photo. I took a picture of it on the peak and placed him smiling in the snow. Then I pulled out the Ziploc bag filled with sacred rice, and an old photo of my own daughter. I looked at it and realized that Alexandra no longer resembled the girl in the photo I'd taken with me to the top of Aconcagua. I took a picture of the photo, then placed it back in my bag and headed down the mountain.

It was early morning, and I'd descended to just below the ice cave when I crossed paths with a fellow lone climber staggering through the wind and the long shadows cast by the clouds over the mountain. He looked tired and unfocused, and I got the impression he was pushing himself too hard. He said his name was Michael and that he was attempting a solo speed ascent.

"You should rest," I told him. "The conditions aren't good up there."

He brushed me off. "Nah, nah," he said. "I'm okay. Done this before."

His determination was more frustrating than noble—not unlike how mine must have seemed to the ranger who'd shaken his head and pointed me toward the ice cave.

"You sure?" I asked. "You really don't look good."

"Yeah, I'm sure."

I've often thought back on that brief encounter and wondered if there was anything more I should have said or done to dissuade him.

"All right, be careful up there," I said.

Two days later, I was standing in the Anchorage airport, waiting for a plane to land to take me back to Canada, when, for the second time in my life, I found myself purchasing a newspaper as the final souvenir of a climb.

The headline on the front page of that day's *Anchorage Daily News* read, "Denali Climber Falls to His Death."

I boarded my plane, sat down in my seat, and began reading Michael's obituary.

CHAPTER 10

THE DEATH NOTE

I was alone, hours removed from the nearest human being, and spitting up blood on the wooden floor of a Chilean shack at the base of the world's highest active volcano. I dragged my body across the floor toward a small wooden desk with a book on top. I tore a piece of paper from the book, laid it out flat on the floor, and began writing what I feared might be my last words.

I began the letter with instructions, written in Spanish, that should it be found resting by my corpse, it should be mailed to a woman in Quebec.

"I feel I'm about to die," I wrote. "Moments ago I tried to stand. My legs gave out. Yellow bile came out of me. Half an hour later, I tried to get up again. I fell to the floor, still trapped in my sleeping bag. I barely had the strength to drag myself to this desk."

I looked over at the cot from which I'd just crawled. There, a green stuffed frog I'd purchased in the Atlanta airport and nick-named Philippe lay on the bed, talking to me. I was hallucinating again. In my mind, the frog had come to save me. I'd brought him with me just to pose for a photo at the summit for Alex and for Annie's girls.

I tilted my head, squinted at the frog and struggled to snap back to reality.

I turned back to the letter at hand.

"I think I'm losing it," I wrote. "I'm scared."

* * *

More than two years had passed since Babu's memorial. I'd returned to my life in Iqaluit, where the only perk was the ample opportunity to test my stamina in the Arctic cold. The practice had served me well in my preparations for Nanga, Everest, and Denali, but by the time I got back from Alaska in July 2002, I wanted out of the Arctic. I'd given the north ten years of my life and was now forty-three years old. I wanted to move closer to home, if for no other reason than to be closer to Alexandra, who was still living with her mother in the Eastern Townships. I requested a transfer to Montreal. I didn't get what I wanted, but I did get closer than I'd been in years. NAV Canada dispatched me to the small town of Roberval, Quebec. I packed most of my belongings—which didn't amount to much more than three suitcases filled with climbing gear and another two filled with clothes and books and magazines about climbing—and departed for Roberval. When I arrived, I bought a couch and a mattress. Then I went out and bought a Volkswagen so that I could drive to Alexandra, and also to the cliff and ice walls that Patrice and I had climbed years earlier.

Annie and I had communicated sporadically by email for a year and a half after our first encounter. She'd reached out to me a few weeks before my forty-second birthday, asking if I had any plans. I told her no, that in reality I kind of hated my birthday. She asked if I'd be interested in joining her for a hike through the Laurentian Mountains, a small but ancient range that cut across Quebec. She knew I liked to hike and thought that experiencing the fall colours would make for a nice time. I considered it a date. I jumped in my Volkswagen and made for the Laurentians.

It didn't take long before she started asking me questions that made me contemplate the direction of my life.

"Why do you insist on climbing a rock, putting yourself in danger, and risking not seeing your daughter again?"

When I realized that I couldn't provide a satisfactory answer to her question in words, I decided to invite her to come with me on a future climb. I was just days away from a rock-climbing trip to the cliffs of Costa Blanca in Spain. It had taken me just over a year to build up enough money to finance another climb, and though it would be substantially less complicated than my last few expeditions, it offered a return to more technical climbing. Annie didn't accompany me on that trip, but it wasn't long before we were making plans for a journey to Mount Kilimanjaro in Tanzania. The highest point in Africa was, by all accounts, a very unadventurous stroll up a modest incline, but I hoped that taking Annie would help to answer some of the more philosophical questions she had about my passion.

I was excited to get to Kilimanjaro, not just for the prospect of climbing with a partner whom I was growing to love, but also because I planned to summit Mount Kenya as well. As the two highest peaks in Africa, both mountains were on my "to climb" list, although it was Mount Kenya, with its multitude of jagged-faced peaks, that excited the climber within.

Having already summitted Aconcagua and Denali, I was slowly working my way through the Seven Summits but still had my eye on the Seven *Second* Summits. Were I to succeed in Africa, there would be ten mountains left on my list. In South America, there was Ojos del Salado (6,893 metres) in Chile, that continent's second-highest peak; in North America, there was Mount Logan (5,959 metres), which rises above the Yukon; in Asia, Mount Everest (8,848 metres) and K2 (8,611 metres), the highest peaks in the world; in Europe, Russia's Mount Elbrus (5,642 metres), and Dykh-Tau (5,205 metres) in the Caucasus Mountains; in Antarctica, Vinson Massif (4,892 metres) and Mount Tyree (4,852 metres); and in Oceania, Indonesia's Puncak Jaya (4,884 metres) and neighbouring Puncak Mandala (4,760 metres). Because people couldn't seem to agree whether Oceania was an actual thing or not, I had Australia's Mount Kosciuszko (2,228 metres) and Mount Townsend (2,209 metres) on my list as well.

I had no idea how many years it would take me to get to the top of all of these mountains, but as I trained for Mount Kenya, I began dreaming of making 2003 the year in which I knocked off as many as possible. I set myself the goal of climbing six mountains that year. I would begin with the African mountains in the winter, then rip it halfway around the world to take a solo stab at Ojos del Salado in the high Chilean Andes. Afterwards, I would return to Roberval to do my job for a few months before taking off for the highest points in Europe.

In retrospect, the schedule I'd set was so ambitious that I was courting disaster, whether I knew it or not.

* * *

There's a story about a leopard frozen at the top of Africa's highest peak. Immortalized in the epigraph of "The Snows of Kilimanjaro," it has long stood as a metaphor for the danger of man's curiosity. But it's more than just a legend. In 1926, a frozen and mummified leopard was found close to the western summit. Its motivations for climbing to that altitude remain a mystery eighty years after its discovery. To some, "curiosity killed the cat." Others believed that the leopard had been lured by the scent of the climbers who'd gone before, leaving a trail in the snow. If the latter theory is true, then the leopard was no better than the men it was stalking. All were chasing a deadly prize.

I'd never actually read the Hemingway story. But I was familiar enough with the legend to think of it as I approached the base of Mount Kenya and came upon the rotting carcass of a leopard that looked like it had fallen to its death from the cliff above. I tried not to take it as an omen. If I stopped to ponder the hidden significance every time I saw a corpse on the side of a mountain, I'd never climb a thing.

It was late February 2003. I'd travelled solo to Nairobi, then taken a bus north through the Kenyan countryside to the ancient mountain from which the country borrowed its name. Soon I was wandering on foot through a village where, for centuries, the local tribes had been raised to worship the mountain, and where houses were still built in a way to ensure that all doors faced it. Before long, I stood at the foot of Mount Kenya's northern face. Its highest peak, the Batian summit, was first climbed by Sir Halford John Mackinder, a nineteenth-century politician and one of the founders of the London School of Economics. Mackinder's expedition made it to the top of Mount Kenya on September 13, 1899, nearly three months after departing Nairobi with the help of sixty-six Swahili and ninety-six local Kikuyu guides and porters to carry their gear. By contrast, I had arrived alone, with all of my gear strapped to my back. I wasn't just looking to repeat Mackinder's success; I wanted to put all the technical skills Pat had taught me to use in order to get to the top of Batian, and *then* I was going to succeed where Mackinder's team had failed. I would tie a line to an anchor at the top of Batian and rappel down its western face, cross a steep 250-metre ridgeline of volcanic rock straight out of Mordor with an equally sinister-sounding name—the Gate of the Mists—leading to the base of Mount Kenya's secondary peak, Nelion. At 5,188 metres, Nelion was eleven metres below Batian but had its own mystique.

Nelion was unclimbed until 1929, when it was approached via the Gate of the Mists by Percy Wyn-Harris and Eric Shipton, arguably the most significant British climbers active between the disappearance of George Mallory in 1924 and the triumph of Sir Edmund Hillary in 1953.

Wyn-Harris was an English knight and a governor of Gambia. Shipton, the son of a Ceylonese colonial tea planter, had travelled to Kenya to become a coffee grower. After successfully summitting the Nelion peak, the two were recruited back in London by Britain's Mount Everest Committee to carry on with attempts to fly the Union Jack atop that mountain. On their first trip to Everest in 1933, Wyn-Harris discovered an ice axe at 8,460 metres along the Northeast Ridge, which was later identified as belonging to Sandy Irvine, who'd gone missing alongside Mallory on June 8, 1924. The axe, which was discovered about twenty metres below the actual ridge, was the only trace of either Mallory or Irvine until 1991, when one of their oxygen tanks was discovered sixty metres farther up the Northeast Ridge. To this day, Irvine's body has not been found. (In 1999, Mallory was discovered lying face down, his hands digging into the side of the mountain some three hundred metres below and one hundred metres east of where Wyn-Harris found the ice axe.) It was Shipton, meanwhile, who, as leader of the 1935 and 1951 Mount Everest Expeditions, gave both Tenzing Norgay and Edmund Hillary their first jobs on Everest. Legend has it that he hired Tenzing because he liked the young Sherpa's ready smile. He hired Hillary on similar grounds, responding to a letter from the enthusiastic young Kiwi who'd written to him expressing interest in risking life and limb to join one of Shipton's expeditions.

Though it was a pleasure to walk in the footsteps of historic company, I wasn't on Mount Kenya to connect with the ghosts of the climbers who'd been there before. Nor was I conscious of all the lives that were connected, in some tangential way, to this mountain.

I wanted to repeat my success on Denali and climb this mountain alone. But the Kenyan government insisted that I be accompanied by one of their country's best climbers. He wasn't at the base of the mountain when I arrived. Nor was he with me later that day when I trekked into the first camp on the mountain, a little shack with a bunk bed. I walked outside the hut, fired up my camp stove, and was midway through boiling water to heat a bag of freeze-dried spaghetti when a local guide came running up to my cabin, screaming and waving his arms madly above his head.

"STOP!" he screamed. "STOP! STOP! STOP!"

I looked up, unsure whether my little propane fire ran counter to some local law. Then I saw a creeping shadow just a few feet away in the bushes. I was still staring at it when the guide reached me, grabbed my arm, and dragged me back into the hut. He slammed the door shut and pointed through a hole in the wall toward the place where the shadow had been but now was not.

"That leopard was going to eat you!" he said.

* * *

His name was Simon and he'd been dispatched to climb with me, as much to save me from the leopard's jaws as to make sure I didn't fall off a cliff. We spent a total of five days together, learning to trust one another as we clipped ourselves on to the same ropes, belaying each other's weight to secure against a fall as we made our way up the southeast face of Nelion before turning toward Batian. It was a beautifully technical climb that forced us up a vertical cliff wall. After a brief rest in a tiny tin-walled bivouac hut near the summit of Nelion, we rapelled down into the Gate of the Mists and carried on for Batian, again engaging in a technical rock climb. It was cloudy by the time we reached the summit of Batian. On a clear day, we would have been able to see Nairobi in the distance, but on this day, we could barely see the other jagged peaks on this mountain. Simon began howling into the clouds like a wolf baying at the moon. I followed suit, wondering as I did whether there was anyone below us who'd be able to hear. It wasn't until we'd rapelled down from Batian that we ran into difficulty. I'd opted not to carry gloves, crampons, or an ice axe with me. My decision seemed sound until we rapelled down to the Diamond Couloir. There, I watched as Simon put on his crampons, grabbed his axe, and started across a vertical wall of ice.

"Don't worry about me," I told him, watching as he clambered away. There was nothing for me to do but punch my fists into the ice, bloodying my knuckles, and kick my boots to get enough purchase to hold my weight on the sheer wall.

My hands were still all cut up, my knuckles looking like I'd been in a street fight, when I went to the Nairobi airport to pick up Annie for our jaunt to the top of Kilimanjaro.

The road between Nairobi and Kilimanjaro is well travelled, yet it remains trapped in another time: it's a red-dirt trail winding through fields of tall grass and sugar cane. The way to the mountain is busy too, with goat herders and tribesmen in ceremonial dress seeking the shade of marula trees. We were still more than an hour's drive from the base of the mountain when it suddenly appeared, its three volcanic cones creating a flattened peak that seemed as crisp and clean as a fresh white tablecloth. I knew, as soon as I saw it rising above the African savannah, why Kilimanjaro had captured the imagination of so many poets.

The Greco-Egyptian writer Claudius Ptolemy (circa AD 100 to 170) wrote of a "great snow mountain" south of the Nile. The mountain seemed to disappear from the Western consciousness with the fall of the Roman Empire but resurfaced in the nineteenth-century writings of a German missionary who wrote of having seen snow in the sky in the heart of Africa. His report seemed so fantastical that the Royal Geographical Society dispatched explorers to confirm the phenomenon's existence. The mountain was further entrenched in Western culture by Ernest Hemingway, who set his most famous short story at its base.

It was certainly breathtaking to behold; its equatorial snows seemed so out of place above the sunburnt countryside. In many ways, Kilimanjaro is as unique a marvel as Everest.

Hans Meyer, a German geographer, and his Austrian climbing partner, Ludwig Purtscheller, were the first to reach Kilimanjaro's summit in 1889. But to believe that is to believe that no member of the tribes that lived near it for millennia ever dared venture up its flanks. That's not to say that Kilimanjaro is an easy climb. Estimates vary, but close to 25,000 people attempt to climb it every year. Forty percent don't make it to the top, and three to seven climbers generally die on the mountain, mostly from altitude sickness. Another thousand are evacuated. So it isn't *that* easy, but with proper acclimatization, ample food and water, and adequate clothing, it may well have been possible to climb Kilimanjaro more than a thousand years ago. It's entirely possible that no one ever tried because it was taboo. The local Maasai believe that the slopes of Kilimanjaro are protected by spirits who freeze anyone who tries to climb it.

We exited our Land Cruiser, grabbed our packs, signed

up for a six-day, five-night all-inclusive trek accompanied by a Tanzanian guide named Festo, and started walking up Kilimanjaro's western flank toward the Shira Ridge. We'd opted for a speedier, less-congested route up Kilimanjaro, partly because we didn't want to get stuck with a horde of trekkers, and partly because it would allow us to approach the peak via the Western Breach, which would give us a modest yet fun scramble and force us to climb on our hands and feet before our summit day.

It was three p.m. by the time we reached our first camp, a palatial tent in comparison to my usual lodgings. A bowl of hot water to wash up awaited each of us. I'd barely cleaned the sweat and dirt of the mountain from my face when a porter arrived with a second bowl, this one containing popcorn. This was a unique type of climb for me, infinitely more luxurious than any of my other expeditions, but I kind of liked it, even if I did wake Annie up in the middle of the night, screaming out in my sleep, "Long live the ice!" The effect of global warming on the snow on top of Kilimanjaro must have been getting to me—that, and guilt for contributing to it.

Two nights later, we were up at 3,800 metres, camped out in a moorland meadow next to a stream, lying on the earth outside our tent, and admiring the stars sprawled out in the sky above. We moved slowly on the third day; Annie was feeling the effects of the altitude as we hiked over volcanic rock, passing what's known as the "Lava Tower," a sort of cork plugged into the side of the mountain, preventing it from spewing out lava. We had a brief rest, then made for a hut on a plateau surrounded by resourceful little cacti that grow out of the blackened earth beneath the snow line. On the fourth day, we reached our final camp, 4,300 metres above the sea. There, as we sat relaxing and talking, we met a sixty-three-year-old German man who'd come by our tent to say hello. He had a joie de vivre that was contagious. I couldn't help but smile at the vigour with which he pushed himself up the mountain as fast as men and women half his age. He told us that Kilimanjaro was his Everest. He wasn't a climber, but he'd always dreamt of "walking through the snows of Kilimanjaro." He had never bothered to try until he was diagnosed with a condition that sounded a lot like Lou Gehrig's disease.

"The doctors say I'll be dead in three years. I figured if I was going to climb this, it was now or never."

His story made me think, for the first time in a long while, about that little boy, Connor, whose picture I'd left on the top of Denali, and of all the little kids I'd met while crossing Canada, raising money for cystic fibrosis research. I didn't even know how many of them were still alive. I lay awake in my sleeping bag that night, looking at Annie, counting in my head all the ways I was lucky in my life. Then I drifted into a short sleep that was interrupted at midnight by a rustle outside our tent. It was Festo, getting ready for our summit push. I woke Annie. She rubbed the sleep from her eyes and got up with a tangled mix of excitement and exhaustion. I told her this was much the same as a midnight summit push from Camp 4 on Everest, except our bodies weren't dying from the extreme elevation. We drank hot chocolate, ate cookies, and headed up into one of those starry nights that can only be fully admired from a mountainside. The cool wind breezed down from the glacier, leaving me chilled as

I slowed my pace to match that of Annie and Festo, who were proceeding up the mountain at about half the speed I would normally have taken. I wasn't as properly attired as they, and though I found it hard not to shiver in their wake, I didn't say anything because I didn't want to ruin the experience for Annie.

This was her Everest too. She'd long dreamt of reaching its summit because, for her, it seemed the limit of what was actually possible. She wanted to know what it was like to climb in high altitude. I watched as she slowed her ascent and began to shiver. Five hours had passed since we'd left camp, and the cold was taking its toll. I called out to Festo, and told him that we had to take shelter from the wind so that Annie could warm up until sunrise. It was most important to me that Annie be able to get to the top of this mountain without being so cold as to ruin the experience. Festo navigated us toward a natural rock shelter to shield us from the wind. I hugged Annie in order to pass on my body heat as we admired the stars above and waited for the sun. She said she was tired and wavering. I told her to wait for the sun; it would be out soon, and once it was, we would be warm all the way up to the summit. She liked that.

We sat on my backpack, cuddled together and watched the sun shoot rays of yellow and red across the African sky. "This is the most beautiful sunrise I've ever seen," she declared.

"Me too."

Shortly after dawn, we carried on for the summit, reaching the outer rim of one of Kilimanjaro's volcanic craters by eight a.m. There, we came upon the lone German with three years to live. He was on his way back from the summit. He'd pushed through the cold of the night and had been the first man of the day to reach the top. I wondered if I'd have moved so fast were I climbing this mountain on my own. I wasn't convinced I would have, and it struck me that this man was climbing as if he were already dead. I could tell by the way he was glowing in the sun that it really meant something to him to know that he'd been able to accomplish this one last dream. He looked at Annie, who was still shivering, and told us, "It's worth every ounce of pain." His words seemed to motivate Annie in a way that mine could not, and soon she was back on her feet, determined to get to the summit as quickly as possible. Thirty minutes later, we were there together. I hugged her while she cried and thanked me for having shared my dream. I told her the very same thing. Without her there, I probably would have just scrambled up to the summit as quickly as possible and never appreciated it for what it was: a mountain as beautiful as any other on Earth.

* * *

I retched up blood from my throat and spat it out on the floor of the hut that I believed would be my tomb. Barely a week had passed since Annie and I had stood atop Kilimanjaro, feeling in love, even if we were both still too afraid to say it. We'd been so close in that moment, but now she was back in Montreal, and I was alone and writing my death letter at the base of a salt-covered mountain halfway around the world.

I'd thought of Annie almost the entire way down to Chile. We'd flown home to Montreal together from Nairobi. But I'd left her there, giving her a kiss and a hug before she retreated back to her life in the city while I carried on with mine, jumping on the first flight out of Montreal to Atlanta for a connecting flight to Santiago. I'd arrived in the city exhausted from two days' worth of flying, having travelled to Chile via Kenya with a circuitous and entirely impractical stop in Montreal. And I'd opted to save time by spending my first night in Chile sleeping on an overnight bus ride north, twisting and turning through the Chilean Andes en route to the small town of Copiapó, a mining town wedged, like most of Chile, between the Andes and the Pacific Ocean. There, I'd walked blurry-eyed straight into town from the bus station to pick up a four-by-four that I'd rented in order to drive into the surrounding hills to get to the base of the world's largest volcano. As I waited at the car rental depot for my four-by-four to arrive, I pulled out my notebook and began writing a list of things I thought Annie would like about Chile. I reached nine before the attendant handed me the keys to a jacked-up Toyota truck with massive tractor tires like the ones for driving over other cars at a demolition derby.

"This should get you to where you're going," the attendant said, pointing to a reserve fuel tank in the bed of the truck.

I knew Ojos del Salado was in a remote part of the country, but I didn't realize that it was so remote that I wouldn't see another human being for hours. The instructions I'd been given by a ranger in Copiapó were clear: "Stick to the main road until you see the mountain in the distance, then point the front of your truck toward the mountain and carry on off the road until you get to the base. There's a hut near the bottom of the mountain where you can sleep. There are no other climbers or trekkers in the area right now, so you'll have the mountain all to yourself."

It seemed like a dream come true to be in a place so remote, until I actually got there. Sometime between when I turned off the road and started bouncing over the dips and gullies of the barren rock and desert landscape surrounding the mountain, my excitement turned to unease. With no tracks in the dirt to guide my way, I simply did as I'd been told and pointed the nose of my truck toward the great peak on the horizon, taking only a passing glance at the strangely mummified carcasses of cows and vultures bleached by the sun and preserved in the salt deposits that lined the countryside. Nevado Ojos del Salado, which literally translates as "Snowy Eyes of Salt," got its name courtesy of the enormous salt lagoons on the mountaintop that, when first viewed from the countryside, must have looked like massive human eyes to the Spanish conquistadors or whoever gave it its name.

I was ill by the time I reached the base of the mountain. I leaned out the driver's side door and spat on the rock below to keep from vomiting. It was no use. I heaved blood and vomit all over the desert ground outside the hut. By the time I dragged my gear from the truck and threw it on the floor of the hut, I was barely strong enough to stand.

I had no idea what was wrong with me. Had the journey here drained my energy? Had the salt air dehydrated me? Had I contracted something in one of the meals I'd eaten on the bus ride from Santiago? I felt my forehead; it was burning up. My legs buckled and I collapsed into a cot. There I lay in a cold sweat, too scared to sleep for fear I'd never wake up. Then came the hallucinations. I knew I was dying when a talking frog told me he was here to save me. I shook the vision from my head, then fell out of the cot, onto the floor, and dragged my body over to the desk with the guest book on it.

I concluded my letter to Annie by writing, "I know now that I never wanted to die alone." Then I placed it on the table next to my cot and coughed more blood into my hand. I lay down but fought to stay awake.

"If I get out of here, things will be different," I told myself. "Things will be different."

I trembled with fever. I did all I could do to keep myself awake, conversing with myself and the little stuffed frog, for fear that sleep would lead to certain death. It was three a.m. when I last checked my watch. Then I passed out.

When I opened my eyes again, it was ten a.m. The sun was peeking through the slats in the wall of the hut. I touched my face to make sure I was still alive. I got up. I walked past the bloodstains on the floor and wondered what in the hell had happened to me. I stepped outside into the sunshine and looked up at Ojos del Salado. I estimated it would take me two days to reach the peak. It would be one hell of an adventure given that I wasn't likely to see another human so long as I was out here. Then I looked down to the truck. I'd parked it with the nose facing away from the mountain, back toward the road that was now out of sight, so I wouldn't get lost when I tried to get out of here.

I was torn. The prudent choice would be to leave this place and head home to recover. But for some reason, I couldn't stop thinking of my father, what he'd say if he'd lived to see me come home without having even given the mountain a try.

"You got sick did you? Thought you were going to die? And

then you walked out on your own two feet? You coward. You didn't even try. Don't tell me that you're done. If you're still standing, you're not done."

It had been a long time since I'd thought about my father, and even longer since I'd let him get to me.

I found myself suited up and heading up the mountain with nine litres of water strapped to my back, alongside everything else I'd need. By day's end, I was urinating a deep shade of yellow. I'd drank a litre of water, but it hadn't made a difference. My body was spent. I looked up from the mountainside at the condors swooping overhead, so beautiful in the sky. It took a while before I realized they were circling over me. I stopped. I turned around. I started the long journey home in defeat.

CHAPTER 11

THE HEART OF THE MOUNTAIN

The only time Annie ever came to visit me in Roberval, she arrived with a friend. She made the five-hour drive from Montreal sometime after my return from Ojos del Salado. I'd considered giving her my death note, but then I thought I should keep it for myself, to analyze the things that had gone through my head in my darkest hour. It seemed like something I should reread. I kept it out on my kitchen counter for a few days upon my return to Roberval. But then I put it away into a box and forgot about it.

There was a knock at the door. I rushed from the kitchen to let Annie into my world. I was ecstatic to see her. She was surprised to see how I lived. She hadn't spent more than five minutes inside my place before asking the most obvious question to anyone's eyes but my own: "Where is all your stuff?"

"What stuff?"

"You know, your stuff."

I looked around my apartment. It didn't seem so barren.

I had a couch. Beside it were some boxes, which doubled as coffee tables. I had a mattress, though no box spring, in my bedroom. A single picture hung on my wall: a mounted poster of K2, which Jacques Olek had given me years earlier and that I brought with me everywhere I moved.

Annie followed me into the kitchen and shook her head when she noticed the empty space next to the countertop where a stove would usually go. "It's like you're camping in this apartment."

I shrugged and smiled. My life was minimalist. I enjoyed knowing that everything I owned could be packed up into the trunk of a Volkswagen Jetta. I didn't want for anything other than human companionship.

Suddenly, I didn't want to be in my apartment anymore, and I got the sense that she didn't either.

"Let's get out of here."

In 2003, Roberval was a small logging town of ten thousand people and very much on the decline. I was there to run an aeronautical study for NAV Canada, who were considering a shutdown of operations in the town. There wasn't much to see or do in town, so we spent most of our time hiking the Laurentians, which had lost much of their size over the years. Among the oldest mountains in the world, the Laurentians stood supreme over North America about 500 million years ago. Then, they were as high as the modern-day Sierra Nevada in eastern California. Now, they are a rocky plateau eroded by glaciers and wind.

The highest point in the Laurentians was just a three-hour drive from my house, but at a modest 1,166 metres, it had never excited me enough to make the journey. We hiked through the hills and valleys of the Laurentians, both of us dreaming of lives that weren't quite as emotionally eroded as the ones we'd been living. We were both carrying baggage and damage from our previous marriages, and neither of us was quite ready to jump into a new life together. So we took it slow. I tried my best not to talk about all the mountains I still wanted to climb, for fear it would bore her or scare her. And I think she tried not to tell me of all the ways she feared I might leave her.

It was a beautiful weekend, and then it was gone.

Sometime later, while sitting alone in my undecorated little apartment, I received a call from a stranger who said he'd gone to university with my little brother Jacques. The stranger's name was Sylvain Bédard. He said he wanted to climb Mont Blanc, the highest peak in all the Alps. I told him that sounded nice and asked how I could be of service. I said I'd never been to Mont Blanc and had never guided anyone anywhere. I hadn't even been to the Alps. He said that was okay. The highest thing he'd ever climbed was Mont Tremblant, and he'd only made it halfway up in three hours. I listened, curious how this seemingly weak and terribly inexperienced climber thought he'd get to the top of Mont Blanc. He'd just conceded, after all, that his biggest mountaineering success was a failed hike up the side of a ski hill in the Laurentians.

"How do you expect to do this exactly?" I asked.

"I don't know," he replied. "I was hoping you could help me."

Mont Blanc hadn't been foremost on my mind, but there was something about it that captured my attention too. That was the mountain on which modern climbing was born. Climbing wasn't really a sport or even an understood pastime until 1786, when Jacques Balmat (a local goat herder) and Michel-Gabriel Paccard (a physician) climbed to the top of Mont Blanc in what was, at the time, a truly inspired quest to do what few in the world believed possible. More than a century later, Eric Shipton, leader of the 1935 and 1951 British Mount Everest Expeditions, wrote of Balmat and Paccard's Mont Blanc summit as "one of the greatest in the annals of mountaineering." Balmat and Paccard had carried out their climb untethered to anything (not even each other). Their only tools on the mountain were their alpenstocks—long wooden poles with an iron spike tip, more commonly found in the hands of a shepherd than a mountaineer. Many of history's greatest climbers had followed in Balmat and Paccard's footsteps to the top of Mont Blanc over the years (including most of the earliest members of Britain's failed Mount Everest Expeditions), albeit with the use of the alpenstock's much more modern replacement: the ice axe. Because of the mountain's proximity to many of the major capitals of Europe, Mont Blanc has, in recent years, been overrun by the thirty thousand climbers who attempt its summit every year. It is one of the most crowded mountains in the world (an average of two hundred people reach the summit on a summer day) as well as one of the most deadly, claiming the lives of an estimated one hundred hikers every year.

I told Sylvain that Mont Blanc had a reputation for being overrun by novice climbing-tourists. He assured me he wasn't "one of those people." Then he told me his story.

When he was thirteen years old, he learned that he had a heart condition that would eventually kill him. He'd made the discovery in the most painful way after his older sister had gone out for a jog and dropped dead. When the doctors tried to figure out why, they found that she had a rare condition in which her heart muscle grew and grew and grew. It was a condition she'd been born with, as had Sylvain. For the next twenty years of his life, he was forced to forego exercise for fear that his heart would grow. But by the time he was thirty-two, his heart was nearly spent. He had tried to have a good life. He was a theatre carpenter and had toured the world with a giant puppet show. He had married an actress and fathered four children, all the while knowing that his heart was dying.

"I've been given a new life," he said, explaining how in the summer of 2000, he'd kissed his wife and kids goodbye, then gone into surgery to have his old heart removed and replaced with that of a donor.

"I've always wanted to climb," he said. "But I was never able to until now. Can you help me?"

I told him he had me at Mont Blanc. Then I jumped in my Volkswagen and drove down to Longueuil to meet him and his family. He introduced me to his five sons, the last of whom had been born after Sylvain got out of the hospital. He explained how he'd seen Mont Blanc years earlier and dreamt of climbing it, knowing he couldn't because of his condition. When he'd woken up in the hospital after the transplant, he told his doctor that he wanted to use his new heart to get to the top of that mountain.

The doctor told him, "Just leave this hospital on your own two feet, and we'll see to the climb later."

"No one with a heart transplant has ever done what I'm trying to do," Sylvain told me. "I want to be the first."

I thought of what Babu might say if he'd been there. I told Sylvain that this wasn't a good enough reason to do it.

"If I can create enough awareness to have just one person sign an organ donation card, then my job will be done," he replied. "And if I can inspire other people waiting for different organ transplants not to give up, then that's a bonus."

"There you go," I said. Then I offered to do something I'd never done before. "I can lead your expedition if you want me to," I said.

The next thing I knew, I was scrambling around my apartment, writing letters to the French government in search of a climbing permit, and looking at potential corporate sponsors to support our climb. I'd been fortunate in my own career to secure a long-standing partnership with The North Face, the San Francisco–based clothing company that specialized in mountaineering gear. The discount they gave me on their gear became essential to the economic feasibility of my expeditions. I had no idea how many companies would want to take the risk of sponsoring a man with a heart condition trying to climb to the top of one of the highest mountains in the world. How little I knew.

Before long, I was sitting in a high-end Montreal restaurant alongside Sylvain and his cardiologist, Dr. Michel White, who had signed on for the climb even before I had. We were being wined and dined by a vice president from a potential sponsor— Merck Frosst, the Canadian subsidiary of one of the largest pharmaceutical companies in the world.

The carpaccio wasn't yet off the table when Sylvain started laying out his plans to the executive in the expensive suit, while

I tried to smooth-talk him with stories of how my grandfather had been the main pharmacist in Lac-Mégantic. The executive listened intently to Sylvain's pitch, then he turned directly to me and asked, "These guys, they don't have any experience. Do you really think they can make it?"

I leaned into his question, exuding more confidence than I actually had: "If they train with me, they can make it."

And just like that, our entire expedition was financed.

But I still had a problem: I was the only experienced climber on a team of five. Sylvain and his cardiologist had recruited a professional photographer with absolutely no climbing experience to document the trip. Meanwhile, a good friend of mine named François had also joined our team. Deathly afraid of heights, François had asked to join the expedition in memory and tribute to his late father, who had also received a heart transplant.

There was no way I could safeguard all their lives by myself. I needed a seasoned climber to serve as a guide on the expedition, so I called Patrice and invited him on what I said might be the most altruistic journey of our lives. I needed Pat, not just to rope himself to two of the climbers on the way up the mountain, but also to help them train and adequately prepare for the adventure while I arranged all the paperwork.

Once that was sorted, I walked into my boss's office and told him I'd need to take a brief leave to take a guy with a new heart to the top of France. I got my leave to lead my first expedition to the Alps. Then I tacked on a few extra weeks so that I could make a quick jaunt over to Russia and take a run at Elbrus and, time permitting, Dykh-Tau as well.

As had become our tradition, I spent the day before my

departure visiting Alexandra. She was twelve years old and beginning to understand more and more about the dangers of what I did in my spare time. If she was worried about me, she showed it only by giving me another necklace to keep me safe on my way up the mountain. Then she hugged me, and I told her again how I loved her more than the stars, and the moon, and even the mountains.

Sylvain was making news even before we arrived at the airport. *Le Journal de Montréal*, the *Globe and Mail*, *La Presse*, Radio-Canada, and several others were keen to cover his attempt to climb. Of all of us, I think Sylvain's cardiologist, Dr. White, was the most concerned about the adventure. There was no telling how Sylvain's heart, which had been cut out of a downed motorcyclist's chest and stitched into his own, would react to the increased altitude. All climbers know that their hearts beat faster and faster at higher altitudes. It was generally understood among doctors that any patient with a heart condition shouldn't even visit high altitudes, let alone exert too much energy, because of the risks involved. Dr. White had helped to keep Sylvain alive in the hospital both before and after his operation. Now he was as much responsible as I was for keeping Sylvain alive on the mountainside. He arrived at the base of Mont Blanc carrying medical instruments and equipment, as well as the burden of having told Sylvain's wife (just as I had) that we would take care of her husband up on the mountainside.

I was confident in my ability to guide our team to the summit, but I was really concerned about his heart. I knew he was strong, but he was taking a cocktail of about thirty pills a day just to keep his heart pumping enough blood to power his body.

He must have sensed my concern, because before we'd even taken our first few steps up the mountain, he took me aside and said, "Gabriel, if we don't make it to the top, I'm okay with that. So long as we do our best."

The heat during the first few days of the climb was enough to make even me question my resolve. We dropped our bags at the base of the Grand Couloir, a cliff face that's less dangerous when it's covered in ice than when it's clear because of the mountain's constant habit of dropping massive rocks down its sides, wiping out climbers as they struggle to get from one side of the Grand Couloir to the other. It was clear of ice when we arrived. We pitched our tents at the base of the couloir, then scampered upwards for a closer view of what we would have to climb come morning. That's when we saw him: an older man crossing the couloir in a lineup of other climbers, all of them trying to time their crossing to coincide with the brief moment when the thirty-five-degree heat wasn't causing the mountain to spit rocks down on them from on high. We were admiring the view surrounding the couloir, looking down at our day's accomplishments, when we heard screaming from the opposite direction. We turned back toward the couloir, only to learn that the older climber had slipped and fallen two hundred metres down the couloir to his death. I looked at Sylvain, who was visibly shaken, then at Dr. White, who was equally unnerved. I reminded them that we didn't actually have to go any higher. They said nothing.

We returned to our tents, started boiling water on our stoves, ate some spaghetti, and talked through the sunset, re-evaluating our purpose on the mountain. The photographer and François were beginning to lose their resolve. They would soon drop out of the climb. But for Patrice, this was his one and only return to the high-altitude mountaineering of his youth. For Dr. White, it was a chance to advance medical science. For Sylvain, it was a means to inspire. For me, it was a break from my previous climbs, which had all been about my own ambitions to get to the top. It didn't matter that I'd secretly wanted to be a guide for several years now or that I'd hoped this trip would help me transition to a life wrapped almost entirely around the mountains. As far as I was concerned, this climb was more about everyone else on my team. And that's what made it special.

Periodically throughout the climb, we'd stop to rest and monitor our hearts. None of us was more surprised than Dr. White to see that his patient was reacting less to the altitude than the rest of us. That discovery, however, meant that it was important to keep Sylvain moving in order to keep his heart, which wasn't beating as heavily as the rest of ours, pumping fast enough to power his body forward.

On our sixth and final day on the mountain, we hiked straight into a blinding fog. Wet snow fell on our faces. Patrice and I guided our way entirely by instinct with barely five metres of visibility. I looked at Sylvain. He was breathing slowly, and his heart had slowed along with our pace. We'd have to get moving again soon if we were going to keep him upright and strong. I was still searching for a clear view when Sylvain leaned in to remind *me* that we didn't actually have to get to the top. For a while, I didn't think we would.

I might as well have mapped out the rest of our route up the mountain with my eyes closed. I couldn't see a thing through the fog. But I started guiding anyhow. "Let's go, guys," I said. "We'll find our way."

I was nervous yet strangely confident. Something inside me seemed to believe that if I simply kept us moving, the fog would reward us for our efforts and dissipate just before we reached the summit. The mountain owed us nothing, but I had faith that our motivations were pure enough that she might show us leniency. I wish I could say there was more to it than that—that my instincts were based on anything more than blind faith. But in the moment, I had nothing else to go on.

By mid-morning, the blanket of fog had dissipated into sporadic pockets. The top of Mont Blanc lay clear within sight. I closed my eyes and thanked the mountain for not letting me lead our team over a cliff to our deaths. I raced forward on our final approach with a camera in my hand so that I could turn around and document the moment when Sylvain and Dr. White reached the summit. I thought I understood just how lucky we were to be there. But as I watched Sylvain break down in tears, I realized that his gratefulness was coming from a much deeper place than mine. He dropped to his knees and pressed his face to the snow. Then he pulled out a picture of his sister and held it in front of him. I thought of my brother Claude. It wasn't long before I was brushing tears from my cheeks as well. Then Sylvain did something I'll never forget. He let go of the photo of his sister and watched as the wind carried her away from the peak.

For the second time in my life, I'd borne witness to a historic first on the mountainside. Sylvain was the first heart transplant recipient to reach the peak of Mont Blanc with full autonomy. It was a beautiful moment, one that kept me reflecting on the loved ones in my life as Patrice and I said goodbye to Dr. White and Sylvain and the rest of the team and then carried on to some of the famous spires of Mont Blanc. I would be alone again by week's end, after boarding a flight to Russia to climb Elbrus. And it would feel strangely empty to be back on a mountain all by myself with no greater purpose than to knock another hill off my list.

* * *

I flew to Moscow first and spent a day wandering around Red Square, before catching a flight to a small town in southwest Russia named Mineralnye Vody, near the Georgian border and the Caucasus Mountains. I jumped into the passenger seat of a four-by-four and made for Elbrus with a very talkative local who spent his days chauffeuring foreign mountaineers to and from the airport, and who missed no opportunity to point out that his family had lived in the area since before the first climber ever summitted any of the mountains that looked down upon his ancestral home.

The base of Europe's largest mountain was awash with police and search and rescue teams. Chris Alexander, a Canadian diplomat from the embassy in Moscow, was also there. Two Canadian brothers had recently wandered off the summit, away from their climbing group, to take a picture of Elbrus's secondary peak just as a freak storm cloud set in. The brothers had gotten lost in the blinding winds and driving rain and snow that pelted the peak at more than one hundred kilometres an hour. The storm had rolled off the Black Sea and wreaked havoc on the mountain for days.

I offered to join one of the search parties, but I was too late. The search was being abandoned.

"We think they wandered blindly into a crevasse near the peak," Alexander told me. "There's not really much hope here anymore."

As the search parties began to disband, talk at the base turned toward what would happen if they couldn't recover or even locate the bodies. I cringed at the thought because I knew what that would mean for the climbers' family back home. It meant no funeral, no death certificate, no closure.

"What day did you say they were last seen?" I asked.

"June 22. Last Sunday."

I did the math in my head. I shivered when I realized that the brothers had disappeared into the fog here on Elbrus at almost the same time as I was leading my team blindly into the fog on Mont Blanc. The parallel gave me the creeps and made me wonder, not for the first time, what kept me safe where others died.

It wasn't often that I allowed myself to dwell on these things while climbing. I felt uneasy reflecting on what had brought me here. Was it vanity? Pride? Genuine curiosity? It troubled me that I no longer knew. I'd warned Sylvain on our descent from Mont Blanc days earlier that he would now have to listen to the mountains calling out to him in his head. "There will be other mountains now that you'll want to climb," I told him. "It will be a struggle to fight the urge to push yourself higher than you are right now." It hadn't occurred to me at the time, but what I was really doing was trying to steer him away from the sirens' call. "The mountains," I'd told him, "have a way of speaking to all of us."

As I loaded my pack onto my back, stretched out my arms, and walked out of base camp, my mind was fixated on the two brothers. I wondered what the mountain had said to them that led them to wander away from their group at the exact moment when the storm clouds rolled in. I beat that question around in my head as I climbed, listening to the wind above and the sound of the rocks crunching beneath my feet. What was it that had drawn me to come here all by myself? Why was I so determined to tackle the Seven Summits?

I carried on for the summit despite the nagging questions in my head. Having already acclimatized the previous week on Mont Blanc, I reached the summit of Elbrus in just two days and with relative ease. I was the only human being there and in a peculiar state of mind. I stared out over Europe from its highest point, catching not a single glimpse of civilization. Facing east, I squinted out over the Caspian Sea and combed the horizon for Asia. But between Asia and me stood a great, white, mountainous wall—the Bezengi Wall, a natural fortress dividing two continents. Anchored by Europe's third-highest mountain, Shkhara, and just across a valley from the slightly higher Dykh-Tau, the wall stood supreme over everything else I could see. I listened to nothing but the gentleness of the wind. It felt like a whisper in my ear. Then I looked west, struggling to calculate the 8,300-kilometre distance between where I stood and the place I called home. I had never felt homeless, but as I stared out over the Caucasus, down into Georgia and out toward the Black Sea and beyond, I felt, for the first time since I began climbing, that my life was stuck in a holding pattern. Somewhere out there was a desolate little apartment that I had no interest in ever returning to again. The wind seemed to whistle as it circled me, and suddenly I was screaming. The sound coming from me was guttural, almost animalistic, the type generally reserved for the release of frustrations. It was strangely calming. Then I stopped, breathed in the mountain air, and screamed again.

"I LOVE YOU, ANNIE!"

I listened as my words echoed through the Caucasus. It was as if the mountains were screaming them back at me, the four words I hadn't yet built up the courage to say to the woman herself.

I stepped down from the peak, feeling more relieved to have screamed my feelings out on the mountaintop than to have climbed to the top. I felt strangely content and ready to descend. But my happiness disappeared the moment I remembered the look of sorrow on the faces of the men and women in the valley below. I halted my descent and took some time to wander around the glacier that draped itself over the peak of Elbrus and down its mighty slopes, searching for clues—a footprint, a dropped axe, anything that might reveal the location of the climbers' bodies. But it was no use. The men were gone and there was nothing that I or anyone else could do to find them up there.

I watched from a distance as Chris Alexander packed up his belongings and left the mountainside, along with members of the climbers' family who'd come here filled with hope for a rescue. I thought of Alex and Annie. This climb had helped me to realize that I had to throw myself into a life with Annie, just as I had thrown myself into a life with the mountains. I was anxious to return home and tell Annie and Alex how much I loved them.

But I returned to the base feeling more sad than happy about this climb. My ascent had been so easy that my success left me feeling hollow, almost guilty.

Emotionally, I was ready to go home, but there was still something holding me to this place. Dykh-Tau and Shkhara were still out there. I felt torn between the competing voices in my head. The mountains on one side, the woman on the other. But there was a third voice in there too. It was fainter now than before, but it was still there. It was my father's voice, and its message was clear: *"Ce n'est pas assez, Gabriel."* ("Still not good enough, Gabriel.")

Why are you trying to please him? I asked myself. *He's dead. I'm not here to please him. I'm here to prove him wrong.*

I travelled deeper into the Caucasus, setting myself up for failure as I journeyed straight into an impenetrable storm at the base of the Bezengi Wall.

CHAPTER 12

BACK IN HILLARY'S FOOTSTEPS

It bothered me, the way she trembled as she cried. But not as much as it bothered me knowing that I was the source of all her pain. That it was the choice I had made that was causing her to shake and sob in public. I had never wanted to hurt her. I had never wanted to hurt anybody.

She was bawling her eyes out now, forcing out the words between deep fits of heaving. "I don't even understand why you climb. Think of your daughter. What am I supposed to say to her if you die?"

I could dangle with one arm from an overhanging cliff and pull myself to within sight of the top of the world, but I'd never been able to address the question of why I climbed, let alone the bigger question: *What if?*

I opened my mouth but no words came out. I placed my hands on her shoulders, tried to wipe away her tears, and told her, "I'll be okay, I'll be okay. Everything is going to be okay." But there wasn't much I could say to calm her. She knew, just as I did, that there was nothing I could do to make sure that everything would actually be okay.

We'd been sitting at a coffee shop in Montréal-Trudeau airport for just under an hour, waiting for the last possible moment before I would be forced to disappear into a security line and make for the gate and the airplane that would begin my long journey back to the Himalaya. Back to Everest. Back to the Death Zone.

It was mid-afternoon on March 12, 2005, and I sat alone with Annie, aware, for the first time, just how damaging the climb could be to those closest to me. I understood her fear. She had good reason to be afraid. But I needed her to be strong. In many ways, I wanted nothing more than to stay with her. And yet I was desperate to leave her so that I could just go, get on my plane, and climb. I had absolutely no idea how to react. So I barely reacted at all.

It was the first time I'd ever seen her cry. I felt terrible. Terrible about myself. Terrible about my life. Terrible about my every single accomplishment on the mountains up to that point. What was it all worth? What was any of this worth? She wasn't telling me to stay. She didn't have to. I knew what she wanted even if she wasn't saying it.

We sat there in silence, both of us wishing this moment would last forever and yet also wishing it had never happened at all.

I hugged her once more. She stole a glance at her watch as she draped her arm over my shoulder.

"You have to go," she said.

I pulled back. "I have to go."

Her eyes were welling up again, but she was fighting back the tears. I breathed deeply, grabbed my bag, held her hand, and repeated the only thing I could think to say: "Everything will be okay."

Then I left her. I was gutted for the entire duration of my thirty-hour journey to Kathmandu and then onwards to Lukla. I felt shaky, cold, lonely, and lost as I exited the plane in Lukla and began retracing my own footsteps back through the rhododendron forest and into the moraines left in the wake of the glacier.

My journey back to Everest had begun with a simple phone call a year earlier, during a brief moment in my life when I'd managed to find relative happiness away from the mountains. It was the dead of summer 2004. More than a year had passed since I'd returned home from Russia, and I'd given as much of myself as possible to what my friends and family called "a normal life." I wanted to settle down with Annie and see if I could replace my urge to climb with the equally thrilling urge to be a real family man, to be there for her, her three daughters, and Alexandra. But it wasn't easy. My work was a five-hour drive from Annie's home in Montreal, and I spent more time that year on the road in my Volkswagen than I did either with her or on any mountainside. For a while, I didn't actually care that I wasn't climbing. Pursuing this new life seemed as great an adventure as any I might have in the Himalaya, the Andes, or the Caucasus. I put my dreams of climbing the Seven Summits and the Seven Second Summits on hold and, for the first time in years, seemed able to go on the Internet without finding myself staring at pictures of K2, Everest, Ojos del Salado, and other mountains. Then came the phone call that changed everything. It was from Sean Egan, the professor from Ottawa whom I'd met at Everest Base Camp four years earlier. Sean and I had become close friends on the mountainside that spring and had kept in touch upon our return. He'd visited me in Iqaluit, where he'd spent his summers working with Inuit and aboriginal youth up on Baffin Island.

I was always pleased to hear his Irish voice. He'd call me periodically to chat about his ongoing research into the psychology of climbers facing extreme physical challenges. I don't know exactly when he decided that in order to complete his research, he would have to face the extreme physical challenge himself. But by the time he called me, he was already committed and funded, not just to take his studies up to the top of Everest, but to become the oldest Canadian ever to do so.

"So you're joining the fucked-up bunch," I teased, reminding him of his earlier description of high-altitude climbers.

He laughed. "I've always said it's the simple things in life that are the hardest things to do."

"So this should be easy then?"

He laughed again, then told me a Buddhist mantra he'd been repeating to his students for years. "We've got to live in the present, Gabriel. You know how it is. The past is gone; the future has not come. There's no good to be had worrying about the things that haven't happened."

It was a long road for both Sean and me to get back to Everest. Sean had built himself a team to help guide him to the top, and at the same time, he was training for what would be the first real mountaineering experience of his life. Meanwhile,

I'd gone through the old motions of scraping together every loose dime I could find to help finance my climb, begging my employer for another leave to take a crack at Everest. Raising the requisite fifty thousand dollars for the climb wasn't easy, but neither was trying to justify my urge to Annie. She knew that climbing was my passion. She'd listened as I explained to her during our earliest days together that "for me, the mountain is like oxygen." But I don't know how well she appreciated that I actually needed to climb to survive. My lack of climbing during the twelve months that followed my return from Russia prevented us from having to deal with what would become the most trying element of our future relationship: the unending struggle to differentiate between passion and obsession. I told her I needed to go back to Everest, and she told me it sounded more like I *wanted* to. I told her there was an absence in my life without the climb, and she told me she understood, then offered up her full emotional support even though I knew she was terrified. I tried to recycle Sean's mantra, the one about how there was no good to be had from worrying about the things that hadn't happened yet. But it did little to settle her fears.

By late March 2005, I was attending an Ottawa fundraising gala in Sean's honour. I hadn't officially joined his expedition and had, instead, opted to return to Everest as part of a small expedition run by Babu's old company, but Sean and I had made plans to time our final ascent up the mountain together so that we might stand at the summit and celebrate our mutual accomplishments as friends. Now he was introducing me to his son, Seamas, a twenty-one-year-old university student whom Sean had referred to as "Seamas the famous."

"His mother and I named him after a little black donkey," Sean liked to say.

I could tell by the way Sean toyed with his son that the two were close. At one point during the party, Seamas took me aside and expressed his concerns for his father.

"I know you and my dad have a special bond. In a lot of ways, he admires you. He doesn't like to fail. That's my biggest concern. That he'll push himself too hard. Please, take care of my dad."

I nodded and assured Seamas that I'd do my best to take care of his father, then told him the same thing I told Annie days later when I left her at the airport.

"Everything will be okay."

* * *

I was hot, exhausted, and demoralized by the time I trekked into Namche Bazaar. Three days had passed since I'd watched Annie fall apart at the airport. I was haunted by it. Sean and his team were days behind me and I was alone, struggling with the image of Annie distraught and shattered. I finally arrived at a cabin on the outskirts of the Sherpa town. I dropped my knapsack on the cot, pointed the antenna on my satellite phone toward a hole in the clouds where I could see stars, and called Annie back in Montreal.

"I don't want to do this," I told her. "I'm coming home. I'll see you soon. It will be better."

Her response surprised me.

"You have to stay there."

"I have no purpose here."

"If you come home, you'll be miserable."

"But I want to be with you."

"I'll be fine," she said, her voice quavering. "You need to do what you went there to do."

I went to bed that night feeling guiltier about my decision to climb than I'd ever felt in my entire life. How was it that this woman was able to say all the right things to keep me out here even when I knew she wanted nothing more than for me to come home? Lying on my cot that night, I asked myself the most unanswerable question of all: *Why am I here? Why are any of us really here?* Then I turned off my headlamp and waited for the dawn.

That morning, I carried on, more confused than enthused. I continued hiking for days up over the moraine until I reached Babu's chorten. I kneeled down next to it, unzipped the top of my pack, and pulled out the rice he'd given me five years earlier. I held the rice in my hand and looked at the keepsakes and mementoes that others had left behind. Babu had touched many lives as a climber. Mine was just one of them.

I placed my hand on his chorten. "Hi, Babu," I said. "It's me, Gabriel." I paused, unsure what more to say. A few trekkers passed by me and I felt self-conscious. It had been eight years since I'd last visited my brother's grave—longer still since I'd last tried to speak to anyone from beyond. I looked over my shoulder to see if anyone else was coming. Then I looked back to the chorten, closed my eyes, and asked Babu to help guide and protect me up on the mountain. And to help protect Sean too.

I got back on my feet and placed a rock on his chorten as a spiritual gesture to keep the bad spirits away.

It was dark when I trekked into Lobuche, the second-last village on the trek to base camp. It was cold and dark as I dropped my bag on the wood plank floor inside a drafty lodge that served as an inn. I was too tired to care about the sound of rodents scurrying beneath the floor. I lay on the cot while snow blew in through the spaces between the wall planks. I filtered the sound of the wind and the rats from my mind, closed my eyes, and concentrated on sleeping. For a few brief moments, I dozed in and out to the sound of a distant cough. It was a constant cough, incessant, almost rhythmic. At first I thought it was just inside my head. Then I opened my eyes and realized it wasn't that distant after all. It was coming from a room down the hall. It was a deep, pained cough. I knew it well. I'd had the same cough five years earlier when my lungs had filled with fluid. For ten minutes, I lay in my bed, listening as the cough got louder and deeper. Then I got up, walked down the hall, and knocked on the door of the room.

A man opened the door. I said hello and told him that I just wanted to meet my neighbours. He said his name was Iain, then pointed to his wife, who was sitting upright on her cot, leaning forward and struggling to breathe. Her name was Helen. They were first-time trekkers from Scotland, trying to fulfill a dream of climbing to Everest Base Camp, but their guides had left them when Helen had trouble keeping up and developed what they'd called "the Khumbu cough."

I listened to her cough as he spoke. It sounded worse than the typical Khumbu cough.

"She started losing her strength a few days ago," Iain said, explaining how he'd watched helplessly, unsure what to do, as his wife deteriorated to the point that she could only climb stairs on her bottom, lifting herself up one stair at a time. "She can't eat or walk."

I nodded calmly. I suspected that his wife had pulmonary edema, but I was no doctor and didn't want to alarm him yet.

I ducked back into my room, pulled out an oximeter, and asked if I could check the oxygen level in Helen's blood. Then I checked her finger, tested it, and found her oxygen was at 27 percent, six points lower than mine had been the night I nearly died.

I told Iain that as far as I was aware, the level of oxygen in his wife's blood was incompatible with life.

"Your wife needs to get to lower elevation immediately," I said.

"The Sherpa here told us to head back in the morning."

"She might be in a coma by morning."

I advised him to pack up their gear, then I walked to a neighbouring hut, found a Sherpa with a grey horse, brushed the frost from the horse's mane, and helped load Helen up onto its back. I advised her husband and their guide to carry on at least to Pheriche.

I barely slept that night, no longer preoccupied with my own existential crises but with the well-being of the two trekkers wandering desperately into the cold night. Maybe Annie was right. Maybe I was supposed to be here after all.

It would be several weeks before I learned of Helen's fate. As soon as the group reached Pheriche, she was placed on oxygen, loaded into a helicopter at dawn, and evacuated to a hospital in Kathmandu. She stayed there for two days, recuperating from what would have been certain death from pulmonary edema.

* * *

The next morning, I rose early, grabbed my gear, and headed for base camp, stopping only when I reached the ridge just an hour's hike from my destination, where Everest revealed herself to me in all her glory. I stopped again, kneeled on the ground, put my hand through the earth, and repeated the personal ceremony that Laurie Skreslet had taught me. I was returning to Everest a very superstitious man. I walked into base camp expecting to see the same circus that had greeted me in 2000, but I found it more or less empty. It was March 24, 2005, and I was the first climber to arrive. The only tents were those of the Sherpa preparing for the pending arrival of climbers from all around the world. I said hello to each and every Sherpa I passed, asked them when the first puja ceremony would be, then pitched my tent close to the spot where I'd pitched it back in 2000. I pulled out my Buddhist prayer flags, strung them over my tent, and began speaking to the mountain. Nothing was as it had been five years earlier. The glacier, which moves a metre per day, had shifted and cracked and melted in all different ways. I sat on the ice and rocks outside my tent and asked Everest to permit my friends and me to climb her. Then I lent my hands and energy to the Sherpa, helping them prepare the rest of base camp. I was still helping them when the radios crackled to life with an SOS from the slopes of neighbouring Pumori. A climber and a Sherpa had become trapped during a storm and were requesting assistance. I was helpless to try to save them. My gear, which had to be carried into camp by porters, had not yet arrived, and I still wasn't properly acclimatized for any higher elevation.

There was nothing that I or any of the porters and cooks at camp could do but look up at the two figures struggling to descend through the clouds on Pumori. It was hard to make out exactly what was happening, but it seemed as though the climber was exhausted and barely able to descend more than ten metres at a time before collapsing to the ground, while the Sherpa tried to get him back on his feet. All through the day, the radios blared with messages of distress until, suddenly, there were no more calls. Just two stationary objects trapped on the mountainside.

It was the worst possible way to begin the season. I retired to my tent, pulled the sacred rice from my bag, and tried not to think about all that I'd just seen and heard.

Hordes of climbers trickled in over the days that followed. They arrived like soldiers from some ancient world, carrying banners bearing their sponsors' logos. I waited patiently for Sean's arrival, reconnecting with Christine Boskoff from Mountain Madness as I waited and getting to know Lhakpa Sherpa, the man I'd come to climb with. He'd been to the summit eight times. Lhakpa was one of the strongest Sherpa on the mountain and well-known for having strapped a client to his back and carried him down to the base all the way from Camp 2. He'd grown up in the shadow of Everest and was recruited by Babu to help set up Nomad Expeditions as one of the most credible outfitters in Nepal.

When finally Sean did trek into camp, he arrived with a two-person film crew in tow. The camera crew had been hired by Rogers Media to chronicle the adventure of the old kinesiology professor with the philosopher's tongue.

He was purple-faced and wheezing from the altitude when

he arrived at base camp, but his excitement at having come this far bordered on euphoria. Sean was a driven man who wanted to inspire his fellow baby boomers back home by sharing his quest to reach the top of the world at the relative old age of sixty-three. He sat in his tent at night, speaking to the camera about the importance of being "responsible to yourself," about his appreciation for Zen, and about the strength of both the mountain and the human spirit. "The only person who can change you is you," he said. He asked me if I would mind sharing my thoughts on camera.

I explained my view on climbing and the romance that I believed had sucked Sean in, but in a good way. "I think that once you start going in the mountains and have the feeling, you can't get rid of it. It's not only a sport; it's something spiritual at the same time. It changes you. You get to know yourself better, and you just want to see many places. With each mountain it's different. You have a different feeling and experience every time. People say Everest is special because it's the tallest, but here you have something special that you don't see everywhere. On other mountains, it's just climbers. This one, it attracts all people. Everyone comes here for a different reason, either to climb the mountain or just to come and see it. It's bigger than life."

I told the camera about the magic I'd felt when I first arrived on the mountain, for that brief period of time when I shared Everest with no one but the Sherpa, before watching as Italians, Iranians, Americans, Russians, British, Germans, Japanese, Koreans, South Africans, and people from other places around the world arrived in our wake.

The cameraman asked me for my thoughts on Sean's chances. "If he can stay healthy and mentally strong, then I think he has a good chance. But in the end, it's Everest that decides. It doesn't matter if you're the best-trained climber and the most fit person on the mountain. It's the mountain that decides who gets to climb and who doesn't."

Sean and I began our acclimatization efforts on our own schedules. I wasn't with him when he reached Camp 1, but I saw him there on my way up toward Camp 2. He'd just completed his first trip through the icefall. I asked him how it had gone, and he confided in me how he'd embarrassed himself by falling off a ladder and dangling over a crevasse. He was able to laugh about it, but I got the sense that it had scared him. His wheezing had turned into a cough, and he was having a tough time eating. "I feel weak," he said. He headed back down to base camp while I carried on to Camp 2.

Two days later, when I got back to base camp, I'd barely taken off my pack when Sean's sirdar, the lead Sherpa in his expedition, came to my tent and asked if I would mind talking some sense into Sean.

"Sean not well," the Sherpa told me. "He cough all the time. I tell him, 'Sean, you need go down now.' But he no listen. He afraid. He go down, he no come back. You talk to him."

I nodded at the Sherpa, rubbed my temples, and gathered my thoughts. If Sean was in a bad state, what would I say? I suspected that he may have been gripped by the same fear that had gripped me five years earlier when I'd sat at base camp with fluid in my lungs, defying the doctor's recommendation for fear that it would mean the end of my own climb. It was Sean who'd helped talk sense into me then, and now I was going to have to try to do the same for him.

It was getting dark as I walked over to his team's dining tent. I could hear Sean inside, hacking away, but I thought it best to be discreet and pretend I couldn't hear him through the canvas. It had been my custom to visit Sean after dinner, sip tea, and chat about life and the expedition. I had a shtick. I'd poke my head through the canvas door sideways, like Kramer entering Jerry's apartment on *Seinfeld*.

This night was more of the same. I poked my head inside the tent. "Anybody home?" I asked, looking around the canvas jokingly.

Sean responded with a fit of coughing.

"You don't sound so good," I said.

He hacked out a deep, phlegmy cough that seemed to crackle inside his chest.

"It's okay, just the flu or a cold or something," he said, forcing the words out quickly before coughing again.

I sat down next to him and his Sherpa. Sean grabbed an extra cup from the table and poured me some tea.

"I'll be okay in a few days," said Sean, again forcing the words out between coughs. Then he smiled, trying hard to mask the discomfort he was in. But there was no masking anything. His face was purple and gaunt.

"You sure you're okay?" I asked him.

"My nose is really stuffed up," he admitted. "And my throat— I can barely eat."

I pulled out some drops of eucalyptus oil, asked his Sherpa to boil us some water, and instructed Sean to drape a towel over

his head and steam his nasal passages with the water and eucalyptus. "I find this helps." He looked at me like I was wasting
his time. "I'm serious. Try it. You'll feel better." He put his head
under the towel and lowered his head toward the bowl for ten
seconds, then sat back up and announced that he was done.

"This is terrible. How do you do this?" he said.

"Get back under there. Fifteen minutes at least."

"That's strong stuff. I can't do it."

"You need to," I said. Then I pushed his head back into
the bowl.

He broke into a fit of coughing and snorting, and then he
blew a chunk of mucus out of his nose.

"See, it's working."

He pulled the towel from his head and announced that he
was done. He still looked terrible.

"You know, if you're serious about climbing this mountain,
you gotta take care of yourself. I think you should go down."

He shook his head and looked at me as if I were betraying
our friendship by making such a suggestion.

"You're tired," I said. "Your saturation is so-so. You don't eat
enough. You need to go down."

He stopped me there. "I'm not ready to say it's over."

"It doesn't mean it's over. It's like me, last time. If you go
down, you're gonna feel better. You're gonna rest. You're gonna
eat better. You're gonna sleep better, and then, when you come
back, you're gonna be stronger and ready to keep going."

For a while, he sat there staring at me. I got the impression
that he was testing me to see if I'd flinch. I didn't.

"Just for a few days, Sean," I said. "You'll come back stronger, get back on schedule. We're still going to stand together on the top of this mountain."

"I'll go down in the morning," he said. "But when I come back, you better not already be on the summit."

I gave him my word, then I hugged him, snapping one last photo of him and his Sherpa before heading back to my tent for the night.

I didn't see Sean leave base camp the next morning, but I understood that he and his Sherpa companion had begun trekking down shortly after dawn, around the same time that I started my own trek back up through the icefall.

The Sherpa was by his side as he sat down on a rock at Dughla and began gasping for breath. A medical helicopter came in for a landing. It was the chopper that had been dispatched to get him off the mountainside.

The wind was deafeningly loud as Sean slipped into cardiac arrest. Clutching at his chest, he shook his head and repeated just two words, over and over.

Then he leaned back over the rock and stared, mouth agape, straight up into the heavens.

"Jesus Christ," he said.

CHAPTER 13

CARRYING SEAN

The manila envelope was unmarked. It weighed nothing and came without any label, explanation, or warning. The envelope arrived by way of a Sherpa I'd never met, who'd carried it into base camp after another Sherpa somewhere down around Dingboche had handed it to him. That Sherpa had been given the unmarked envelope by yet another Sherpa somewhere around Lukla. In fact, it had been carried all the way from the banks of the Bagmati River in Kathmandu with the explicit, albeit "verbal," instructions that it be brought to a French Canadian named Gabriel, who lived in a North Face tent with prayer flags draped over it, pitched right on the edge of the Khumbu's tail. Carefully, I opened the envelope and slowly realized what was inside.

It was just a few days since Sean had keeled over in Dughla. The only witness to his death, a young Sherpa named Lhakpa Tsheri Sherpa, who'd go on to be named National Geographic 2012 Adventurer of the Year, had done everything possible to revive Sean in the moments after he'd collapsed. But it was no use. The same helicopter that had been dispatched to help evacuate him was used to carry his body to a morgue in Kathmandu, where he was put on ice until his son and daughter arrived from Ottawa. His son arrived via London, while his daughter had boarded a flight in Montreal, accompanied by Annie, who'd opted to be with me at base camp as I struggled to come to terms with Sean's death. Annie had been by Sean's children's side as the professor's body was taken down to the banks of the Bagmati, a holy river for both Buddhists and Hindus. His remains were placed on kindling and kerosene packs at the side of the river. It was Seamas, the boy who'd asked me to take care of his father, who'd carried the torch to his body and who, along with his sister, had decided to place one-third of Sean's ashes into an envelope, handed it to a Sherpa, and asked that it be brought to me so that I might fulfill Sean's dream of reaching the top of Everest.

The cremated remains of my friend were now in my hand.

Annie was already with me at base camp when the envelope arrived. It was her first time there, and though it wasn't her favourite place, she felt it was important to be by my side. We sat inside my tent, talking about Sean and his children and what lay ahead and what lay behind for both them and us. For a while, I was afraid to step outside or pick up the satellite phone. Back home, my mother and everyone else I knew would have read about how Sean had become the third Canadian to die on Everest. He had joined Blair Griffiths, the CBC cameraman who'd been crushed to death in the icefall twenty-three years earlier, and Roger Marshall, who'd fallen while trying to descend solo after an unsuccessful attempt up the extremely difficult and rarely climbed Hornbein Couloir. This steep and narrow route up the mountain's northern face was named after Thomas Hornbein, the American who first reached the top via the couloir in 1963. I knew what the newspapers and television networks back home were saying—that the sixty-three-year-old kinesiology professor was playing with death when the mountain claimed him. Sean had always been such a positive character, and he'd come out here to try to inspire others. I worried that his death would now serve to do the opposite. Now I was scared. My fear was amplified four days after Sean's heart attack. I was at base camp when a thirty-nine-year-old American climber took off with his brother into the icefall. He'd been in the middle of switching his carabiners on the fixed line when he slipped and fell ten metres into a crevasse. He died of hypothermia while his brother and others looked down on him in horror, unable to mount a rescue before it was too late. The entire incident had occurred not that far from my tent.

It was both excruciating and calming to have Annie with me at base camp while all of this unfolded. She wasn't completely acclimatized, having rushed to my side before I pushed off for the summit. We lay awake, listening to the mountain and admiring the stars through the vent, while I worked up the physical and emotional strength to climb.

If she was as concerned for me in that moment as she had been weeks earlier at the airport, she masked her fear well.

I began my final preparations to leave base camp. On the floor of the tent, I laid out my *khata*, the ceremonial silk scarf the Sherpa had given me as part of the puja. Then I grabbed the envelope with Sean's ashes, poured them onto one end of the scarf and knotted it so they wouldn't fall out. On the other end, I did the same with some of the rice Babu had given me.

Neither Annie nor I really spoke or slept much on our last night together at base camp. I was too deep inside my mind, building the confidence required for the climb, and she was too focused on being there for me to distract me from that task.

It was two thirty in the morning when I got up and dressed. I climbed out of my tent and into the cold Himalayan night. In the dining tent, I ate some breakfast and put on my helmet and my harness. I grabbed my jumar (the hand-held mechanical device that attaches to a climber's harness, slides upwards on a rope, and locks into place to hold a climber's weight), slings (sewn loops of webbing used to hitch on to anchors during the climb), and ice axe, then made for the site of our expedition's puja. I lit some juniper, placed my hand on an altar of stone and rock, faced the mountain, and asked her to please be kind with me.

The stars seemed to circle above as I spoke to her. "I'd like your permission to dance on your summit," I said. Then I closed my eyes, took a deep breath, and carried on.

Annie walked with me to the edge of the icefall, where Lhakpa, the Sherpa who would climb with me up the mountain, stood silently waiting. I nodded at him, then hugged Annie goodbye, looked toward the icefall, and began my climb. I took off slowly, careful not to look back in case I caught a glimpse of Annie watching me as I navigated my way through the most dangerous part of the mountain. For four days, Lhakpa and I climbed at our own pace, each of us focused on our next steps, hardly ever within speaking distance of one another, except when we stumbled, exhausted and frozen stiff, into camp. The mountain seemed to have opened her arms to us, granting us a twelve-hour window of clear skies on our summit day, but the climb was still taxing and perilous.

It was shortly before midnight on May 29 (fifty-two years to the day that Sir Edmund Hillary and Tenzing Norgay first summitted this mountain) when I radioed down to Annie from Camp 4. We were on the edge of the Death Zone, and I wanted her to know that I was okay.

We were about to depart on my summit push. I felt uncharacteristically strong at this altitude—physically, mentally, and emotionally. I'd placed the scarf with Sean's ashes in the top of my pack. I looked at it next to me in my tent and felt strangely calm.

"How do you feel?" Annie asked me over the radio from base camp.

I told her I felt like Sean was actually with me. I didn't want to be cocky, but I told her it seemed like even Everest wanted me to succeed.

I turned off the radio and looked at Lhakpa, who was pumped up and ready to go. He nodded and we put on our oxygen masks and headed up from the South Col, the Milky Way lighting up the ridge before us. It was crisp and gorgeous as the dawn filtered through the valleys of the Nepalese countryside below. The first rays of sunlight hit our backs as we made for the Hillary Step, the twelve-metre vertical rock face that marks the last technical challenge before the summit. There were only a few climbers and Sherpa ahead of us, and I thanked the mountain for having led us here ahead of the usual mass of climbers that bottleneck at this very spot. Then I leaned forward into the Hillary Step, placed my hands on the chiselled rock that protruded out one side, kicked my crampons into the ice right next to the rock, and scrambled up the last real obstacle between me and the summit. When I got to the top of the Hillary Step, I looked at the last seventy metres between me and the top of the world. I stopped there, caught my breath, then reached into the top of my pack, pulling out the scarf with Sean's ashes. I draped it around my neck and spoke to him from inside my oxygen mask.

"Well, Sean, we wanted to get here together," I said.

I'd spent so long dreaming of this moment that I assumed I'd be an emotional mess, especially with the added element of carrying Sean's ashes as high as any other human being had ever climbed. I don't know how long it took me to make those last few steps toward the summit. Time felt as if it were slowing all around me. I began counting my breaths between steps. Eight full gasps for every step.

The peak of the Earth soon revealed itself. Prayer flags, photographs, and mementoes from the men and women who'd stood there before lay frozen in the snow. A lone Sherpa stood just a few steps from the summit, one hand on a radio, the other on a cigarette. I peered at him through my goggles as he puffed away in the thin air. I was mesmerized by him as I struggled for breath within my oxygen mask, noting, even in that moment, how humbling this whole experience was.

The smoking Sherpa was smiling and nodding at me with approval as I passed him. Then he shouted into his radio, "Base camp, base camp. Gabriel summit!" I paused in awe while

Lhakpa joined me. I waited for some rush of fulfillment to crash over me. Instead, I felt a wave of relief.

I spoke once more to Sean. "Okay, Sean. It's done." Then I removed my oxygen mask, breathed in the mountain air, and cried. Several minutes passed before I removed the scarf from my neck, tied it to a tripod that had been left on the summit, and then reached down into the snow and picked up a small rock.

"I have given you my friend," I said. "And I would like this rock."

Then I sat down in the snow, took out a photo of Annie, her three daughters, and Alexandra, and wept again. I had asked the mountain for just two minutes on her summit so that I might dance. She gave me an hour instead. But I didn't feel like dancing. I tried to think of everyone in my life who had helped get me here. I thought of my mother back in Lac-Mégantic. It was nighttime there. I thought of the candle she'd have kept lit for me in the cathedral in the centre of my hometown. It would be flickering now in the dark. I thought of Claude and of Sylvain's sister. Of Patrice, Jacques, Babu, and Sean. I thought of my father and whether this would constitute an A+ in his mind. But most of all, I thought of Annie, 3,500 vertical metres below. I knew she'd be counting the minutes that I was up here, and would be waiting in angst until word got back to her that we were on our way down.

* * *

It would be another two days before I got back to the base of the mountain. My face was chapped and peeling from the sun and the wind. My mind and body were exhausted. Annie was waiting right at the base of the icefall, alongside a cook with a celebratory beer and a fresh *khata* for me when I arrived. Annie hugged me, then remarked that I had no expression on my face.

"You look like the walking dead," she said.

I nodded. It still hadn't set in that I'd actually just been to the top of Everest. I hugged her again, then told her I was ready to go home.

It would be two weeks before I got back to Montreal to visit Alexandra. I was ecstatic to see her, even if she did seem somewhat put off by the change in my appearance. I tried to tell her what it had felt like to stand atop the world. She seemed more interested in hugging me than listening to my stories. Then I thanked her for a poem she'd written and sent to me while I was away. The words had moved me to tears when I read them in my tent before pushing up the mountain.

She was fourteen years old; I had no idea how she'd grown up so fast.

We all miss you so,
But for me it is different
I have never felt this kind of pain,
Before I was too small,
But now as I grow I'm realizing,
How bad I miss you when you are gone,
I am one of the few people in the world who feels this,
But we suffer it,
No matter what, because we love you,
and want to make you happy.

Inside we have so many fears,
diseases, getting lost, and worst of all,
the fear of death,
which will keep you from coming back,
We hope you achieve what you came for,
but the important thing for me,
is for you to come back alive,
and all live happily ever after.

I just want you to know,
we will always accept your choices,
whatever they will be
even if they break our hearts
know that we do all this
because we love you.

CHAPTER 14

IDOL WORSHIP

I know a man who once made an astronaut choke up by asking what seemed a simple question: "What's the worst part of being an astronaut?"

The astronaut said nothing. For a few moments, the two sat in silence until the man tried again.

"Is it leaving your family to wander off into space?"

"No," said the astronaut, his voice cracking as he spoke. "The worst part's actually when you come home. And you sit down at the dinner table and one of your children asks you, 'Dad, what was it like to look down at the Earth from a window in space? Or head out of the shuttle on a spacewalk?' And you realize it doesn't matter what you say, because they'll never really understand."

* * *

Whatever high I may have felt after having stood atop the world started to disappear the moment I got into my Volkswagen in

Montreal and began the five-hour drive back to Roberval. And it was completely gone by the time I turned the key to my apartment and wandered inside with a carton of milk, a tin of coffee beans, and the few other groceries I'd picked up on my way back into town. I sat down next to the boxes on my sofa, looked at the white walls that enclosed my life, and started dreaming of my next adventure. There was little about my life up in Roberval that I liked.

I took solace in knowing that my days in this small town were numbered. The airport tower would soon be shuttered and my work here complete. I requested that I be transferred to Montreal. This job had been good to me, but I was done with working in remote communities. My pay had afforded me the opportunity to climb whatever mountains I chose, and my bosses had, but for the rare occasion, granted me the leaves required to climb around the world. But in return, I'd spent the last decade of my life in the far north, stunting my ability to rebuild a family life or do anything, really, other than work and climb.

It was Annie who pointed out that I didn't really live to work or work to live. Instead, I'd fallen into a pattern of life where I just sort of lived to climb and, therefore, worked to climb as well. I wasn't sure if she thought it was a character flaw or an affirmation that I was living my life according to the credo of *The Little Prince*, which I'd first read shortly after my brother Claude's death: "Make your life a dream, and the dream a reality."

I was frustrated, disappointed, and short of options when I was told that instead of going to Montreal, I was to be redeployed to Sept-Îles. Going back to the town where my career began would mean moving 450 kilometres farther away from the life I was hoping to forge with Annie in Montreal.

So I quit. I handed in my resignation, donated my couch, cutlery, and mattress to a local church, packed the rest of my life into the trunk of my Volkswagen, and made for Montreal. Annie and her daughters accepted me into their life with open arms. Soon, my climbing gear and boxes of old climbing journals were dumped into a closet. For the first time in twelve years, I lived in a home with people and things in it. On holidays, I'd drive out to Cowansville, pick up Alexandra, and bring her to Montreal for family suppers.

I was happy but scared. I'd given up the security of a job that guaranteed me a really good salary and an irreplaceable pension. I was forty-five years old—nowhere near retirement and an awkward age at which to reinvent myself and begin a second career. But I wasn't as concerned about how I might afford to grow old as I was about how I might finance my passion for climbing.

Not many people made a lucrative living as professional climbers. Those who did were an elite group whose members relied heavily on sponsorships, guiding, and the lecture circuit. In Canada, the "pros" consisted of men like Laurie Skreslet (who was by then a well-seasoned guide on Aconcagua) and Patrick Morrow, who, as a photographer, climbed to the top of Everest two days after Skreslet; he went on to become the first person to climb to the top of all eight mountains on the contentious list of the Seven Summits. I say "contentious" because opinions differ on whether the highest point in the Australian continent was Kosciuszko (the mountain Dick Bass had claimed in his quest for the Seven Summits) or the significantly more difficult Puncak Jaya in Indonesia.

I was an accomplished climber, but I had yet to break the same kind of ground as Skreslet or Morrow. Still, my expeditions over the previous decade had gotten me into The North Face family. The San Francisco–based outdoor clothing company had started outfitting American climbers in the 1960s; by the time I came around to the sport, The North Face was a global brand. I was on my way to becoming one of their official athletes. Once that happened, they would pay me to wear their gear on my expeditions, and in return, I'd help them grow their brand. They had sponsored me as an expedition leader for Sylvain on Mont Blanc. Another source of income was the public stage. I wasn't particularly at ease in front of a crowd, but people seemed to gravitate toward my stories, especially the ones about the faulty zipper that nearly killed me, and about my journey up the mountain carrying Sean. So I built myself a website, branded myself as a public and motivational speaker for hire, and started addressing corporations and students across Canada and the United States.

It never took long before those who listened to my talks asked me when I was going to climb K2. Everyone, even non-climbers, knew that K2 was a much more dangerous climb than Mount Everest. Everest was dangerous, but at least it was relatively solid. K2 was covered in loose shale and had a reputation for dropping chunks of rock and ice from its sides and wiping climbers clear of its flanks. By 2005, roughly 2,500 people had summitted Everest, while only about 250 had reached the top of K2. There was roughly one dead climber on K2 for every four successful summiteers.

I wasn't yet prepared mentally, physically, or emotionally for K2. I was just starting my new life with Annie, and I knew that if I started talking about K2 at the dinner table, she'd start second-guessing what she'd gotten herself into.

I decided to look instead toward Oceania, Australia, and Antarctica.

The plan was simple: I'd spend the winter trying to grow my new business as a public speaker while also pitching myself and my plan for my next few expeditions to my sponsors in the hope they'd offer their support. In the spring, I would lead my first trek to Everest Base Camp—I'd safely ferry mountain-enthusiasts who weren't part of "the fucked-up bunch" (to quote Sean Egan) to base camp and back down to Lukla for a fee. It would be my first experience as a Himalayan guide and would help to bring in some added cash. If it all worked out, I'd return to Quebec in the summer, visit my mother back home in Lac-Mégantic, and use the hills and mountains that surrounded her house as a training ground for the fall, when I'd depart for the Far East on my next real climb.

Annie, wanting to relive her success on Kilimanjaro three years earlier, signed on to join me for the morning stroll up Mount Kosciuszko in Australia. As far as climbing goes, Kosciuszko was a joke. The pitch and height of the mountain were actually less impressive than that of Quito. We "climbed" the mountain via the only legal route possible: over the remnants of an old road that once led vehicles up to a lookout point just a few metres from the summit and that now serves as an environ-mentally friendly trail meant to keep tourists from trampling the grass on the mountainside. We laughed as we heel-toed it up the road, passing octogenarians in Velcro shoes and parents pushing strollers.

"Isn't this fun?" Annie asked when we got to the top.

"Yup," I said. "If we hurry, we can make it back into town in time for lunch."

If it hadn't been for Annie's companionship on that climb, I might not even remember it, that little trek having been immediately preceded and followed by two far more memorable experiences.

The first involved a brief foray into a jungle conflict zone teeming with warring cannibals on the island of New Guinea. That was a hell of a trip. The second involved a deep and thought-provoking conversation over rye whisky in the company of Sir Edmund Hillary on the north island of New Zealand.

* * *

Of all the mountains included in the Seven Summits, Puncak Jaya, or the Carstensz Pyramid, the highest point on Mount Carstensz, is perhaps the least climbed and requires by far the most amount of technical skill, even if, at 4,884 metres, the Pyramid can be climbed in just one day. But it's not the technical challenge that keeps potential climbers away; the reality is that getting to the Pyramid is often harder than climbing it. Unless you're able to chopper straight to base camp, you have to hack your way through wild jungle, passing through the traditional homelands of different cannibal tribes who remained isolated from the rest of the world until climbers started arriving in the 1960s. Given the remoteness of the mountain and the potential for getting shot by an arrow while approaching it from any of its sides, it is not surprising that the Pyramid, which was first sighted by Jan Carstensz (the Dutch explorer who gave it his name) in 1623, went unseen by Western eyes for two centuries after its discovery. As was the case after the initial sighting of Kilimanjaro, few in Europe actually believed the report Carstensz brought back about a jagged vertical wall rising out of the jungle with snow on its top. The difficulties of actually accessing the many spires of Mount Carstensz persisted well into the twentieth century; as a result, it was not climbed until 1936, when a trio of Dutch climbers set out to scale what was then the highest point in the Dutch empire. They succeeded in reaching the summit of a snow-covered peak called Ngga Pulu (about 4,900 metres), located on the north rim of the jagged wall. It would be another twenty-six years before anyone else managed to get back to the top of the mountain. By that time, the ice on Ngga Pulu had melted away, revealing a rocky spire that was actually nineteen metres shorter than the peak of one of its neighbours, which was known as the Carstensz Pyramid and later renamed Puncak Jaya by the Indonesian government.

In 1962, the first man stepped on the Pyramid's top. His name was Heinrich Harrer, the Austrian climber portrayed by Brad Pitt in the movie *Seven Years in Tibet*. Harrer had been well-known in the climbing world since 1938, when he and three others climbed the north face of the Eiger in Switzerland, considered one of the most daring climbs to this day. Harrer wrote about his experiences in Tibet after escaping a British POW camp; he was taken prisoner while returning from a failed attempt up Nanga Parbat in British India at the outbreak of the

Second World War. He was pushing fifty when he got to the top of the Pyramid. He passed away at the age of ninety-three just a few months before I set out to retrace his footsteps in New Guinea.

I knew almost nothing about the area or the Pyramid, but I'd heard how difficult and dangerous it could be to actually get to the base of the mountain, so I hired Christine Boskoff and her Seattle-based outfitter, Mountain Madness, to facilitate the trip. After two seasons with Boskoff on Everest, I considered her a friend. And though she wasn't personally joining me on the Pyramid, she and I had made plans to climb to the top of Vinson Massif in Antarctica three months later. With Mountain Madness taking care of the particulars of our trip, I allowed a novice climber and friend from home to accompany me on the mountain.

The Carstensz Pyramid was nowhere to be seen as our plane touched down in the nearest town, Sugapa. It was blisteringly hot when we exited the plane onto the tarmac. We'd barely grabbed our gear when we were stopped by official-looking men with AK-47s dangling from their shoulders. They told us that if we went into the jungle, we'd definitely get ourselves killed. The tribes that lined the route to the mountain were at war with one another; we were told they'd shoot us with arrows, whether they knew we were climbers or not.

"Cannibals," one soldier said. "Chop you up and eat you."

It had been thirty years since the last Westerner was reported killed and eaten by the cannibals of New Guinea, but the soldier's warning was enough to dissuade us from our planned trek. So we stayed in the village for the better part of a week, spending almost all of our time either sitting in a small house with an armed military guard at our doorstep, or on the tarmac, where we sat on our backpacks waiting for a plane to break through the clouds overhead and deliver a pilot, any pilot, who could fly the Russian-made helicopter that would take us to the mountain. When we weren't literally sitting around, watching the local militia practise martial arts on the tarmac, we wandered around the village under the armed protection of the Indonesian military, whose presence led us to believe that this village wasn't much safer than the jungle.

When a pilot finally arrived, we climbed into the chopper and lifted off in the direction of base camp—that is, until the mist in the sky turned a darker shade of grey, forcing us to abort our approach and fly back to Sugapa. Though the GPS in the cockpit said we were 0.16 kilometres away from our destination, we couldn't see it at all. After three or four fruitless trips between base camp and the village, we finally made it. After touching down at 4,300 metres, we jumped out, watched as our chopper lifted off, and took a quick look at our surroundings. The base camp was a damp place, with lush grass and dark green moss that disappeared into the misty valley beneath us, and the greyness of Carstensz's vertical pitch directly above.

We left base camp in the darkness of night, hoping that if the weather held, we'd get to the top and back in time to catch that day's chopper ride back to the village. Soon, we were climbing through pouring rain that quickly began to freeze. Our ascent was delayed slightly when, while trying to navigate an overhanging wall, my left foot broke off a piece of the cliff wall and I was left dangling by one arm over oblivion, with no way to go any farther up the overhang. I had no choice but to climb back down to the nearest fixed line and jumar my way up over the wall just like everybody else. At the summit, with snow and rain pelting our faces and turning to ice on the rocks beneath our feet, we took a quick photograph, looked at each other, said, "Yup, we did it," then started back down.

We were back in Sugapa by nightfall that same day. I'd scratched another of the Seven Summits from my list but was already preparing for the true highlight of this trip: a planned meeting with Sir Edmund Hillary.

* * *

They say you should never meet your heroes, because when you do, they almost always let you down. I thought of that as I stood with Annie at the carousel in Auckland Airport, waiting for our luggage to arrive and wondering if the world's most famous climber would be anywhere near as kind and inspiring as his reputation.

The second child of a journalist-turned-beekeeper, Hillary was hardened by his father's fists as a young man. His father, Percival Augustus Hillary, was, by all accounts, extremely damaged by his experiences in the First World War. Percival had served in Gallipoli, where he was badly wounded, and he returned to New Zealand, suffering from what was then known simply as shell shock. Sir Edmund spoke often of how his father's beatings had changed his nature as a child. The stories resonated with me for obvious reasons. "My father had grown some very good grapes along the side of the house, and there was one particularly good bunch that was just coming ripe," one of Hillary's often repeated stories began. "One morning they had disappeared and he automatically thought of me, and I denied it, so over to the woodshed, and I got a really good thumping that day."

Hillary said the beatings made him stronger, if also humble and somewhat insecure. He grew up believing himself ugly and never had many friends. He dropped out of university after just two years of study to help his aging father with his beekeeping business. By then, the beatings had stopped, but the damage had been done. The only place where he seemed to really feel good about himself was in the mountains; he'd discovered he had a passion for climbing as a young adult still trying to find his place in the world. When World War II broke out, he became a navigator on flying boats. He spent long hours sitting on the side of a tarmac in Fiji, reading books about far more accomplished mountaineers than himself and their adventures in the Himalaya. It was only after a chance encounter with Harry Ayres, another Kiwi climber eight years his senior, that Hillary actually learned how to climb himself. Ayres was a seasoned guide and a master of technical climbing who had also had a terrible relationship with his father. Hillary always credited Ayres with having given him the training required to become the world's most famous mountaineer, though Hillary admitted he never attained anywhere near the same level of technical grace on rock or ice as Ayres. Climbing behind Ayres, Hillary reached the top of New Zealand's highest mountain in 1948 before moving on to the French Alps to continue his indoctrination in the sport. He was never the best technical climber or the fastest, but he was a solid all-around mountaineer and a nice guy who everyone seemed to like to have around on an expedition.

I knew Hillary's story as well as any admirer could without having met him. I'd read in his memoirs about how, two years after first seeing Everest and stepping onto the Khumbu Glacier, he had returned as part of a much larger expedition filled with many climbers more accomplished than he. And how, by sheer will and perseverance (as well as a touch of luck and good weather), he and the equally, if not even more, admirable Tenzing Norgay reached the summit on May 29, 1953, on the eve of Queen Elizabeth II's coronation. The young queen offered him a knighthood immediately after his feat.

I'd found it interesting how, after summitting Everest, he described his return to base camp as "a touching and unforgettable moment, but somehow a sad one too." He'd been quoted in his later years as saying he was racked by guilt over what had become of the mountain and the surrounding Khumbu as hordes of climbers sullied the area with garbage.

We grabbed our bags, jumped in a car, and began cutting across New Zealand en route to White's Beach on the Tasman Sea, where Hillary had built himself a cottage as a retreat from the world. We watched the countryside from the back seat of the car, passing rolling hills as far as the eye could see and endless flocks of sheep. We arrived at an apartment and dropped off our bags before carrying on to Hillary's cottage.

There was so much I wanted to talk with him about. My only fear was that his advanced age (he was eighty-six at the time) and distinct lack of ego would make him quiet in our company.

There's a lesson in humility in the story of Dick Bass, the poetry-reciting Texas billionaire who pioneered the quest for the Seven Summits. The story goes that he sat down next to a stranger on a flight across America and went on and on in great detail about his adventures on all seven continents throughout the entire flight. It wasn't until the plane was about to land that Bass realized he hadn't even asked the stranger's name while going on about himself. "That's okay," the stranger replied. "I'm Neil Armstrong."

Despite his fame and accomplishments on Everest, Hillary was as down-to-earth an icon as any—the exact opposite of Dick Bass. Of all his positive traits, it was his humility that I admired the most.

I'd felt a kinship with him because of his history with his father, his views on mountaineering, and the modesty with which he spoke of his successes. He wasn't as good a climber as Hermann Buhl or Reinhold Messner or Babu Chiri Sherpa or even Tenzing Norgay. But he'd left his mark on the world none-theless, not just by getting to the top of Everest, but by going back into the valley below for years to help build the Himalayan Trust and establish infrastructure to support the Sherpa community.

When we stepped out of the car, it was bright and sunny, and the ocean waves were rolling gently over the beach beyond Hillary's cottage. We headed for his neighbour's door, since it was, after all, Hillary's neighbour, a man named Ben Van Toledo, who'd actually invited us down here to visit. I'd met Ben on Everest that spring. Ben had cut his forehead at a party in Lukla. The doctor attached to my team had stitched him up and spread two Band-Aids like a cross over his forehead. I photographed the wound and sent the picture to him via email as a joke. We became friends, and Ben told me that Hillary was his neighbour. I'd been reading a book called *Just Ask* at the time and thought, *What the hell, I'll ask if Sir Ed and his wife might be willing to meet and talk with me if I ever find my way to New Zealand.* Ben said he'd put forward the question. The response came quickly by email with the subject line "YESSSSSSS," followed by a brief explanation: "Sir Ed and Lady June are waiting for you."

We arrived at Ben's cottage and relaxed by the seashore, waiting for dinner and Hillary's arrival. I'd admired him for so long and from such a distance that I still didn't believe this would happen.

I was anxious as I anticipated his knock at the patio door. I caught his shadow first, moving slowly toward the cottage. He was tall and cut an impressive figure, though he now walked with a cane. His greatest climbs of late were the steps outside his cottage. But that didn't matter. He was Sir Edmund Hillary.

Annie and I watched in awe as he came to the door. Ben made the requisite introductions. Then I pulled out a bottle of Canadian whisky and presented it to Sir Ed. It wasn't the finest stuff in the world, but I knew Hillary liked a dram a day, and so I'd brought it as a gift from Canada. He thanked me, then handed the bottle to Ben to pour us a drink. He and I retired like old-fashioned gentlemen to the living room of Ben's cottage, leaving Annie and the others to chat in the kitchen.

We were barely out of the kitchen when Lady June looked at her husband and me.

"They're all selfish," she said. Then she looked to Annie as if for affirmation. "But we wouldn't choose them any other way. Would we?"

It was a question Annie would ask herself over and over in the coming years.

I followed Hillary into the living room and held his whisky while he lowered himself slowly into a chair. He was gracious, albeit shaky, as I handed him his drink. The first thing I'd noticed when I shook his hand earlier was the size of his palm. I fixated on it again as he gripped the glass. His hands had once pulled him to the top of the world, and though they were now eighty-six years old, they were still thick and powerful. I watched as he held his whisky glass in both hands, shaking, as he raised the glass to his lips. He lowered the glass and thanked me again for the kind gift. He struck me as content, happy even. I knew people often said that all climbers eventually look the same. Their eyes droop with the inherent sadness that permeates their sport, while their skin withers and betrays the effects of numerous sunburns, frostbite, and oxygen deprivation. In some ways, I was beginning to look the part, but Hillary was different. He hadn't lost the grace or the smile of the gentleman who once inspired the world.

For an hour, we shared stories of our lives, yet we barely spoke of climbing. He talked about his foundation and his affection for the Sherpa. I told him of mine as well. He seemed most happy when he spoke of his mother and how she'd helped him to the top of Everest. "You know the scarf in all the photos?" he asked. "The striped one I wore on my head on my way up Everest? Those were actually my pyjamas. My mother sewed them into a scarf." I liked that story. It made me think of my own mother and all the candles she'd lit for me over the years.

Toward the end of our conversation, I asked him a question: "What was your greatest achievement?"

"It wasn't anything I did on the mountain," Hillary replied.

CHAPTER 15

LEADING MEN INTO THE DEATH ZONE

The city of Montreal was just waking up, and cars and trucks were beginning to back up on the bridge into the *centre-ville*. It was a cold and frosty morning. I'd woken at my new home on L'Île-des-Soeurs, a quiet little island haven in the middle of the St. Lawrence River within sight of the city, jumped in my car, and headed south and east, away from traffic and into the dawn, en route to an ice wall in northern Vermont. The mercury was dipping just below zero, and I was taking advantage of the cold. In less than a month, I'd be stepping out of a plane and onto a glacier runway in Antarctica. I was still sporting the vestiges of the tan I'd picked up on the beach outside Sir Edmund Hillary's cottage. I needed to get my body tuned to the cold. There wasn't much else that concerned me about my next climb. But I wanted to at least enjoy it. I was, after all, going to be paying big bucks just to get to the top of the bottom of the world.

It felt good to be back on ice. Back in training mode. Back in my element. It was nearly dark by the time I got off the wall. I stretched out my legs, checked the time, and just stood there for a moment, letting the sweat cool on my back before jumping in my car and heading home.

Nearly a month had passed since I'd last heard from Christine Boskoff. She was to be my climbing partner on Vinson Massif. Her last email had been strangely cryptic. She'd given barely any details other than that she was in China with her climbing partner, Charlie Fowler, and they had just been forced off some mountain because of scary ice conditions.

"All sorted for Vinson," she wrote, referring to our upcoming Antarctica climb. "Looking forward to it already. Off now for a 20,000-ft peak up a new route. Speak soon."

I figured she must have been on some secret first ascent. There was no other reason not to name the mountain. But I thought little of it. We weren't that close and I just assumed she'd been sending out dozens of emails at a time before disappearing back into whatever remote corner of China she was climbing in.

I emailed her back but didn't get any response. I guess none of her other friends did either. But now an email from one of her Mountain Madness colleagues seemed to indicate a problem.

"Christine's missing," the email read. "Hasn't been heard from since November 8. Not entirely sure where she is or where to look." This didn't sound good. I checked my old emails again to verify the date of our last correspondence. It was from November 8 as well.

I began searching the Internet for news. The details were rather grim. Christine and Charlie had last been seen passing through a seven-hundred-year-old monastery in southwest China. But they didn't have the proper permits required to climb in the region, and so they kept their plans to summit an unclimbed face of Genyen Massif (a mountain held to be holy by Buddhist monks, who travel great distances to pray at its base) so secret that none of her friends or family knew where to tell investigators to look after the two missed their flight home to the United States. That flight was on December 4. More than three weeks had passed since they'd last been seen.

For the rest of the month, I was glued to my email and following the news reports coming out of Sichuan as American and Chinese climbers set out to search the towns and trailheads near several unclimbed six-thousand-metre peaks in the area. The search zone, which was the size of Colorado, seemed huge, and as the date on the calendar drew closer to the New Year, I began losing faith that Christine and I would be meeting on that Antarctic glacier as planned.

I knew she was dead the moment I learned that they'd found her partner half-covered in snow, the apparent victim of an avalanche. He hadn't been roped to Boskoff at the time of his death, and though her body hadn't been found yet, I knew there was no chance that she'd survived. I cancelled my plans for Vinson Massif.

Boskoff had been the leader of one of the world's more recognizable mountain outfitters. She had kept Mountain Madness alive after its founder, Scott Fischer, died in the 1996 Everest disaster. She'd become a regular fixture at base camp in the years since purchasing the company from his estate. Her death would resonate throughout base camp that spring.

* * *

There was no way to convince Annie that the financial merits of leading an expedition to the top of Everest outweighed the risks involved. She knew well enough that it didn't matter how safe you were on the mountainside or how many times you'd actually been to the top of Everest; it was the same gamble every time.

"You've already been to the top," she argued. "What point is there now in going back? You've got your conferences. You've got your trekkers paying you to go to base camp. Why risk all of this just to go back?"

There wasn't much I could say other than explain to her that in order to maintain my sponsorship deals and differentiate myself from the other climbers offering themselves up as public speakers, I had to go back. I had to take my experiences and push them one step further. It was either that or make an attempt at K2. There wasn't much else I could think to do with myself that spring.

I tried to rationalize my decision to go back by explaining that it wasn't a selfish gesture. "I'm not just climbing for me this time," I said. "I'm helping others fulfill their dreams."

That winter passed quickly, and before either of us knew it, it was March 25, 2007, and we were back at the airport, this time accompanied by Alexandra and Annie's three daughters. Annie's youngest, Amy, peppered my cheek with seventy kisses, one for each of the days I would be away on the mountainside. I was surprised to see that Annie and Alexandra held up better than the others, though it made me wonder if maybe they'd just been hardened by the previous times I'd left them.

I took my responsibilities as a guide very seriously. Having almost always climbed with just my own life in my hands, the weight of having others depending on me and my knowledge of the mountain made me feel anxious and kept me awake on the flights to London and Kathmandu. I had assembled a small, nimble team, inspired by, and still associated with, Babu's Nomad Expeditions, whose Sherpa would be lending invaluable assistance to get us to the top. I was also fortunate to have Garry Hartlin, a communications specialist based in Pembroke, Ontario, joining our team as a sort of base camp manager. I'd gotten to know Garry two years earlier when he'd been serving in a similar role for Ben Webster's team. When Sean had died, Garry was the one to relay the message to me up on the mountain. Garry was a master at reading the weather patterns circulating the mountain and had helped navigate me through the volatility of the weather on Everest after Sean's death.

Our team consisted of four Canadians and five Sherpa. Not one of the Canadians had any Himalayan experience. I'd been lured back to the mountain in part by a young filmmaker from Ottawa named Elia Saikaly. He was the cameraman who had followed Sean to base camp in 2005. Elia had been moved by the experience and had gone back to Everest the following year, retracing Sean's footsteps all the way up to Camp 1. I'd helped him prepare for that initial climb in 2006, outfitting him and teaching him about gear that he didn't really know how to use.

He'd survived his first foray above base camp, and I was happy for that. I'd lost enough friends on this mountain and didn't want to lose another one. Now Elia wanted to film all the way up to the top of Everest in order to finish the adventure that Sean had begun. Sean had preached the need for fulfillment in life. That message had touched the young filmmaker, who'd been a lost child, running away from his family at the age of fourteen and spending a portion of his youth living on the streets of Ottawa before finding his way into foster care and taking on what he thought was his calling as a weightlifter. Elia was a powerful specimen, having broken a world powerlifting record at the age of seventeen, but he had absolutely no climbing experience to speak of when he hired me to take him to the top of Everest on Sean's behalf. I was hesitant at first. Everest already had too many climbers clogging up its slopes. Still, the kid's passion and motivation impressed me. I took him on as a client, along with two men from Montreal.

I was already exhausted by the time we arrived in Kathmandu, and unsure of my decision even before I laid eyes on the mountain. There, I met with Babu's former business partner, who was also named Babu. This Babu had kept the company, Nomad Expeditions, in operation after Babu Chiri Sherpa's death. He would be our man in Kathmandu, supplying us with Sherpa guides.

Among those joining us from Kathmandu was Lhakpa Nuru, the young Sherpa who'd climbed with me during my first ascent in 2005. His presence gave me more confidence. Like many modern-day Sherpa, Lhakpa had been born into a life that, for better or worse, revolved around the mountain. He said he loved to climb, which was fortunate because the mountain provided the best livelihood for the Sherpa in the area, even if it wasn't always the best life.

I watched as Babu walked out of the foyer of my hotel and back into the congested streets of Kathmandu. I was already indebted to him for his support. We were all indebted to the Sherpa for their support. I thought of what Hillary had told me about his greatest achievement in life not being on the mountain, but in the schools and hospitals he had tried to fund for the Sherpa people. He may have felt guilty for opening the Khumbu up to so many egotistical tourists, but he'd done more than anyone to help the inhabitants of the area. Babu had tried to do the same. After Sean died, his sponsor had pursued a similar goal, raising money to build a school in Kathmandu in Sean's honour. Part of what I liked about Elia's plan was that it would help to raise awareness about Sean's school and continue to fund it beyond its construction.

The anxiety I felt about being an expedition leader on Everest was amplified the moment I learned that one of my climbers had forgotten his crampons back in Montreal and was now scrambling to buy a replacement pair in Kathmandu.

That sinking feeling came again during the trek to base camp, when Elia went on ahead, paying no mind to the rest of our group. I knew he was strong, but I had some concerns when I watched as he disappeared up ahead without bothering to look back to ensure that the rest of us were okay. He stopped only when he couldn't find the trail and needed me to point him in the right direction. Little did I know, he was actually trying to find a quiet place to be alone and apologize to the mountain for a previous transgression. (The year before, he'd laughed and joked with a Sherpa in the icefall while filming the site of a rescue helicopter crash from 1973.)

We were a week into our trek when we reached Dughla. I stopped, as I always did, next to Babu's chorten, but this time I asked him for guidance on how to safeguard the lives of the men in my care. We'd just passed the helipad and the rock on which Sean had died, and now we were at his chorten. Kneeling down by the memorial for Sean brought back a wave of emotions and made me realize how very different this climb already felt from the one Sean and I had set out to accomplish two years earlier. I brushed a tear from my face and placed a small stone atop his chorten.

As I stood there talking to Sean via the mound of sacred rocks piled in his honour, I had no idea that the weeks ahead would push me even further than the weeks behind had done. Entrusted with the lives of three men with barely enough experience to participate in a trek, I was now leading them into the Death Zone.

Just before we reached base camp, I took Elia aside and asked him if he wanted to take part in my little ritual with the mountain. It seemed fitting that I impart to him what Laurie Skreslet had imparted to me. At base camp, I pitched my tent as close to my usual spot as possible, unpacked my gear in the same orderly fashion I always did, and placed a photo of Annie and the girls next to my pillow. I put my sacred rice, along with the weathered old photo of Alex that had been with me on every journey on every mountain ever since Aconcagua, inside my climbing pack. When I was done, I went out to check on Elia, who'd seemed almost emotional upon entering base camp, having retraced Sean's footsteps to the very place where he'd last seen him two years earlier.

I tried to pass on to Elia all the knowledge that Babu had passed on to me. I explained to him that even if he wasn't religious, there was a place for spirituality on the mountain. He seemed ready and open to take in all aspects of the climb. He was growing on me as a friend and as a prospective partner on the mountain.

The sky was a beautiful blue without a cloud to be seen as the lamas smudged flour on our cheeks and handed us rice to throw on one another. The blessings completed, we convened in our dining tent to go over the next day's plan. I had adopted the same strategy employed by Babu in 2000 for how we would acclimatize for the summit: three rotations to different altitudes before our final summit attempt from Camp 4, just below the Death Zone.

For the next three weeks, we climbed back and forth through the icefall, over the Western Cwm all the way up to Camp 3, and Elia never lagged too far behind my lead. All the while, we heard reports of a stray dog somewhere up on the mountain. He'd been sighted at Camp 2—having clawed his way up through the snow and ice to 6,500 metres above the sea—the camp near which Babu had died, and where I'd nearly died seven years earlier.

It was one month to the day since our expedition began, when we stumbled, exhausted, into Camp 4, passing the old weather-beaten tent that doubled as a tomb for the unknown climber. I was nervous as I lay in my tent that night, knowing that I had to be mindful that nine lives (including my own) were now in my care. Our bodies were deteriorating rapidly as we slept, and they would begin to literally die just a few steps out of camp as we crossed into the Death Zone. I'd been combatting a terrible headache ever since Camp 2, but I'd experienced a weird hallucinatory vision in the night: an old Sherpa visited me inside my head to tell me to remember to drink more water. I'd awoken startled, unsure for the moment who had visited me. He'd had no discernable face. I forced as much water down my throat as possible and passed out. When I awoke, my head was clear. I ate some chocolate and popped half a Viagra pill. It was all the rage on the mountain that spring. The drug, which promotes erections by opening the tiny veins and arteries to the penis, has a similar effect on the lungs at high altitudes, helping to stave off hypoxia. Elia followed me out into the night. It was clear and beautiful, still and cold. The stars illuminated our path all the way up the South Col.

The Sherpa and I had planned for a nine thirty p.m. departure from Camp 4. If all went according to plan, we would be on the summit by five thirty in the morning, just in time for the sunrise. Then we'd head back to Camp 4 by one p.m. and onward to Camp 2 by six p.m. All told, we would spend fourteen and a half hours in the Death Zone. It is widely understood among all high-altitude climbers and guides that because of the rapid deterioration of mind and body above eight thousand metres, it's best to get to the summit and back as quickly as possible. Most deaths near the summit occur during descent, after sixteen hours in the Death Zone, when many climbers' cognitive functions become even more impaired than their bodies are.

From his place in our base camp tent 2.7 vertical kilometres

below, Garry Hartlin sat monitoring the weather patterns circling the mountain. I radioed down for guidance. There were
no storms in the forecast.

We were already down a Sherpa before we left Camp 4.
Elia's Sherpa had woken up too sick to risk the push for the
summit. The rest of us climbed through the night, untethered
to one another but attached to the fixed line as we moved up the
Southeast Ridge. The wind picked up as we went. It didn't take
long for Elia to fall back behind us. He was carrying all his camera gear, plus the oxygen his Sherpa would have carried for him.
I kept in radio contact with him until he lost his radio. Then I
had no way to direct him through the obstacles that lay before
him. He was on his own.

There was a group out in front of us, moving painfully
slowly up the South Col. We passed them only to learn, as the
wind and snow pelted us in the face, why they'd been climbing
so slowly. The weather was changing quickly, blowing snow
over the fixed line and forcing our Sherpa and me to dig out the
rope and re-fix every anchor as we went. It was still dark when
the team we'd passed abandoned their climb and turned back
for Camp 4, leaving just us and one other team still pushing for
the summit. I didn't know where the other team was, only that
they were somewhere up above. I was encouraged to know that
we weren't the only fools still up here. The wind was deafening now, penetrating the down in our snowsuits and leaving us
chilled to the core. I checked my watch. It was three a.m. and
we were at 8,300 metres—halfway between Camp 4 and the
summit—just below the Balcony, a small, flat spot below the
ridge where we could rest and huddle in the cold.

I estimated that Elia was by now an hour's climb behind us. I gathered the rest of the team around. "We can't keep going like this," I said. "It's getting too dangerous up here. We can either go back or huddle here and wait for the wind to die down." All agreed that we'd wait it out. We huddled together in the snow, our faces buried inside our arms. I radioed down to Garry, alerting him of the situation. He said the weather seemed to be breaking up above. I struggled not to shiver. Elia arrived shortly before dawn. He'd lost his radio but had found his way to us with the help of Phinzo, one of two Sherpa who'd been hired by the oldest member of my team to increase his chances of making it to the top. He huddled next to us, exhausted and cold.

"Guys!" I shouted. "Look at that." The sun was rising, breaking through the storm as the wind died down. I rose to my feet, took a look around, and realized, in the light of day, that we'd spent the night within sight of a few bodies forever left on the mountainside. I checked to make sure that everyone in the team was still strong, then we kept moving. We were still 450 metres shy of the summit, and though we were already six hours off schedule, we would be okay so long as we could make it to the summit by noon. That would give us enough time to make it back to Camp 4 before darkness set in. My greatest concern now was the amount of oxygen we were consuming up on the mountain. We weren't too far away from the Balcony when one of my clients opted to turn around. His feet were frozen and he was being forced to decide between making the summit and losing his toes. He chose to save his toes.

It was late morning by the time we reached the South

Summit. The lone team that had been ahead of us in the night had already reached the top and passed us on their way back down to Camp 4. I was now the only expedition leader on the mountain currently trying to guide his men higher into the Death Zone. I believed that Elia had turned around also, since he'd waved to me an hour or so earlier, signalling a return to Camp 4. Only the oldest of my clients and his Sherpa were still following Lhakpa and me up the mountain. Lhakpa and I had the energy required to push on up the last one hundred metres over the Hillary Step and to the peak, but I was no longer confident that my client would survive the descent if he continued to follow us. I looked at Lhakpa and told him, "I think we're done."

He tilted his head at me. "Gabriel, we so close. It right there."

"I know. I know. But I don't want to go to the top, then turn around and pass dead bodies from my team below. I go down. You want to summit, you go summit. I go down."

Lhakpa nodded. He understood.

I turned my attention to the man, who was staggering forward at a painfully slow pace. He didn't have the energy he needed to take him to the top and back at a reasonable speed. He'd be out of oxygen before he got back to the Balcony, and we'd be climbing down in the dark, pushing twenty-four hours in the Death Zone.

I ran through the possibilities of what I might have to say or do to stop him from carrying on if he refused to abandon his ascent. He was a proud man who had given his all just to get to where he was. I thought of myself five years earlier, exhausted but pushing forward blindly until Babu tapped me on the shoulder and told me what I already knew: "If you keep going, you're going to die."

He looked at me, exhausted and flushed. I pulled off my mask to talk to him.

"How you feeling? You feel good?"

He nodded, then collapsed into the snow beside us for a break. I knew he wouldn't admit defeat himself. And I knew if I kept going, he'd keep following me until he died.

I breathed in the cold, thin air.

"The expedition is over," I said. "I'm going down. But if you want to go up, I'll let you go up with your Sherpa."

I figured it would be easier for him to follow me knowing that I was the one giving up, not him.

He didn't even pause. "Ah no, Gabriel. I'm done."

I patted him on the shoulder, nodded at Lhakpa, and together, we all started back down.

It took us about an hour just to get back to within sight of the Balcony. I was the last man heading down on the fixed line, keeping my team in front of me as I went. I watched them disappear around a corner of rock. I took one last look up toward the summit, said my goodbye to the most beautiful view in the world, then turned back toward the bend in the ridge. And there, to my horror, was Elia. Standing directly in front of me on his way up. I was shocked. Completely and utterly shocked. He had come out of nowhere and was all by himself.

I stared at him, surprise, concern, and a touch of anxiety churning over in my empty stomach. He looked through me with expressionless eyes. I could tell he was still set on getting to the summit. I could also tell he wouldn't survive up here without me. It was just before noon, and we were at least a three-hour climb from the top.

He was twice my size, still built like that powerlifter who'd set a record just a few years earlier. I stared at him for a good long while, then raised my goggles and unclipped my oxygen mask.

"Elia, what are you doing here?"

"I'm going up."

"But I saw you turn around."

"What?"

"Hours ago, you waved your hand at me and said you were turning around."

He looked at me, confused. "No. That was Phinzo," he said, explaining that it was one of the Sherpa who'd turned around, not him. "I thought you understood. I would have called you, but I lost my radio," he said. Then he took another step closer, pulling his body weight up on the fixed line. I watched as his ascender got closer to mine.

"Elia," I said, "the expedition is over."

He didn't say anything. He just continued looking at me, staring blankly from behind his goggles. He took a step closer, his right hand gripped to his ascender. He slid his ascender farther up the fixed line. I gripped mine and slid it down toward his, blocking its way up the line. We stood like that for a moment.

I could see how much this meant to him. "Elia," I said, "you're two hundred metres from your death. We can't make it."

In that moment, I was scared. I was scared that I might be wrong to stop him, scared that I might be right, and scared what would happen if he forced his way past. Summit fever can do terrible things to a climber's psyche. It can blind him to danger and make him throw away his humanity. It's what leads some men to step over the dying bodies of their fellow climbers in order to make sure they reach the summit.

"Elia, we can't. It's too dangerous now. There's only us up here. We've spent too much time up here already. We have to go back."

I watched as he lowered his head and looked down at how far he'd come. He stared down into the Khumbu Valley and out over Nepal for a good long while. I didn't know what he was going to do next. Then he looked back up, nodded, and broke into tears. I started crying too.

Chapter 16

THE OTHER SIDE OF THE MOUNTAIN

I closed the trunk and watched as Annie pulled away. There was no chance she was going to come to the airport. Not after all the previous times. It was easier on both of us to make our goodbye as brief as possible. And when she went home, she did as she had to do: put me as far out of sight as possible. She'd ensure that my personal belongings (I still didn't really have much, other than clothes and a few books) were neatly stored in a closet that she dared not open. She knew if she did, it would bring on a wave of anxiety, anger, and fear. She called this "the dark side of the mountain." The dark side of my obsession.

I gave my bags one last look as they disappeared on the conveyor belt at Montréal-Trudeau airport. There was more than just my usual climbing gear in those bags. I'd packed two priceless tokens of memorabilia: a Montreal Canadiens one-hundredth anniversary flag signed by every member of the current team, as well as an ice axe bearing the signature of my childhood hero, Guy Lafleur. The plan was for me to carry the flag and the axe to the top of Everest and then bring them both back to be sold at auction to raise money for the Montreal Canadiens Children's Foundation. Perhaps it wouldn't have the same drama as bringing Sean's ashes to the top of the mountain, but the Canadiens seemed to be enthused about it, as was their broadcaster, RDS, who'd agreed to broadcast clips from my summit attempt over their network during the NHL playoffs. They'd also had me on one of their sports shows to explain the challenge that lay ahead.

That's where I met the man who would later save my life. I was in the makeup room, getting foundation dabbed on my weather-beaten cheeks, when I noticed a little bald guy next to me, chatting up his makeup artist. He cracked a joke, I laughed, and the next thing I knew, I'd made a new friend. His name was Sylvain Guimond. He was a multi-millionaire who'd made his fortune in biomechanics, having developed a computer program that tracked the movements of pro athletes like Tiger Woods and John Smoltz to get the most out of their bodies while causing the least amount of strain. Sylvain was a fortunate man in more ways than one. He'd woken up in New York on the morning of September 11, 2001, and began his commute to the World Trade Center, where he was supposed to put his system to work on the New York Rangers. A last-minute call from Glen Sather redirected him to Madison Square Garden instead and saved his life.

He'd sold his company at the age of thirty-eight, then completed a Ph.D. in sports psychology. Now he was making his name working with speed and figure skaters in the lead-up to the 2010 Olympics. His main clients were Bryce Davison and Jessica Dubé, who were still reeling from a 2007 accident in which Davison had sliced Dubé's face with his skate during a routine spin. She took eighty-three stitches to the cheek and nose and was left with a very visible scar. Davison's scar was deeper. He was gripped by post-traumatic stress disorder (PTSD) and couldn't get through their routine without the fear that he was about to cut his partner's face off again. That's where Sylvain came in. He'd been working on the skater's psyche to help him overcome the accident that haunted him on the ice and off.

My makeup complete, I reached for my phone and took down Sylvain's number.

"I'd like to keep in touch with you," I told him. "I might need you someday."

"I've always wanted to work with a climber," he said. "I bet you've seen some stuff."

It was my turn to go on camera. I spoke of my upcoming plan to bring the Canadiens' flag to the top of Everest and to do so with the help of an ice axe signed by my childhood hero. In so doing, I would join a very small and elite list of climbers who had summitted Everest from both its Nepalese and Tibetan faces.

I'd always wanted to try Everest via the North Col. It might as well have been a completely different mountain than the one I'd climbed before. With its own base camp, its own set of unique obstacles, and its own mystique, the route up Everest's northern face, which follows in the footsteps of George Mallory, has long been considered a more strenuous climb than the more frequently travelled route, the one taken by Sir Edmund Hillary up the Southeast Ridge. The two routes aren't even in the same country.

Before inheriting its name from Sir George Everest (a Welsh geographer and surveyor-general of India from 1830 to 1843), the three-sided pyramid that sits supreme on the border of Tibet and Nepal was known by three very different names. To the Nepalese familiar with its southwest face, the mountain was known as Deva-dhunga, the "Seat of God" (it was later changed to Sagarmatha, "Goddess of the Sky.") To the Tibetans, who lived in the shadow of its weather-beaten North and Kangshung Faces, it was Jomolungma, "Goddess, Mother of the World." Its third name was given to it by the British, who obsessively mapped the region in order to better understand the defensive wall of mountains that stood like a natural fortress between the British Raj and its imperial neighbours to the north. To the British, the mountain was simply known as Peak XV—that is, of course, until they decided that it was far too special to have just a numeric name.

Sir Everest (whose name was actually pronounced "Eve-rest," not "Ever-est") had retired from his post as surveyor-general of India and settled back into a noble life in England when the Great Trigonometrical Survey, a sixty-year project undertaken on behalf of the Survey of India, discovered that Peak XV was actually the highest point in the Himalaya and, by consequence, the highest point on Earth. Because of its newfound status as Earth's third pole, it was decided that the mountain needed a better name. Rumour has it that the seventy-five-year-old Everest objected to giving his name to the mountain, but that didn't matter to the British any more than the fact that the locals already had two names for it.

For sixty-nine years after its discovery as the world's highest peak in 1852, Everest remained off limits to foreign climbers. The kingdoms of both Nepal and Tibet had closed their borders to the West. It was Tibet, under diplomatic pressure from the British in 1921, which opened its borders first. And it's for that reason that the first eight Western expeditions to the mountain were made via its inhospitable northern face.

Many know the story of George Mallory, the most distinguished member of the first three expeditions to the mountain. For Mallory, getting to the top of Everest was an obsession. He was known for climbing like a man on a one-way trip, which is less romantic than it is suicidal and ultimately tragic, given that he had three young children. Though Mallory may have gotten farther up the mountain than anyone else on those early climbs, he would never have been able to do so were it not for the help of an overlooked and largely forgotten Canadian.

Born in Ottawa in April 1890, Sir Edward Oliver Wheeler was the son of the co-founder of the Alpine Club of Canada. His father had helped map and delineate the mountainous border between the provinces of British Columbia and Alberta. Wheeler got his start as a mountaineer climbing in Banff National Park before studying engineering at the Royal Military College of Canada. A decorated soldier during the First World War, he joined the Survey of India after the armistice and relocated to Delhi. When Mallory and company set out from London on the first British Mount Everest Expedition, Wheeler was chosen to help them survey both the mountain and the surrounding area in order to find an actual way to the summit. It was Wheeler who mapped the team's journey up the East Rongbuk Glacier. And it was Wheeler who first discovered the North Col, a steep wall of ice and snow that cut across the top of the East Rongbuk Glacier, creating a sharp-edged pass between Everest and neighbouring Changtse in Tibet. It rose gradually all the way up to the Northeast Ridge, creating a natural route to the summit. Shortly after making his discovery, Wheeler led Mallory and a third member of the expedition to the North Col, and in doing so, they became the first men to actually set foot on Everest.

The following year, Everest claimed its first victims. Seven Gurkha porters were killed when Mallory and his men accidentally triggered an avalanche while trying to get back to the North Col by going straight up an icy slope instead of taking a safer, more roundabout approach. The avalanche, which began with what Mallory described as "an explosion of untamped gunpowder," put an end to the 1922 expedition.

Mallory, who was a schoolteacher, spent the better part of the next year trying to raise support for a return to the mountain. It was while on a publicity tour for his third expedition that he famously responded to a journalist's question. Asked why he would even bother to climb Everest, Mallory replied, "Because it is there."

He made his final summit push on June 8, 1924. He was last spotted "going strongly for the top" by a fellow member of that expedition who was watching from a far-away lookout. Mallory was tethered to his climbing partner, Sandy Irvine, and it was believed at the time that the two had reached the Second Step, the largest of three prominent cliff faces that bar all attempts at summitting via the Northeast Ridge. Forty metres in height, the last five of which are more or less vertical, it is the most technically demanding part of the entire climb. And it's located just 240 metres shy of the summit, well inside the Death Zone.

Whether Mallory and Irvine made it to the summit might forever remain a mystery because the climbers soon disappeared behind a cloud and were never seen alive again. Mallory remained lost on the mountain until 1999, when he was found clinging to its side, having fallen into the Great Couloir, an immense and steep gorge, just below the North Col. It's believed he fell off the ridge while trying to descend, broke his leg, and then waited for death. Irvine is still up there somewhere. Many climbers have theories as to where they might find him. And I'm no different, which is one of the reasons why I wanted to climb the North Col to begin with, and why, to this day, I intend to go back.

The British organized four more expeditions to the north side of the mountain, none of which managed to get any closer to the summit than they had in 1924. The mountain was left alone during World War II and wasn't attempted again until 1947, when an inadequately provisioned Canadian engineer and mountaineer took a wild and unsuccessful stab at the mountain. Accompanied by two Sherpa, one of which happened to be Tenzing Norgay, the expedition never made it to the North Col due to terrible weather. The next time anyone set foot on the mountain, they did so via Nepal. It wasn't until 1960, seven years after Sir Edmund Hillary's ascent from the south, that a Chinese team finally made it to the summit via the North Col.

Though the north face had been tamed in recent years (the Chinese bolted a ladder to the mountain at the Second Step to make it less of an imposing and deadly obstacle), my desire to summit from it was unchecked. To summit Everest from its north and south sides would help set me apart by putting me on a short list of Everest climbers who had reached the summit via two of its sides. It felt, in some twisted, weird way, as if my previous climb up the Southeast Ridge hadn't amounted to anything more than an A.

And because I was still my father's son, I needed an A+.

* * *

Kathmandu was abuzz with the usual chaos when I arrived. I'd spent the better part of the last two days in the air, but now I was sitting, bleary-eyed, on a couch next to Miss Elizabeth Hawley, the keeper of the mountains. I told her of my plan to lead an expedition of three to the top of Everest via the Northeast Ridge.

I had two friends coming with me on this expedition. The first was Elia Saikaly, who was more eager than ever to get to the summit. Elia and I had grown close on the mountainside back in 2007, despite his own difficulties accepting that I'd made him turn around. He'd struggled with feelings of failure after that climb, but he'd completed his film about Sean and had been looking for a chance at redemption on the mountain. When I told him I was going to the north side and could use a film-maker, he signed right up. We were soon joined by a very young and successful entrepreneur from Montreal named Luc Poirier.

Luc wasn't the most experienced climber, but he had the passion. He'd been to the top of Kilimanjaro and had nearly succeeded on Aconcagua. He knew he couldn't get to the top of Everest by himself and had hired me for my logistics and experience.

For five days we sat in Kathmandu, waiting for the Chinese government to approve our passage into Tibet. We weren't alone. All other climbers trying to approach the mountain from the north were delayed passage. Rumours circulated the city that the Chinese government was trying to quickly clean up a mess of human casualties from the previous year, when they shut down the mountain while a thirty-one-man team carried the Olympic Torch up to the summit. No one knew what was really going on.

We were already behind schedule by the time we got clearance to cross the border by Jeep and make our way over the Tibetan plateau before dropping south into the northern reaches of the Himalaya. We spent the better part of two days clinging to the roll bars of the Jeep as we drove slowly over many of the same rough-cut rocks that the first British explorers had traversed all those years ago. We might have been making our way to base camp with the help of a mechanized vehicle, but we were doing it without a caravan of three hundred yaks, fifty mules, and one hundred porters, like the ones that had travelled alongside those first expeditions.

I was puking my guts out by the time we reached base camp. My entire body had been weakened by a horrendous case of food poisoning I picked up in the thousand-year-old Tibetan town of Tingri. I'd thought I was mounting a recovery by the time we left the town, but I was now unable to stand, and I collapsed into my tent to shiver and sweat until I regained enough strength to eat and talk. I still wasn't in the greatest shape to climb.

Everest's Tibetan base camp was nearly empty when we arrived, the majority of the would-be summitteers having opted to approach the mountain via Nepal in order to avoid delays brought on by Chinese bureaucracy. We sat at base camp like stationary objects, and soon learned that our sirdar was an alcoholic set on extracting as much money as possible from Luc. There was little to be admired or enjoyed about our time at the base. Situated on gravel moraines left by the retraction of the Rongbuk Glacier, which is said to have shrunk by roughly one hundred vertical metres in the ninety years since its discovery, Everest's North Base Camp has the same allure as a gravel parking lot. I was eager to get on with the twenty-one-kilometre trek over the melting remnants of the Rongbuk to the Advanced Base Camp (ABC) at 6,400 metres. We were now within striking distance of the North Col, which begins at seven thousand metres and intersects with the Northeast Ridge higher up above. I was out of breath, weak, and struggling to eat, drink, or sleep by the time we reached ABC. I knew my body wasn't acclimatizing properly, but I was shocked when the oxygen saturation in my blood dipped down to 39 percent. It hadn't been that low since the time I'd gone hypothermic in the night after the zipper on my sleeping bag broke. And now I was at the same altitude on the other side of the mountain. There were so few climbers on the mountain that the nearest doctor I could locate to discuss the situation with was Dr. White, who'd climbed with me on Mont Blanc. He was at home in Montreal, and only reachable when the sky was clear enough for me to get a signal on my satellite phone. Exhausted, shivering and sweating at the same time, I peered out the flap of my tent toward the moon and dialed the phone, hoping that the weather would hold long enough that I might get a diagnosis from the doctor. I told him of my predicament: there were men on the mountain waiting for me to guide them to the summit, but I wasn't acclimatizing.

"Your body is probably not reacting properly because of the food poisoning," Dr. White explained.

When I told him my saturation level, he advised me to get right off the mountain and head down into the valley before it was too late.

I listened, but I wasn't ready to accept defeat.

"I'm at 6,400 metres right now. What if I go down to 5,700 for forty-eight to seventy-two hours?" I suggested. "My saturation should bounce back. If it gets to 70 down there, do you think it's worth coming back up?"

He listened quietly. I knew I was being somewhat crazy to even suggest it.

"If it doesn't get up to 70, what are you going to do? Honestly, are you going to turn around?"

I paused for a moment.

"Yes."

"Then go down and see what happens."

It was nine p.m., not a good time to try to descend back to base camp. I popped half a Diamox (a pill that helps prevent epileptic seizures but also serves to combat altitude sickness) but puked the pill out as soon as I swallowed it. I was feeling desperate and tried to keep myself awake until morning for fear of edema. It was no use.

I awoke in a panic, my heart racing. I checked my watch—I'd been asleep for nearly three hours. I felt like I was having a heart attack. I checked my saturation. It was 31 percent. I cried out for Elia, but the wind was so strong that my voice couldn't carry even the few metres from my tent to his. He couldn't hear me. I rummaged through my summit gear in the tent, found the oxygen mask I'd brought up to wear in the Death Zone, strapped it to my face, and began to breathe. My heart slowly calmed; my eyes closed and I drifted off. Seven hours passed until I awoke again. My oxygen saturation level had risen to 69, still below that of the other climbers even after my night spent with the mask strapped to my face.

I knew that without an oxygen mask strapped to my face, my saturation would plummet back into the danger zone. I alerted Elia that I was heading down to recover but advised him and Luc to continue with their acclimatization along with their Sherpa while I tried to sort out what was wrong with me.

I left Elia and Luc with our Sherpa at ABC, grabbed a stove, some fuel, and a tent and headed back down to the lower elevation. I was popping Tylenol and sleeping pills to make sure I would sleep. I passed out the moment I pitched my tent at 5,735 metres, waking only when my urine soaked my sleeping bag and got so cold that I could no longer sleep. I jolted back to life, confused, mortified to find that I was so out of it I'd spilled my pee bottle in my sleeping bag. I stripped naked and slept in a small, dry part of the bag. For the next three days, I recovered slowly, monitoring my saturation levels obsessively until they reached about 70 percent. When I wasn't monitoring, I was writing to Annie, thanking her for supporting me even when it was difficult for her, and trying to explain all the reasons why I felt I had to get to the top of this mountain again.

"No matter how light I climb, I always bring a photo of you and the girls with me to the top of any mountain," I wrote. "The Sherpa, they always travel with a photo of the Dalai Lama in their pocket, because His Holiness is their one true guide. I always carry you."

When I finished writing to Annie, I wrote to God, although in that moment I had replaced God with the mountain. I asked for safe guidance in the days ahead. I knew I was still in rough shape, but there was no way I was going to abandon this climb. Not without at least strapping on my crampons and taking my first few steps on the North Col.

I was still weak when I decided to head back up to regroup with Elia and Luc. I sent a message up the mountain with a Sherpa, asking Elia to prep two protein bars, two chocolate bars, and two energy drinks for my arrival.

Whatever struggles I was having with my own body, they were nothing compared to the growing shit show that was engulfing the mountain. I rejoined Elia and Luc at ABC only to learn that teams of Sherpa had revolted against other expeditions. Everyone seemed to be heading down the mountain. Meanwhile, a ferocious wind began battering the North Col. The storm destroyed our tents in the night and ripped away the anchors that fixed the lines to the mountainside, leaving us to cling nervously to the ropes as we struggled upwards to continue our acclimatization. No matter what I did, I couldn't get higher than ABC without supplemental oxygen. My body was completely spent. At one point, I was having so much trouble putting on my crampon that I looked at Elia and said, "I can't believe I'm doing the thing I hate the most."

"What do you mean?" Elia asked.

"I'm going up when I should be going down."

He looked through his goggles at my tired eyes as I tried to focus on anything other than the climb. My relentlessness was becoming dangerous. I didn't know what was wrong with my mind any more than I knew what was wrong with my body. I'd become what Jacques had warned me about all those years ago. I was like Captain Ahab pushing myself and my crew to the end of the world, and for what?

The wind began to howl louder, halting our ascent midway up the North Col and nearly ripping us from the mountainside. When I saw a gap in the line, I gripped Luc's pack and tried to keep us both from blowing away with the monsoon until we reached the next section of rope. I felt more vulnerable than I had in years, as if my life, as well as Luc's, depended on my weakening ability to hold my grip. When finally we went back down to Camp 1 to regroup, Luc announced he'd had enough. I understood him entirely. And yet I refused to follow him out as he made his way back home to his family in Montreal.

It was May 12, 2009, and as I walked among the tents at base camp, I spotted a man sipping tea. He was an infamous climber, well-known throughout the community for having abandoned his tent-mate, who was deathly ill with edema, in 2007. He'd decided to leave the man to die so that he could carry on with his summit. I was confronting the climber about his actions when an energetic young man materialized from out of nowhere and calmed me down by asking if I wanted to have a cup of tea with him. His name was Frank Ziebarth, and he was wearing a hat that read, "Fuck the Fake Shit." He asked me how my climb was going. I told him terrible. He said he was having his own difficulties too, but that he was feeling strong and determined to reach the summit.

"This will be my fifth and last eight-thousander," he said.

"Your last?" I asked.

"I'm retiring."

He was twenty-nine years old and looking to settle down. He said he'd come to the mountain with a plan to reach the summit without oxygen and then unfurl a banner from his jacket, asking his girlfriend to marry him.

Frank was immediately likeable. One cup of tea turned into a pot of tea and then into a friendly conversation that spread out over several days. He was born in Germany, began rock climbing in his youth, and had had his eyes set on Everest for as long as he could remember.

He said he'd been with his girlfriend for six years. They'd fallen in love in Germany and then relocated to Calgary.

"She's a rock climber too," he said.

"Ah," I said. "So she understands?"

He laughed. "Do they ever really understand? I was dreaming about Everest before I even met her. But after this, I'm done."

There was a maturity to him that I found inspiring. Here was a man, twenty-nine years old, probably the strongest climber on this side of the mountain, a fitness guru with a purist's heart. He'd already climbed five of the world's fourteen highest mountains, and he was out here on his last climb, willing to give it all up for the woman he loved.

"That's gotta be quite some girl," I said.

We exchanged contact information. I snapped his picture and told him I hoped we could keep in touch, maybe do some ice and rock climbing back in Canada, little stuff, just to keep him in shape after his "retirement." Then I wished him good luck on the mountainside. Fewer than 2 percent of the climbers who had reached Everest's summit had done so without supplementary oxygen, and I knew he was in for a hell of a struggle.

"Whatever you do, don't sit down," I said.

He laughed. He'd heard it all before.

Pushing hard for the summit, he was gone by the time I woke up the next morning. He was still up there a week later when Elia and I felt good enough to break out again onto the North Col. It was May 28, well past the date when the monsoon usually hit Everest, shutting down the climbing season by pummelling the mountainside with storm after storm. I was anxious not to give up. Our Sherpa were no longer willing to go up the mountain with us, and we watched as teams of climbers gave up their attempts for the summit and headed back down to base camp. The only other climber, besides Elia and me, still crazy enough to be taking off from ABC this late in the season was a Peruvian named Richard, who, like Frank, had been trying to get to the top without oxygen. He opted to stick with us in order to better both his chances and ours.

I was still reeling from the food poisoning, and sucking on oxygen at seven thousand metres just to keep myself upright. It wasn't long before the weather began to change, and soon we were climbing into a storm just inside the Death Zone. As we crossed the eight-thousand-metre threshold, I looked at my oxygen regulator and saw that my last bottle was nearly empty. I'd been sucking on gas for nearly two days, and I knew that the moment I took off the mask, I would be in serious trouble. My mind and body would begin to die almost immediately. I felt like one of those doomed astronauts in the movies, floating through space with a compromised space suit.

"You're going to have to get me more oxygen, or I'm going to be in trouble," I said.

"You're out again already?" Elia exclaimed.

I nodded, then pointed upwards. "There should be some tanks stashed at Camp 3. I'll keep coming up, but you're going to have to bring me some down, or I'm dead."

He looked at me, wondering whether he should really leave me in such a dangerous state. Then he put his hand on my shoulder, told me he'd be back as soon as he found some oxygen, and hurried on up the col toward Camp 3, which was still an hour's climb away.

I watched him disappear from sight, counting my every breath, trying desperately to limit the number of inhalations required between each step. But it was no use.

I was stuck. I knew I should have already gone down, but if I turned around now on my own, I wouldn't stand a chance. And if I just sat there, I'd risk falling asleep and freezing to death in the gathering storm. I had no choice but to keep pushing on into the fog and ice and hope that Elia would find at least one canister with oxygen in it and then come back and find me before my gas ran out.

My tank was completely empty and I was about to fall over

by the time I stumbled into Camp 3, the highest camp on the North Col, three hundred vertical metres inside the Death Zone, yet still a long and arduous journey, mostly sideways across the Northeast Ridge, to the summit. Elia had scavenged a few half-empty bottles of oxygen by the time I arrived. He gave me one and I screwed it into my oxygenator and sucked back. The camp was abandoned. We had no food, no fuel, and no shelter. Our Sherpa had left a stash of food and oxygen under a rock somewhere, but in the blinding blizzard, we could find nothing. Without Sherpa support, we were reliant on the scattered detritus we could find in the camp for sustenance. We were like scavengers, searching through discarded oxygen bottles and food stashes in order to resupply and continue our ascent. The snow was really coming down now, the wind howling as the temperature dipped below minus twenty-five degrees. Elia combed through the snow on his hands and knees, gathering decade-old packages of freeze-dried meatballs, along with whatever half-empty canisters of oxygen he could find. There was no telling how old the canisters were. Just as there was no telling where our tent was supposed to be. I began pawing through the shredded remnants of old camps. I spotted a bright yellow patch of fabric off in the distance, protruding from beneath a layer of snow. It was fifty metres away, across a cliff-faced traverse. With my ice axe in hand, I cut across the cliff, kicking my crampons into the ice wall until I could reach the tent. I tucked it into my pack and went back across the cliff to Elia. Then we pitched the tent in the dark. The wind was so strong that I could barely get the tent upright, so I threw my backpack inside to weigh it down and then crawled inside along

Full of energy with Elia Saikaly at Camp 1 on Everest's south side in 2007. Elia and I had returned to Everest to complete a documentary about our late friend Sean Egan.

Sunset at Camp 4 on Everest in 2007. It's views like this that attract many to the Death Zone.

One of the more difficult night of my life. Fighting frostbite and exhaustion at 8,300 metres on Everest's North Col, 2009. Those are socks on my hands.

Babu Chiri Sherpa, at centre in purple, with his team after his record-setting speed ascent in 2000.

Babu Chiri Sherpa (seen here in 2000) was a mentor to me and probably the most respected Sherpa since Tenzing Norgay.

In good company at the top of the world in 2005 with my trusted companion and friend Lhakpa Nuru

ooking down at the North Col, George Mallory's route up Everest's north face, 2009.

At the top of Everest for the second time, 2010.

Looking out over Tibet from inside the Death Zone on Everest, 2009.

Exiting the water in last place after a 3.8-kilometre swim during my second Ironman, 2012. Learning to swim at age fifty taught me that while you may never conquer some fears, you can learn to live with them.

I don't know how many avalanches I've seen in my life, or how many I've photographed. It's hard not to stare at them when you hear them rumble. Nanga Parbat, 2013.

Assessing the damage at Camp 1 on Nanga Parbat after it was hit by yet another avalanche, 2013.

In the meadow at Nanga Parbat Base Camp, days before the Taliban massacre, 2013.

My friend Ernie Marksaitis training in Chamonix, 2012, in preparation for Nanga Parbat.

At Everest Base Camp the day after the earthquake in 2015. Most of the survivors had already been evacuated. Emotionally and physically exhausted, I was waiting for a helicopter to take me back to Lukla.

With Amy again—still climbing with me after all these years!—and her sister Kelsey, 2015.

With my daughter, Alexandra, and my granddaughter, Rosie, in 2016. Seeing Alex become a mother has helped me understand the personal toll of being a climber.

It's not always easy staying in shape for the climb. Training with Kelsey over Christmas break in Florida, 2014.

Searching for the best route to the top of the unclimbed Tenzing and Hillary Peaks, 2016.

with Elia. Exhausted, we just sat there staring at each other, our headlamps barely strong enough to cut through the darkness. It wasn't until I shifted my weight to the back of the tent that I realized I'd pitched it so that it was dangling over a cliff.

We were both groggy to the point of collapse. It would have taken nothing more than an errant shift of body weight for us to accidentally flip the tent over the cliff, sending us bouncing down the Great Couloir to our deaths. "This isn't good," I said, understating the obvious. Yet neither of us seemed able to find the strength to move. We were sitting upright and nodding off, both of us knowing full well that if we accidentally leaned back in our sleep, we'd be falling before we even woke up. But we were so exhausted and starved for oxygen that it was difficult to concentrate, let alone calculate risk or think through our actions with any sort of rational understanding.

"I'm so tired," I said.

For a moment, we just sat there, both of us wondering if we could survive the night if we didn't move for the next eight hours.

Elia nodded and closed his eyes.

I was slowly drifting off to sleep when I was startled back to life by the realization that my decisions were going to kill us.

"This is crazy," I said. "I need to pull this shit together. We need to get everything out of the tent, slowly."

We pushed our bags back through the door, followed by all the canisters of oxygen Elia had gathered. Then we crawled out. The moment I dragged my leg out of the tent, it took off with the wind and disappeared downward into the clouds above Tibet. Without our weight to anchor it down, it might as well have been a kite. Yet it had no lift in the thin air.

I watched it in a state of shock.

"I think we're fucked," I said.

We sat in the snow, the altitude and our exhaustion increasingly hampering our cognitive abilities. We knew we should be searching around for another tent, but instead we just sat there, exposed to the blizzard. The snow had gathered thickly on our bodies by the time Richard arrived. He'd been climbing slowly through the storm, hoping that we'd have a shelter built and soup boiling upon his arrival.

I told Richard my thoughts on the situation: "Richard, we're completely fucked."

He looked at me in a way that made me realize that he wasn't yet ready to give up on life. It was enough to snap me back to reality. We desperately needed to resume our search for another tent. We spread out, the three of us never more than three metres apart, and began patting through the snow until finally we found the collapsed remnants of some long-abandoned lodging. We pitched the tent and crawled inside. Extreme fatigue was beginning to mess with my mind. My feet felt so cold that I took off my boots and put my feet inside my down mitts to warm them up. Then I put my hands in my socks to keep them from freezing. I sat there spaced out in the cold, the thin tent material the only layer between the ice and my snowsuit. Unconsciously cuddling up to Richard in order to steal his body heat, I slept in fifteen-minute bursts.

When morning came and I realized we had not died, I unzipped the tent and took a look outside. The monsoon clouds were gathering in the distance but at lower altitude. The wind was still high, blowing snow off the mountain and into our tent.

I thought of Frank as I gathered up handfuls of snow and began melting it on my stove. He was still up there on the Northeast Ridge. He'd been up there all night.

For nine hours, I melted snow, trying to create at least three litres of water for each of us so that we could combat the altitude and survive the climb to the summit and back. Each of us knew full well that we should already have turned around, and yet we remained focused with a singular determination to finish what we were already referring to as "the climb from hell."

Water duty complete, I laid out the plan for the summit.

"If the weather's clear tonight, we'll leave at ten p.m.," I said. "It will be a long haul, but we should get to the Second Step by two a.m. and, hopefully, the summit by seven a.m."

I closed my eyes and fell asleep once more. I awoke at ten p.m. to Elia shaking my arm. I was still exhausted. I stumbled outside, sat down on a rock, and looked up at the moon over Everest. It was a perfect night. I reached for my crampons and nearly keeled over into the snow.

I was still too exhausted to stand. I shook my head at Elia. "I'm not ready for this," I said. Then I crawled back into the tent and passed out again. At midnight, I got my second wind. I suited up and, together, the three of us began making our way from the North Col onto the Northeast Ridge. We were alone: three men staggering slowly through waist-deep snow, unfixed to anything, knowing full well that the dead on this mountain outnumbered us. It was blisteringly cold as we made for the ridge, just a few hundred metres above the snow basin where George Mallory still lay, clinging to the mountain. It was impossible not to think of him and the other dead up here.

I was just starting to get some momentum when I looked down at my foot in the snow and realized I'd lost a crampon. A strange relief rushed over my body. There was no way I'd make it to the summit without a crampon. I knew if we kept going, I'd slip and fall and end up in the Grand Couloir myself.

"No more," I whispered to myself and the mountain.

Then I shouted out to Elia. I was just shaking my head when he turned around.

"No more."

CHAPTER 17

BACK ON TOP

There's an image that's been seared into my mind for a few years now. It's the face of a man I barely knew but considered a friend nonetheless. I can still see him in the night when I close my eyes. He doesn't smile. He doesn't scream. He just looks at me from beneath a layer of frost-covered flesh. When he visits me, I don't sleep. He remains as I left him, seated near the top of the world, trapped in the Death Zone.

Before I tell the story of that friend and his small place in the larger narrative of my life, let me explain that it's because of that man that I now have a different definition than most people of what is commonly referred to as the Death Zone.

In order to understand what I'm trying to say, you have to believe that I have never climbed a mountain in order to stroke my ego or to say that I did it. On some level, I climb for the same reason an otherwise fully functioning man steps outside his office to fill his lungs with the smoke he knows could one day kill him. I climb because I'm weak. And I can't not climb.

And so I dragged myself back. To that place high in the sky where man was not built to survive. There, on the North Col, that frozen ridge that divides your world from mine, I found myself caught in yet another snowstorm in the dark of night. A year had passed since I lost my crampon in the snow and forced myself to turn around, exactly one year since I was last here with Elia and Richard. And though neither of them was with me now, I had been drawn back. Haunted by my own defeat.

* * *

Standing motionless in a cloud 8,300 metres above Tibet, setting out from Camp 3, an oxygen mask pressed to my face, I took a deep breath of compressed gas and wondered how many more steps it would take before I'd poke my head above the storm and begin seeing stars. I was just a few hours shy of the Earth's summit and feeling deceptively strong. My blood was turning to sludge; my brain and lungs were slowly swelling as my heart pounded against my chest. I was dying, but I felt inspired. Optimistic even. I was three hundred metres into the Death Zone, yet still hours away from my goal.

Lhakpa, the Nepalese Sherpa with whom I'd climbed many times, stood in the falling snow lit up by my headlamp. We'd been climbing for thirteen days. We'd crossed into Tibet to follow in my own footsteps and then push beyond the place where I'd acknowledged defeat. There was no fame to be had this time, no media interest in my ascent. It was just us and the mountain and the ghost of the previous year.

But now we were stuck in a traffic jam of climbers. We were

like statues slowly disappearing under the snow. The only difference between our bodies and the frozen corpses on the mountainside were the flickers of light coming from our foreheads.

A nudge on the rope from the South African at my back encouraged me to take one more step closer to the peak, but the traffic jam ahead still left me with nowhere to go. It was just before dawn on May 24, 2010. We'd begun this final ascent shortly after midnight, when the thunder and lightning below stopped terrorizing our climb. We'd crossed into the Death Zone eighteen hours earlier. I still felt strong, but I knew that as we stood in line, unable to move, the chances of joining Mallory up here for eternity increased with every minute. Frustrated, energized, and giving in to a momentary fit of summit fever, I unhooked from the rope connecting us with the other climbers and followed Lhakpa as he found his way around the stationary bodies standing in the snow. Free from the lineup, we trudged up the mountain, our crampons clinging to the ice beneath the snow under our feet as we passed the First Step, a wall of boulders marked by the body of an unidentified climber known only for the green of his boots. Then we got to the arduous Second Step, where Mallory was likely forced to turn around in defeat. Up the ladder we climbed and onwards into the fog until we reached the Third Step— a ten-metre cliff wall just 138 metres from the top.

That's when I saw him: my friend and countryman Frank Ziebarth, sitting at the base of the last true obstacle on our way to the summit. The night had turned into a grey morning, and he was resting in the falling snow. He was sitting barely an arm's length from the path to the top. The orange of his jacket was getting quickly covered up with white. He'd managed to summit without oxygen, but it had nearly killed him. He'd barely begun his descent when he had to sit down to catch his breath.

I avoided looking directly at him. There was nothing I or anyone could do to help him now. I stared into the rock wall beside him and whispered down to him, "I'll be back, Frank." Then I lifted my arms above me, grabbed hold of the cliff wall, and continued for the top.

Lhakpa was already above the wall, waiting for me to join him. With our crampons digging into the mountain's side, we took turns leading each other until we found ourselves with nothing left to climb. It was nine a.m. and we were standing on the barren tabletop marked by Buddhist prayer flags and sobbing men kneeling in the snow. I stuck my ice axe next to Everest's peak, pulled off my mask and gasped for whatever oxygen my lungs could pull from the air.

At 8,848 metres above the sea, every breath I drew outside my mask was slowly suffocating me. But I didn't think of that. I was too busy taking in the beauty of the moment. I'd been fantasizing about getting back to this place ever since I'd left it. Now I was one of a select group of people to summit Everest from both its southern and northern face. I looked down on the world and wept at the thought that no other human on Earth stood higher in the sky. I pulled out my satellite phone, called Annie, and texted Alexandra and the girls in Montreal. It was the middle of the night where they were. I was full of joy the moment I heard Annie's voice on the phone.

I sat down in the snow and stared into the clouds that spread out over the Tibetan plateau under my feet. Then I spoke to the mountain.

"Thank you," I said, "for letting me get back here."

Then I looked to my right, to the very place where, five years earlier, I'd strapped the *khata* with Sean's ashes to a Chinese tripod. I looked for it, but it was nowhere to be found. Perhaps it had been swept off the mountain by the winter jet stream and its hurricane-force wind or buried under a fresh layer of ice and snow.

Seated above the world, the lack of oxygen slowly distorting my mind into a state of ecstasy, I wanted to stay here for as long as possible. I knew I was in danger, that hypoxia would soon render me delusional. I'd been up here for over two hours, and with every passing minute at the summit, my body grew weaker and my chances of surviving the descent got worse. If I didn't get moving, I'd soon become nothing more than a preserved corpse frozen to the summit. While a steady flow of climbers approached me from both the north and south, I got up, took one last look at the peak of our world, and said, "I'll see you again." Then I reattached my mask, filled my lungs with some much-needed oxygen, nodded at Lhakpa, and started back down.

When we got to the top of the Third Step, I turned my back to the clouds, squeezed the toes of my boots into the mountain, and climbed down to the base of the wall. Frank was still there, exactly where I'd left him hours earlier. I looked at Lhakpa, told him to carry on without me, and then sat down by my friend's side.

Frank had been sitting there for just over a year. He'd climbed to the top without oxygen, but he'd been so focused on that goal, he'd refused help from everyone else on the mountain, even as it became clear to those around him that he wasn't going to make it. When he sat down to catch his breath at the base of the wall, he slipped into a coma and died. His death was a result of high-altitude cerebral edema. But it was entirely self-imposed. He'd succumbed to the one danger that scared me the most, the one you can't see: the danger from within.

Frank's face was masked by a twenty-centimetre layer of fresh snow. A year earlier, just before his death, he'd told me how he planned to stand on the summit with a banner above his head, asking his girlfriend to marry him. Now I'd been asked by that same girlfriend to remove his corpse from the well-worn path to the summit. She didn't like the fact that people stopped to look at him on their way up the mountain.

I looked at the orange of his jacket, barely visible now beneath the snow. Then I found myself speaking to him from behind my mask.

"Why'd you do it?" I asked. "Why'd you sit down? You killed yourself. Christina asked me to move you. She misses you. I'm sorry. I don't want to do this. But I have to. I told her I would."

Exhausted and with little time and oxygen left, I put my arms around his body and tried to move him. I couldn't. His body had frozen to the mountainside. I tried the only other thing I could think of. I started searching for the banner and his camera so that I could bring them home to his girlfriend so she could see what he saw before he died. Rummaging through a dead man's pockets, I found nothing but an extra pair of gloves. When I began looking around his collar, a layer of snow fell to his chest, and suddenly I was staring at the face of the man I once knew.

My mind froze and I began gasping inside my mask. I don't know how long I stood there staring at him. Soon, I was reaching for whatever snow I could find, packing it back into place. But there was no covering up what I'd just seen.

Turning away from my friend, I stumbled down the mountain until, finally, I looked over my shoulder and found his body had disappeared into the cloud.

Six years on, his frost-covered face remains exactly where it's been ever since that day: trapped inside my head. If only it were alone in there, I might not be writing this today.

CHAPTER 18

VARYING DEGREES OF HIGH

I squeezed my eyes shut as tightly as I could and tried to block out the image of Frank's face from my mind, but it was no use. He was in there and I couldn't get him out. I was back at Advanced Base Camp, having just come down from the top of the world both literally and figuratively. I was in a dark and lonely place.

I felt like a complete and utter failure for not having been able to move Frank's body.

I was alone now in my tent, spiralling into a depressed state, when I reached for the phone and called Annie. I told her I didn't feel right and that I was sad and anxious. We hadn't spoken much about Frank, but somehow she knew that seeing him on the mountain might mess me up.

"I don't know what's wrong with me," I said.

"You should call Sylvain," she replied. Sylvain was the sports psychologist I'd met the previous year, the one who'd been working with the figure skater to overcome the trauma of having almost taken his partner's face off with his skate.

It seemed potentially expensive to dial up a therapist from the mountainside and start hashing out the source of the demons inside my head. But I felt like I was stuck. I didn't even want to leave my tent. The prospect of going back down to base camp and arriving home to face the media and Frank's fiancée made my stomach and head hurt.

"I really think you should call him," Annie said.

I dug through my journal for the psychologist's number. I punched the digits into the satellite phone and stared at it, second-guessing myself before I pressed call. I knew I was cracking. I'd seen one too many horrible things on this mountain, and now I was crying into my hands and telling myself to keep it together. What would my father think if he could see me now? *All fucked up in a tent because you looked a dead man in the face? Get over yourself, Gabriel. How about I tell you about the time I watched my friend explode beside me?*

I put the phone back down by my side and tried to concentrate on wiping Frank from my mind. It didn't work. As soon as I closed my eyes, he was right there again. I picked up the satellite phone and hit call.

Sylvain was in his car somewhere between his office and home when I reached him. We'd barely gotten past hello when I began laying it out.

"Sylvain, I'm really stuck here," I said. "I haven't slept in four days, and I can't go up and I can't come down. I'm stuck."

He pulled his car off the road and asked me to explain.

"What's wrong here, Gabriel?" he said.

I told him about Frank, the story of how he died, and how his fiancée had asked me to move his body to preserve his dignity.

"I told her I'd move him," I said. "But I didn't move him. I couldn't. I just couldn't."

I was speaking fast and anxiously. Sylvain made me pause. We hadn't been speaking long, but already he knew what to say.

"Gabriel, just a second. You have to understand why you went there. You went there to summit. You summitted."

"That doesn't matter. I told Christina I'd move the body. I didn't move the body. He's still there. He's right fucking there on the walk up to the mountain."

"Lucky for him."

"What do you mean?"

"What would it accomplish to have moved his body?"

"It would have given his fiancée peace."

"You've given her that peace already."

"No," I said. "I failed."

"Gabriel, you've preserved the link between the two of them."

"What are you talking about?"

"You have seen him and you've spoken to her. You've united them in a way you didn't even know was possible."

My mind was slowly coming around to Sylvain's point.

"What did Frank do for you when you saw him?" he asked.

I thought about the question for a moment. Then I thought about all that had gone through my head when I first spotted Frank, resting at the base of the Third Step.

"He reminded me of how careful I have to be."

"And do you think he reminds others of the same thing?"

"I hope so."

"So his death has meaning right now, Gabriel. His death has meaning."

"But I told her I'd move him."

"And lucky for you, the mountain wouldn't let you move him. Otherwise Frank's failure would have no meaning."

"But what about the camera?"

"That's not what she needs, Gabriel. She doesn't need to see the last things he saw. She needs to know that you've seen Frank. That he's okay where he is and that he's serving a purpose. She needs closure, and you can give that to her. She needs to know that he's not just up on the side of some cliff somewhere, but seated where he sat himself down, sending a message to everyone else who climbs up there."

It had taken a few minutes, but I was starting to see Sylvain's point.

"In some ways, it's as if he's still alive," Sylvain added.

"But he's not alive."

"What is it to be alive, Gabriel?"

I didn't put much thought into my answer. "To breathe," I said.

"No," he replied. "To be alive is to get into the heart and mind of those who see us. Not getting the camera is a positive. You have preserved his privacy."

I thanked Sylvain for taking my call. He said he wanted to see me as soon as I got home. Then I closed my eyes.

* * *

I returned home to the opposite of a hero's welcome. Annie was obviously pleased that I'd come back safely, but it was time for me to get back to the chores of our daily life. I'd been gone for nearly two months, roaming a mountainside while she carried on with her life, all the while preparing, mentally, for the prospect that I would get myself killed in the process. It was emotionally exhausting for her to put me far enough out of her mind that she didn't just sit by the phone and worry the entire time I was away. She bore the brunt of that stress inside, trying hard not to show it. But it was always there.

The laundry basket was waiting for me when I arrived, filled and ready for my attention. It was a subtle reminder that I was back in the real world. I threw the contents into the washing machine, then went upstairs and slept for what felt like two days. Annie's youngest daughter came into the bedroom and climbed onto my back. I was so tired, I barely moved. She just stood there, between my shoulder blades, laughing.

It felt good to be home. I was relieved to have gotten to the top of Everest once more. In many ways, it felt like the greatest accomplishment of my career. And yet it left me at an impasse. Where do you go when you've already been to the top of the world, twice?

I wrote a letter to Frank's girlfriend. I chose my words carefully, trying to capture the essence of everything Sylvain had told me during my breakdown at the base of the North Col. I told her I'd seen Frank, that he looked peaceful in his place on the mountain, and that he was receiving the proper respect from the men and women who passed by him. I let her know that I'd tried to move him, and how sorry I was to have failed her. Then I tried to reassure her by telling her that Frank's life and death would have an impact on every climber who passed him from now until eternity. That he wouldn't grow old on the mountain. He would remain there, exactly as he was. Then I apologized once more and signed off.

I hadn't been home long before I got an invitation to appear on a Quebec-based television show, to be interviewed by a journalist with a reputation for putting his guests in the hot seat. I knew that going on TV would help me attract new clients as a public speaker, but I was afraid what would happen if the interviewer began posing questions about the dead on the mountain. Though I'd slept well immediately upon my return to Montreal, the subsequent nights had been difficult. I still lay awake in bed with Frank's face staring back at me inside my head. Some nights I found myself staring instead at my reflection in the bathroom mirror, unsure what I was really looking at. I accepted the invitation to appear on the show. Then I called Sylvain and asked him to come with me. I wanted him to stand with me in the corridor backstage before the taping, to keep my mind from venturing into that dark corner where I didn't want it to go. The last thing I wanted was to be asked a difficult question that would trigger something within my head and make me relive my moments with Frank on national television. That wouldn't be good for anyone other than the journalist.

Backstage, Sylvain peppered me with questions about the dead bodies and the selfishness of the entire sport to prep me for the interview. He asked me how I or anyone could possibly justify the waste of human life on Everest.

I responded, "The greater waste would be to live in fear. A lot of tragedies have occurred on Everest. I don't deny that, but none of us ever go to any mountain expecting to die. We go expecting to live our lives to the fullest. I know that's hard to understand. But there's a certain breed of human who will always live that way. And I've become one of them."

Sylvain nodded with encouragement.

"You can do this."

Minutes later, when the same question was asked on camera, I was able to give more or less the same answer.

* * *

I was forty-nine years old, one mountain short of completing the Seven Summits, and busier than ever as a speaker. Yet I felt like a fake. Not because of any unclimbed peaks, but because I was preaching about "fear" and the importance of taking control of your own life, yet I'd spent the last thirty-nine years completely terrified of water. I'd never recovered from the time my father had watched me struggle for breath in our swimming pool. On beach vacations with Annie and the girls, I'd never venture more than ankle-deep into the sea, and even that was difficult. I hated the water. It reminded me of my father.

One day, I told Annie, "I'm going to tackle my personal Everest. I'm going to compete in an Ironman."

She asked me if I'd even heard what I'd said. "You know they swim in the Ironman, right?"

"I know."

"I don't think you know what you're getting yourself into." She was puzzled. "You want to do this where?"

"In the Gulf of Mexico."

"When?"

I gave myself one year to train for the Ironman. One year to first break the fear in my mind, learn to swim, and then perfect the front crawl. It wasn't the "Ironman" label that attracted me, or the fact that the endurance race—a 3.86-kilometre swim followed by a 180.25-kilometre bike ride and a full 42.2-kilometre marathon—was considered the most difficult one-day sporting event in the world. It was the challenge of the swim that really got me.

In many ways, I was setting myself up for failure. But I felt like this was my A+. Like I owed it to myself to do the one thing my father probably died believing I'd never do.

I thought of him as I stood ankle-deep on the stairs of a shallow pool, my personal swimming coach encouraging me to step slowly into the water. A group of retirees was wading around and looking at me with curiosity while a team of competitive swimmers entered the real pool to do some laps. I felt ridiculous and humbled.

I stood in waist-deep water, clinging to the wall, while my coach encouraged me to gently lower my body so that my shoulders were in the water, and then to bob my head without screaming. It seemed like forever before I felt safe in that shallow pool. And as soon as I did, my coach moved me out of it and into the one that was four metres deep.

I was terrified as I lowered my body slowly into the deep pool, my hands still clinging to the wall while my coach shouted out words of encouragement. "Now let go of the wall and paddle out a few feet into the water." Feeling courageous, I thrashed my body out a few feet, then scrambled back. "Very good, Gabriel! Now do the same thing but dunk your head." I gave that a go, and before I knew it, I was sinking in a panic, screaming underwater until I felt the arm of a lifeguard wrap around my wrist and pull me back above the surface. My coach saw the horror on my face. She pulled out a wetsuit and told me to put it on. She said the wetsuit would help me float if I was in trouble. Then she trained me to float on my back like a starfish. "If ever you're in a panic or tired, this is what you do. It won't matter if you're in the pool or in the ocean. So long as you're on your back, you'll be able to float." From that day on, I couldn't get in the water without my wetsuit. To my coach, I was a fascinating challenge. It seemed I was only comfortable so long as I was moving. If I stopped propelling myself forward, I'd begin to thrash about the pool, and then the only question was whether I'd remember to roll over on my back before I started sinking to the bottom. She never quite figured out why my brain refused to let me just tread water, and neither did I. Almost every day for six months, I'd arrive at the pool, put on my goggles and my wetsuit, and stand at the edge of the water, breathing deeply and building myself up for the final moment when she would yell and I would jump. I swam lengths until I was completely gassed. And when that moment came, I'd roll over on my back and float like a starfish, staring at the ceiling, concentrating on everything above and nothing below.

By the time November rolled around, I could swim. But I wasn't fast, and I wasn't pretty—my foot paddling had been likened to that of a mountain goat by more than one person.

I arrived in Florida five days before the Ironman. I still hadn't dipped more than a toe into the ocean, so I made my way to the beach, looked out on the Gulf of Mexico, and watched as the waves crashed into the shore. I was terrified. For two days, I stared at the water, wanting to go in but unable to bring myself to do it. On the third, I rushed into the water and started working on my crawl. I was like Forrest Gump—once I started going, I couldn't stop. But eventually I had to. And when I did, I started to freak out again. I still couldn't tread water.

Race day came, and I put on my wetsuit and made for the beach. The air was cold and I was scared. I stared out at the Gulf, surrounded by 2,402 other competitors. The gun fired and I sprinted into the water, one man in a herd of humans rushing into the sea. I dove into the waves and began my strokes. For the next two hours, two minutes and thirty-seven seconds, I crawled just below the surface, falling farther and farther behind the pack as I struggled against the open waters of the Gulf. I narrowed my focus in on my crawl. "Three strokes, breathe on the right. Three strokes, breathe on the left. Repeat." When I began to panic, I restarted my count, reminding myself that every stroke I made or breath I took got me a little bit closer to the shore. It didn't matter that I was the 2,365th competitor to finish the swim. All that mattered was that I was out of the water. Then I jumped on the bike and began the five-and-a-half-hour process of singling out 719 competitors in front of me, hunting them down one by one and passing them. And when I was done that, I proceeded on foot for another four and a half hours and chased down yet another 413 racers. And when I crossed the finish line after twelve and a half hours, I was in the 1,134th position out of 2,402 competitors. But I didn't really care, because I'd made it to the end of the swim. And because of that, I felt like I'd won.

When I tell people the story of my Ironman experience, they ask me if I still swim. And the answer is no. I remain as uncomfortable in the water as I was the day my father let me drop to the bottom of the pool. I may have faced my fear, but I hadn't erased it from my memory. If someone were to ask me if I could swim, I'd honestly have to think about my answer for a moment. Because if I got pushed off a cliff right now and fell into the water, I might very well just freak out and drown.

It took a few weeks before my body recovered from the physiological trauma caused by the Ironman. But once the pain went away, I began thinking again about what I would do next.

I'd put my plans for the Seven Summits on temporary hold after Christine Boskoff's death, but I revived them when Annie's father, of all people, expressed an interest in trying to become the oldest man to ever climb Vinson Massif. He was seventy-seven years old when he looked at me over the family dinner table on Christmas Day and said he'd been inspired by my exploits to try to push himself to a higher level. I started training him for the expedition, and he was on his way to financing what he called "the next great adventure of his life" when he was diagnosed with Alzheimer's disease and was forced to give up on the dream. I wasn't interested in doling out the money to climb Vinson by myself, so I gave up as well until Elia reached out to me, asking if I'd be interested in starring in the pilot of a reality show set on the Seven Summits. Elia, whose family had immigrated to Canada via Lebanon, had begun work on a proposed television show that would unite seven novice climbers from seven different Arab countries to form a single team to attempt each of the Seven Summits. He needed an expedition leader. I signed up and we began work on the pilot, which took us to Mount Toubkal in the Atlas Mountains of Morocco. There, I led a team of Jordanian, Lebanese, Palestinian, Algerian, Moroccan, Iraqi, and Egyptian climbers to the highest point in the Arab world. All the while, we were being followed by a camera crew, which never seemed to rest, not even when one of the climbers fell unconscious on the floor of a refuge partway up the mountain. For a while, my only hope of building up the cash required to get to Antarctica was wrapped up in that proposed TV series. And when the show wasn't picked up, I put Vinson, along with Antarctica's second-highest peak, out of my mind yet again.

* * *

By the spring of 2012, I was back in the Khumbu Valley, not just as an expedition leader, but as the head of my own climbing outfit. Mine would be the first-ever Quebec commercial expedition, not so different from the operations of Mountain Madness, Adventure Consultants, or any of the other established outfitters at base camp, except in size. Having always attached myself to small teams, I opted to set my own team up in the same manner. I called my outfit "The Dream Team." It would consist of eight trekkers who'd hired me to guide them no higher than base camp. Among the trekkers was a young doctor named Eric Contant, who'd wanted me to lead him to Everest ever since he'd seen me onstage during my first-ever public performance in Sherbrooke back in 2006. Eric had become a good friend, a fellow Ironman, and the on-call doctor attached to my team. The trekkers were joined by three client climbers who had hired me to help direct them up to the summit of the mountain. Two of the three client climbers attached to my team were millionaires. Paul was a Kiwi-born investment banker living in the UK. Pierre was a Montreal-based property mogul originally from France. My third client was a humble government worker from Ottawa named Nathalie. They were all accomplished enough climbers to get to the top without needing me to suit up and guide them. I wasn't interested in guiding anyone who didn't have the skills required to get themselves up the mountain. I'd screened my clients carefully. I didn't want to be like one of those outfitters who accepted anyone so long as they had enough money. And I wasn't that interested in risking my life to get someone with no experience up to the top, even if they did want to pay me the going rate of $125,000 for a private guide.

The rest of the team consisted of twenty local porters and yak herders who would help carry our required gear to base camp, as well as two cooks, one to be stationed with me at base camp, and the other up at Camp 2. Last and most important were the three Sherpa I had hired to accompany the client climbers to the summit. There was no one I wanted on my team more than Lhakpa, the Sherpa who'd been with me during my two summits and who had, by now, been to the top fourteen times. I trusted him more than anyone else on the mountain. He'd recommended two other Sherpa to join us, Namgyal and Pema. In addition to being one of his country's finest climbers, Namgyal was a Buddhist lama. I liked him immediately. He had an aura of calm about him that he transferred on to others with his gentle demeanour. I also liked listening to him recite prayers in his tent at base camp and high up on the mountainside. Pema had been on my team in 2009, during my troubled

climb on the north side. He'd earned my respect when he res-
cued a Norwegian climber who'd been missing in the Death
Zone for nearly seventy-two hours. I felt confident in Namgyal,
Lhakpa, and Pema's abilities to take care of my clients up on the
mountain while I guided from below. I'd spent a decade reading weather patterns and navigating planes in and out of air-
ports. I felt as well equipped as anyone to manage a team from
base camp.

That year, the mountain was the busiest I'd ever seen it.
Massive teams sponsored by National Geographic, The North
Face, and others were already set up by the time the Sherpa
and I picked the spot for the ten main tents that would make
up our camp. We held our puja with the lamas reciting prayers
from three-century-old Tibetan tomes. We asked for forgive-
ness from the mountain for the damage our tools were about
to do to its crust, then we asked for Sagarmatha's mercy. Up
above, teams of Sherpa worked day and night to fix a new line
through the icefall and into the Death Zone, noting as they did
that something seemed off in the Western Cwm. A mild winter
had left the mountain's rocks exposed to the sun, and as the
Sherpa began their ascent, they were plagued by falling rocks,
which left them believing that Sagarmatha was angry. That
view was reinforced when three Sherpa died in rapid succes-
sion. The first, a Sherpa who'd been to the summit ten times,
got drunk and dropped dead at base camp. I tried not to watch
as his friends and countrymen carried his body out of camp.
Three days later, another Sherpa fell from a ladder in the icefall.
He'd been overconfident, trying to race a friend back down to
base camp, and was navigating the icefall without being clipped

on to anything. Then, a cook higher up the mountain suffered a stroke. Their deaths cast a pall over the established teams at base camp, but all the while, the expeditions kept advancing up the Western Cwm. My team had just cleared Camp 1 when an avalanche swooped in behind them and wiped it out, sweeping another Sherpa into a crevasse. After that, I put our expedition on hold. It was windy up on the mountain—129 kilometres per hour, according to the calculations I'd been given by Garry Hartlin, who was helping me monitor the weather from his computer back home in Canada. Every day, I examined reports that seemed to indicate that the jet stream was just sitting on top of the mountain. There would probably be one window to summit, that window would be small, and the path to the top would be overcrowded.

There were a number of teams at base camp that I'd never heard of, run by people I'd never seen before. Their presence, and disorganized nature, made the rest of us uneasy. I liaised closely with the two Everest leaders I'd come to respect and trust the most in previous years—Tim Rippel from British Columbia, who'd been running his own expedition company for more than twenty-five years, and Russell Brice, a Kiwi climber who was one of the most respected and experienced expedition leaders in the entire business. Brice had been telling me for days that he had a feeling something bad was going to happen up on the mountain if the conditions didn't improve quickly. "I might pull my team out of here," he said. "This season is turning into a mess. I don't want to lose anybody up there."

Brice was the most established veteran at base camp. His operation was ninety people strong and included thirty Sherpa.

But I understood his concerns. I shared them, but with a smaller team, I believed I could keep tabs on my group in the face of a pending disaster.

I was still trying to figure out what Brice's withdrawal would mean to the rest of us, when I called home to Annie only to learn that Alexandra was pregnant. I couldn't believe what I'd heard. How had my daughter grown up so quickly? I still had a picture of her as a little girl in my knapsack. I tried to reach her myself but couldn't get through. I wanted to congratulate her even though I was, in all honesty, angry. She was twenty-one years old and had only a high school diploma, while her boy-friend was still trying to get his. I feared what the future would hold for her as much as I feared what the future would hold for my team on this mountain. I lay awake in my tent that night, thinking of my daughter, slowly grasping the newfound reality that she wasn't the only one growing old. I was about to become a grandfather.

I was struggling to reach Alexandra by phone when word reached my tent that Brice had officially shut down all his teams and was evacuating his people to Kathmandu. I understood his decision entirely. I'd known Brice for years. He'd based his decision to leave on his own experience. I had to base my decision on my own. Brice had deemed himself unable to safeguard ninety lives, but I still felt confident in my ability to take care of the seven who were relying on me. With his team's absence, the risks of getting to the summit changed. There were still three weeks left until the monsoon. The icefall was dangerous but no more so than usual. The Sherpa had begun moving the route between Camp 3 and 4 to get it away from the falling rocks. I met immediately with Tim Rippel. Neither of us was yet ready to crush our clients' aspirations on the mountain. I instructed my team to head down into the valley to rest up while I stayed at base camp to try to figure out our summit window and see if our team's Sherpa could help secure the lines up the mountain.

Being forthright with every climber on my team, I explained that the conditions up above were going to be extremely difficult to handle. The mountain was going to be crowded, and people were likely going to die if they weren't following a plan. All my climbers decided they would give this season their all. And so I began my final preparations to direct them into the most notorious traffic jam in the mountain's history.

I sat my team down before their summit push and explained, "You're going to hear three thousand strategies from other climbers. I don't care about their strategies. We are sticking with our own. My goal is to get you to the summit and back here. That's my goal. You need to trust me, and I will get you home."

On the morning of May 14, 2012, I awoke to the sounds of two hundred Sherpa and climbers leaving base camp. They were all starting their final push at the same time, as one mass, anticipating a morning summit on May 18. I held my team back—not the most popular decision, but one I hoped would keep them from getting trapped in the Death Zone, lined up behind two hundred climbers. It took every ounce of experience, as well as my faith in Garry's ability to read the weather from halfway around the world, to determine that our summit window would still be open by the time my climbers got within striking distance of the top. I'd earmarked May 19 for my team. That afternoon, I held a two-hour meeting, going over every element of our plan for the summit. I reminded the climbers of the importance of turnaround times, and showed them exactly where their oxygen stashes had been placed on the mountain by the Sherpa. I told them not to worry about the teams that had already pushed on ahead, and reminded them that we weren't racing anyone to the summit. Then I laid out the plan. They would head to Camp 2 in the morning, and they would stay there until I got more intel on what was transpiring higher up on the mountain. I didn't want my team anywhere near the traffic jam pushing for May 18. "If any of you want to join that mass, you're welcome to. But my strategy is to hold you back." They all understood.

The next morning, over a two a.m. breakfast, I reminded them, "Just do what we've been doing, stick to our plan, and you'll all be fine." Then I stood under the stars and watched as Lhakpa led our climbers into the icefall.

Back in our base camp headquarters, I sipped tea, monitored all information coming off the mountain, and fielded calls from the families of the climbers I'd just watched disappear into the icefall. They'd all been reading blogs about the crowds and predicting a disaster. For two days, my team climbed through gale-force winds, all the while checking in with me. I could see on the weather charts that the four-day window remained open. When I wasn't liaising with my team up on the mountain or trying to calm their families, I was listening to a busy signal on the other end of Alexandra's phone. And when there was absolutely nothing else to do, I sat on a stationary bike I'd lugged up in pieces on the back of a yak all the way from Lukla so that I could train for my second Ironman.

By May 17, my climbers were all at Camp 3, but one of

them was sick, struggling with stomach problems. I told him to lie low, recover his strength, and wait it out as the mass of climbers pushed on for the summit. The next morning, Lhakpa and the rest of my team were resting easy at Camp 3, seven hundred metres beneath the Death Zone, asking if they should stay there or push on for Camp 4. I called Tim. He had climbers up at Camp 4 and said that the bad weather was pushing most of the planned summits back to the following day. I didn't like the sound of that. I began hearing rumours that there were so many people up at Camp 4 that the Sherpa were going to try securing a second fixed line from the Hillary Step up to the summit. The weather report was getting worse by the hour as well. The window was closing and there wasn't much hope for a summit after May 19. I alerted my team: "Your best bet is going to be to work your way in front of that group of climbers." My climbers were better rested than the mass, having been able to climb at their own pace and rest properly.

Still, I was nervous. The entire game plan had changed very quickly. I made it clear to my team members: "If at any time any of you find yourselves stuck in the middle of the traffic jam, don't get caught up with what others are doing. You must remember your turnaround time." It wasn't worth dying in a lineup just to get to the top of the world. With that said, I directed my team to push up to the South Col and get some rest at Camp 4, but to prepare to depart by eight p.m. to avoid the traffic that would be leaving at midnight. If they could head out from Camp 4 ahead of the crowd, they'd reach the Hillary Step in advance of the lineup. It wasn't the strategy I'd held from the start, but it was now the safest option other than abandoning our climb.

At eleven thirty p.m., Pierre called down to base with a garbled transmission saying they were just leaving Camp 4. They'd rested a bit longer than I'd instructed and were already getting bogged down in traffic. Then the radio went dead and I couldn't hear anything more.

I began to get antsy. The weather was holding, but half the crowd from the day before had camped out on the South Col overnight and waited for May 19 to summit. I had a terrible feeling that my team would be trapped in a logjam of climbers below the Hillary Step, forced to stand still in the Death Zone for three hours just to take a single step forward. I wasn't the only base camp manager having radio problems. None of the other teams had been able to dispatch any transmissions back to base that night. It was 9:35 a.m. when Lhakpa's voice finally began crackling out of my radio. He said that he and Paul were safe and sound at the base of the Hillary Step. They were caught in traffic, but the majority of the climbers were behind them. They'd departed Camp 4 at eleven thirty p.m. and expected to reach the summit by noon. He hadn't seen the other four members of the team but knew they were behind him somewhere.

"People, lots of people up here. Everywhere. Harder and harder to move," Lhakpa said over the radio.

I stuck a pin on a map of the mountain sprawled out in my command tent. It marked Paul and Lhakpa's place and time. Next, I heard from Nathalie, who reported that she wasn't too far behind Paul and that she'd managed to get to the Hillary Step ahead of most of the other climbers, but she was still in traffic. I asked her how she felt. She said she was strong, so I told her to go for it, but if she started to falter or found herself stationary for too long, she would have to turn around.

It took a while before I heard from Pierre. He hadn't been able to move up the mountain at the same speed as the others. He was sick and had already vomited three times in the night. He was now in sight of the Hillary Step, but he was heeding my earlier warnings and giving up on his climb. "I can see the summit. There are too many people. I gave my kids a promise," he said. "I told them I'd come home. I just want to see them again. I'm done." I told him I understood, made sure that his Sherpa stayed with him, and then monitored his progress back down the mountain.

By eleven a.m., I knew that my team members were all on the move, four of them going up, two of them coming down. I checked in with Tim, who said he had had climbers stuck at the base of the Hillary Step for more than two hours and that he was starting to worry about the amount of oxygen his clients were consuming.

Tim was now directing his people back down after hearing that members of other teams were just standing there, refusing to give up yet unable to move forward. We had fears that the lessons of 1996 were being ignored, and that the bottleneck at the Hillary Step that had slowed everyone's ascent during that year's disaster was happening again, and our teams were going to have to navigate through it. I had every faith that my team would heed the strict turnaround time I'd given them, but without any means of reaching them, I had no actual way of knowing what was going on. I was powerless and I didn't like it.

I was beginning to hear reports that climbers who'd been on

the summit at 7:40 a.m. had gotten stuck at the Hillary Step for eight hours on descent. "There's a lot of fucked-up people up here," I remember hearing one of Tim's guides say.

It was noon before I received word via our team's cook stationed at Camp 2 that Lhakpa, Namgyal, Nathalie, and Paul were all now standing on the summit. They were alone up there, enjoying the moment. I was relieved to hear it but unable to reach them and tell them to get moving.

For two hours, I sat by my radio, unable to reach anyone on my team, and willed the radio to come to life with news from any member of my team while I tried to keep a tally on what else was going on up the mountain—who was where and in what condition.

It was nearly six thirty p.m. by the time I got word via Pierre that Nathalie and Paul were back at Camp 4 with their Sherpa guides.

They were still in the Death Zone, but at least they'd be safe in their tents, where hot tea and extra oxygen bottles were available to get them through the night.

As the sun went down and the mountain went dark, news came that there were several climbers still out above the Balcony. The disaster we'd all been fearing was about to unfurl.

I woke up the next morning to news from my cook that a Canadian woman was dead. I was pretty sure I knew who it was. There had been a Canadian woman at base camp, a client I'd never seen before attached to a team I'd never heard of, who'd pitched her tent next to a giant poster of herself. She was smiling on the poster, dressed in her snowsuit with a mountain superimposed in the background. Everyone at base camp knew she wasn't really a climber. I didn't know much about her. But I soon found out that she was a Toronto woman who'd spent more than eighteen hours getting from Camp 4 to the summit. She'd exhausted her every breath just getting there, refusing her Sherpa's pleas to turn around hours earlier. What we didn't know then was that she'd re-mortgaged her house to pay for the $100,000 trip, put off having children with her husband, and abandoned her career in the hope that summitting Everest would change her life. She hadn't actually climbed anything before. She was far too inexperienced to be on the mountain, and she'd placed herself and others in jeopardy. She was exactly the type of client I feared and feared for. She'd apparently collapsed just below the south Balcony. Her last words to her Sherpa, uttered after nearly twenty-five hours in the Death Zone, were "Save me." She was still attached to the fixed line, her headlamp still lit, when she slumped over and died.

She wasn't the only person who had died up near the summit that night. A sixty-one-year-old German and a forty-four-year-old South Korean had succumbed in the night, as well as a fifty-five-year-old Chinese climber. But it was the Canadian woman, Shriya Shah-Klorfine, whose face and name would soon be splashed across the Internet. She was young, attractive, and extremely naive. It was only a matter of time before the media began running with the story. The newspapers and TV stations were quick to call, searching for pictures of the long lineups on Everest. They would all want to capture the death march and criticize the sport.

I walked over to Shah-Klorfine's expedition's headquarters. There I found a young base camp manager, nervously chain-smoking in the back of his tent. His cellular phone was ringing by his side. He looked at it but refused to pick it up. It was a newspaper calling. The news had already spread.

I told him I'd heard that one of his clients was dead on the mountain. He didn't say anything, just kept smoking. I could see he was in shock. Then his phone started ringing again. He looked at it, then shook his head.

"It's her husband," he said. "I can't talk to him. I can't talk to him."

"Does he know anything yet?" I asked.

He shrugged his shoulders and kept on smoking.

"You have to pick up that phone," I said. "He can't learn this from the media."

He just kept on smoking. I shook my head, reached for the phone, and began the most difficult conversation of my entire life.

CHAPTER 19

A MOST AMBITIOUS PLAN

The media was eager to talk to me before I'd even gotten on the plane back to Montreal. They all wanted to run a story about how greedy outfitters and novice climbers had brought about this most recent tragedy. There was much to be said, but I kept my mouth shut. Seven climbers and three Sherpa had just died. Who was I to criticize anyone?

I slipped back into regular life rather quickly. I went to visit Alexandra as soon as I could. She was already seven months pregnant. I was no longer upset. The disaster on the mountain had helped me realize it wasn't worth being upset about anything. She was my daughter and that was all that mattered. So I offered my support.

"If you need a place to stay, you've always got a place with me," I said. Then I hugged her. There wasn't much more I could think of to say other than to ask about potential names and dates.

My mother in Lac-Mégantic was happier than I'd ever seen her. She still took great joy in knowing just how many people could trace their existence back to her and my father. I visited her after most of my expeditions. I stuck around town for a few days, running from one end of the main drag to the other and then taking off into the hills that surrounded the lake. It had been forty-seven years since I'd called Lac-Mégantic my home, but the city's Chamber of Commerce had named me an ambassador for the city years earlier, so I tried to spend chunks of my summers in town, using it as a sort of personal base camp. Having spent fifty-eight days in a tent at Everest Base Camp, I desperately needed to get moving. I hadn't swum in nearly two years, but I'd signed myself up for another Ironman competition and only had a month to prepare. It was important to whip myself into shape quickly—not just for the Ironman, but for what I had planned after that.

I'd left Everest knowing that I wouldn't be coming back for the 2013 season. I had other mountains to climb. I'd been putting off K2 long enough. I'd decided that if I didn't climb it soon, I might never get to it.

The mountain had always been on my radar, ever since Jacques Olek had given me the laminated poster that still hung in a storage room dedicated to my gear in the basement of our house. I looked at it every time I grabbed my gear. It taunted me. I knew that if I climbed K2, I'd never again have to listen to anyone tell me that Everest wasn't good enough. I also knew that attempting to climb it was only going to get harder to justify. I was now pushing fifty-three and about to become a grandfather. I was in fantastic shape, but I could feel my age catching up with me. My eyesight, which had been perfect my entire life, was starting to go, and it freaked me out, especially after Annie explained that the eye muscles are often the first part of a person to really show their age.

I'd been talking about climbing K2 for as long as I could remember. I'd felt close to doing it back in 2007. I'd told Garry Hartlin as much one night at Everest Base Camp. He hadn't been supportive. Few people were.

"Gabriel," he said, "K2 is a young man's mountain. When you're twenty-five years old, that's one thing. You're getting too old for that. You've still got all your fingers and toes. You should think this one through. That mountain kills a lot of people."

I nodded. I understood what he was saying, but I also knew I had the experience required to counterbalance my age. My only real impediment had been the lack of a climbing partner.

Shortly before departing Everest Base Camp in 2012, I'd befriended an American climber named Marty Schmidt. Schmidt was an extremely strong alpinist. He'd grown up in California, climbing in the Sierra Nevada as a teenager. He'd been a pilot in the United States Air Force, but he'd always said the mountain high was better than any high he'd reached in the cockpit. He climbed his first major peak in 1983, when he summitted Denali. Five years later, he named his first-born son after the mountain. He'd worked as a guide in the Andes and the Himalaya, where he summitted five of the eight-thousanders. The year before I met him, he'd created a new route to the top of Denali with his son in tow. They called the new route "Dad and Son."

I liked everything I knew about Marty. He'd made two attempts on K2, and when he told me he was heading back with his son, we decided I would join them. We made plans to meet in northern Pakistan in July 2013. Ours would be an alpine-style push, a quick drive for the summit. None of us wanted to spend more time than necessary on K2's slopes. Everest was dangerous, but at least it was relatively solid. K2 was covered in loose shale and had a reputation for dropping chunks of rock and ice from its sides. We'd begun talking about ways to acclimatize somewhere other than K2. We'd need a mountain almost as high but with a lower death rate. Marty and Denali had decided on Broad Peak, the twelfth-highest mountain in the world. It was right on the border between Pakistan and China. I had a different plan. I'd do my acclimatization on Nanga Parbat, which I'd been wanting to climb ever since I'd seen it back in 1998. It didn't matter that its two nicknames were the Man-eater and Killer Mountain. Likewise, it didn't concern me that Nanga Parbat was now situated in a part of the world the US State Department advised avoiding due to a heightened threat of terrorist attacks.

* * *

I spent the summer of 2012 liaising with other climbers I knew, searching for a partner for Nanga and K2. The climbs would be the two most technical and challenging of my life. I needed someone I could trust in every way imaginable. I found that partner through a mutual friend named Nina Adjanin, a Serbian climber whom I'd met on Everest in 2009. Nina had been planning her own expedition to Nanga Parbat and suggested I reach out to a Lithuanian she knew who'd already had some success on the mountains in Pakistan. His name was Ernestas Marksaitis.

"You two seem like the same people," she said. "I think you'll get along well."

Ernestas, or Ernie, as I came to call him, was a forty-four-year-old father of two. He'd grown up in Lithuania's green plains and low hills, far from any mountains. He'd discovered a passion for climbing at the age of thirty-eight and soon quit his government job in order to pursue climbing full-time. He was a gregarious prankster who would crack a joke at any altitude. He'd gotten his start climbing in the Tatra Mountains of Slovakia and Poland before moving on to the Alps. He'd been to the top of Denali and was part of an expedition to Dhaulagiri, the world's seventh-highest mountain, in 2008. He'd been a mathematician and a university lecturer in a previous life and was now teaching himself how to speak Urdu. He'd fallen completely in love with the Karakoram Range and wanted to interact not just with the mountains, but with the people in the valleys as well. He didn't have much money and climbed mostly without oxygen because of the expense (a single oxygen tank can cost upwards of $450, and a climber can go through any number of tanks on a single Himalayan climb). Ernie was a purist at heart. He preferred climbing solo, and in the alpine style, when possible. He'd done so on Broad Peak in the summer of 2012 before joining up with a Polish climber for a stab at K2. He'd gotten to seven thousand metres on that climb, but was forced to turn around and give up his summit push when someone stole his tent. He was still pissed about that when I met him.

I enjoyed listening to him talk about his experiences on K2.

It helped me to visualize the climb ahead. I'd studied the mountain for years and knew the route we would take well enough to know what parts of it scared me. The one that made me the most nervous was the infamous Bottleneck, the narrow couloir where climbers are forced to traverse an ice wall with a pitch at 8,400 metres. The couloir, which can only be traversed one climber at a time, is located directly below a massive overhang of ice and snow the size of an apartment building. No climber in his right mind wanted to spend more time than necessary crossing the one-hundred-metre traverse under the overhead serac, which has a reputation for dropping large chunks of ice, especially in the midday heat. In 2008, ice fell from the serac and killed eight climbers over the course of two days. The climbers had been descending from the summit through the Bottleneck when the serac started crumbling above them. Over the next two seasons, not a single climber made it to the top of the mountain.

There were countless ways to get killed on K2, all the more reason to spend as little time as possible on its sides. And so, over email, Ernie and I hashed out a plan that would see us spend thirty days on Nanga Parbat, acclimatizing on our way up that mountain, before heading north for a climb on K2.

Our plans were set. But I dreaded sharing them with Annie.

I'd stopped speaking of K2 around her years earlier because I knew how much it bothered her. I broached it casually, telling her over coffee one morning that I was thinking about climbing it. I expected she might challenge me and remind me that I was getting older. But years of living with me had helped her anticipate my actions before I made them. She said that every year with me seemed to be the same. It was like I was on a cycle. I came back from every climb feeling great, whether I'd summitted or not. The post-climb bliss would begin to wear off by the end of summer. Come fall, I'd throw myself into conferences, but unless I had another climb to look forward to, I became depressed. Christmas would come and I'd escape into planning mode for another great adventure in the spring. Then I'd become happy again as I built up to my departure. It was an emotional roller coaster with seasonal highs and seasonal lows. She'd ask me whether this cycle was ever going to stop, and I'd remind her that this was who I was. Then we'd debate the difference between passion and obsession, and she'd ponder Lady June Hillary's words to her back in 2006: "They're all selfish. But we wouldn't choose them any other way." When I told Annie of my plans for Nanga and K2, she just sort of nodded.

But there was one more impediment to my departure that I hadn't foreseen. It weighed 4.3 kilograms and went by the name of Rosie.

I'd been at home, working on notes for a conference, when my phone rang. Alexandra had just given birth. I grabbed my keys, hollered up to Annie, rushed out to my truck, and rocketed over the bridge into Montreal to the hospital to meet a beautiful, bald little creature. I had thought I was prepared for this moment until someone called me Grandpa, and suddenly I got choked up thinking of a similar moment twenty-two years earlier, when I'd held Alexandra for the first time. I looked up from my granddaughter and into Alexandra's eyes. It had been years since we'd been really close, since we'd sat on the hood of my truck and had our picnic dinners under the northern lights together, since we'd had our last father-daughter phone call and stared up at the same sky, thousands of kilometres apart, talking about all the things she wanted to see and do in her life. It seemed an eternity since she'd written me that poem I'd carried with me to the top of the world. She'd been just a kid then; now she was a mother. How had so much time and distance passed between us?

It was harder to leave her now than it had ever been before. I didn't like the idea of not being there as she started her own family. It was a feeling I struggled to explain. In some ways, she needed me less now than she ever had. But there was something about seeing her so enamoured with her own daughter that made me question our entire relationship.

I wasn't regretting my decision to go to Nanga Parbat and K2 so much as I was dreading the trip. I was about to take on the two deadliest mountains of my career. I'd invested money and lined up a climbing partner. We'd both booked our tickets, and here I was holding my granddaughter, remembering what it meant to be a parent and feeling sick to my stomach at the thought of another climb. I felt torn in a way that I hadn't felt before.

I stopped sleeping. Frank's face came back. I started picturing Alexandra, Annie, and Annie's daughters on the other end of that phone call I'd had with the widower, imagining what it would be like for them to answer that call and hear someone say, "I'm sorry, but Gabriel didn't make it back."

Sean, Babu, Christine, Frank, the falling men on Aconcagua and Mont Blanc, the body in the tent on Everest, the old man on Denali who'd refused to rest, the Frenchman—they were all in my head.

Nothing felt clear anymore.

I made my usual pre-departure trip to the notary's office to update my last will and testament. While I was there, the notary offered some unexpected advice: "You should think of something other than money and property to leave to your daughter in case you die."

"What do you mean?" I asked.

"Something personal. Something that has meaning only to her."

I thought about it. I still didn't really have any personal belongings other than the sacred rice, pictures of Annie and the girls, and a few rocks from some of the mountains I'd summitted.

Annie wasn't sure what I should do but said she thought the notary was right. "Maybe you should write something for her," she said. We didn't talk much about my parenting skills. I knew her view. She'd shared it a few times when she'd made it clear that she was glad I wasn't the father of her girls. It was hard on them to see me leave for the mountains as it was. Annie wouldn't have been able to bear it if the emotional pain of her daughters had had the added dimension of a biological connection. I knew that for her, a father was someone who had to be there for his children. Always. Period.

We stopped at a stationery store. I ran inside and grabbed two notebooks, a yellow one for me and a pink one for Alexandra. I'd decided that I'd write a journal just for her, and try to chronicle my view on our lives both together and apart. I'd take it with me on the mountainside, along with the hope that if I died, the book would somehow find its way back to her.

* * *

285

My bags were packed. But I still wasn't ready to go. I began reaching out to friends both distant and close, letting them know how much they meant to me. I'd never done such a thing before, never gone to the mountain expecting to die. I called my mother and thanked her for always lighting those candles for me. I told her I'd see her as soon as I got back. I called Sylvain Guimond and thanked him for all his help teaching me to let go of the sense of failure that had crippled me after seeing Frank. I reached out to Patrice and told him how much I missed the days when he and I were just young men travelling the world. I texted Alexandra daily to see how she was. I spent as much time as possible with her and Rosie, going to the park or just hanging out doing nothing. I hugged Annie extra tight at night but tried not to tell her just how much I was going to miss her on this expedition. I didn't want her to get as worried as I was. I reached out to Elia. We'd been through so much on the mountain together that I considered him my little brother. He was heading back to Everest, and I wanted him to know how much he meant to me and to wish him good luck. But I still wasn't ready to go. I still needed to talk to someone, to empty my brain into another person's head before departure. I called up Eric Contant, the doctor who'd trekked with my team to Everest the year before and with whom I'd trained and competed in the Ironman at Mont Tremblant. Eric had become a close friend over the previous year. I'd been training him for the mountains. He had become a novice climber, working on ice and rock. I'd become his mentor, doing for him what Marcello, Patrice, and Babu had done for me. Two nights before my planned departure, I invited Eric over for dinner.

We had a delightful evening, chatting and laughing. Then Eric and I went outside for a walk.

"You know," I began, "these mountains are really dangerous. I just want you to know. I might die. I want to tell you that I really appreciate you, I love you as a friend, and if anything happens, it's important to know that."

Eric nodded. I'd never spoken to him like this before. I felt ambivalent as I spoke, as if my heart wasn't really set on what I was about to do.

"I don't want to miss my granddaughter's life," I said. "I want to watch her grow up."

Then Eric piped up. "Gabriel," he said, "you have to either go or not go. You can't go halfway. If you're going to do this, you have to do it with everything. There are only two options here."

I stopped walking and just stood there. I was more unsure about my abilities as a climber than ever before.

"I know," I said.

CHAPTER 20

KILLER MOUNTAIN

The meadow was lush and green and beautiful, a pleasant canopy of grass and edelweiss. It was the perfect place to drop our bags, pitch our tents, and catch our breath. I was tired but exhilarated. A week had passed since I'd left Montreal, since I'd rushed home from a conference in Pittsburgh, packed my bags, had a quick sushi lunch with Annie, and ridden to the airport to stare at the back of her car as she drove off, unsure if she was looking back at me too.

I'd spent almost two days in transit just getting to Islamabad. As with my previous visit, the airport was crawling with armed police. It was 3:10 a.m. when I touched down in Pakistan. Ernie was at the airport to greet me. He was tall and slim, with a bald head, and I spotted him immediately as he hobnobbed jovially with a couple of Russian and Ukrainian climbers who'd just gotten off other flights and were also attached to our expedition. I gravitated toward him. He recognized me and started speaking to me in Russian. He knew I wouldn't understand a word he was saying, and that was his point. He was all smiles and jokes from the get-go. He led us, bleary-eyed and confused, from the airport to our hotel, a safe haven where I dropped my bags and tried to sleep. We divvied up our gear between what we'd need for Nanga and what we'd need for K2.

The city was the same unnerving mess of organized chaos that I remembered from sixteen years earlier. We departed just before midnight on the day I arrived. We were a group of twelve international climbers, all attached to one expedition without a clear leader or plan. We boarded a brand new bus and headed out for the Karakoram Highway, looking, I'm sure, like a group of Western tourists heading out for a midnight jaunt into Taliban territory. Every few kilometres that we travelled, we came upon a police checkpoint. And at every checkpoint, an armed officer got on our bus and travelled with us to the next checkpoint. It seemed there was always someone on the bus whom we'd barely just met, carrying an AK-47.

The Karakoram was even more breathtaking than I remembered. We made our final approach to the Hilalay Bridge in a convoy of topless Land Cruisers, twisting through the desert valleys and snaking our way toward the end of the road. Then we climbed out and began the trek behind a caravan of porters and chefs and emaciated beef cattle with caged poultry strapped to their backs, marching to their own slaughter, up through a landscape scarred by centuries of landslides and glacial retraction, until we reached the meadow that would be our base camp.

From our grassy perch at 4,100 metres, Ernie and I stared up at the mountain, crisp and white above the greenness of the meadow. It felt as if the grass beneath us was bowing down to the pristine canvas that rose out over the distance. The mountain seemed so untouched and magnificent. I was as much in awe of Nanga Parbat now as I had been when I first saw it in the winter of 1998. We sat in silence, both of us admiring its beauty, listening as a distant crack echoed around us. We watched as Nanga Parbat released a wall of ice and snow from its side. Even in that moment, as a deadly avalanche rushed down onto the glacier, sprinkling the meadow with powder, the mountain still seemed peaceful. But I knew it wasn't. The death rate on Nanga Parbat was only marginally lower than on K2, and we both knew the days ahead would be trying and rife with danger.

We'd chosen to ascend Nanga from its western side, known to the locals as the Diamir Face. It was on this face that the great Reinhold Messner had lost his brother. The mountain may have been beautiful, but she wasn't called the Man-eater for nothing. She had a well-earned reputation for not giving up the bodies of the dead.

We would be following in the footsteps of Toni Kinshofer, a German mountaineer who had lost all his toes and one of his climbing partners on his way to the top in 1962. We'd be managing risks as soon as we departed base camp. First, we'd have to scale the Diama Glacier to reach Camp 1, avoiding hidden crevasses, before entering a corridor prone to avalanches. There, we'd pitch our tents next to an overhanging cliff and hope it would protect us by redirecting an avalanche should snow begin to slide down the corridor. Then we'd climb for the better part of a day through the couloir, scaling ice and rock, dodging even more crevasses, all the while exposed to avalanches, until we reached a three-hundred-metre vertical wall known as the Kinshofer Wall. On top of that wall, we'd find Camp 2. By that point, we'd be at 5,900 metres and would begin to suffer from altitude sickness. We'd be forced to return to base camp to acclimatize before climbing back and moving on to Camp 3, which was a further 1,100 metres up the mountain at a forty-degree incline. From there, we'd look forward to a scenic yet treacherous trek through another avalanche zone to Camp 4. Then, with our brains and bodies starved for oxygen, our digestive systems shutting down, and our heart rates speeding up, we'd cross into the Death Zone and make for the top. On the summit, with temperatures dipping to twenty degrees below zero, we'd rejoice and maybe even cry. We'd look to the north and see K2 waiting for us in the distance. Then we'd snap our selfies, alone and together, take out the photographs of our families, kiss them, and turn around to try to get back down via the same route we had come up.

Though we'd be climbing as a pair, we'd never be entirely alone on the mountain. There were twenty climbers in our expedition, and at least twice as many in other groups. Though some of them were quite strong, including members of the Russian National Climbing Team, others seemed ill-prepared for the task. They lacked supplementary oxygen; only five of us had arrived with enough to get us to the top or serve as backup in case of an emergency. To make things worse, there weren't enough radios, and some climbers were already looking to make money off their colleagues by charging a hefty fee to lay down the fixed line on the mountain. The unease I'd felt before departing Montreal was quickly coming back.

I spent that first night at base camp alone in my tent with

my headlamp on, writing feverishly to Alexandra in the pink notebook I'd bought before coming to Pakistan. I began with the most pressing details, and an assurance that I still loved her more than the stars, more than the clouds, more than every-thing—even this mountain. Then I turned out the headlamp and lay awake in the cold.

The sky was tranquil and blue by the time I got out of my tent, grabbed my gear, and met up with Ernie for a six a.m. breakfast and a six thirty a.m. departure upwards to Camp 1. We were the first ones up, breaking the trail over the glacier and into the couloir to dump our gear and pitch our tents. We positioned our tents carefully, staking them into the snow as close to the base of the overhanging cliff wall as possible. Then we headed back down to base camp. For the next three days, it was the same. We made our way up and down between base camp and Camp 1, Ernie and I working alongside two Russian climbers to fix a line through a minefield of crevasses. When that was done, we began working our way up to the base of the Kinshofer Wall, breaking trail for those who followed and working our way toward the three-hundred-metre cliff wall that stood as the most technically imposing barrier between us and the summit. But we were forced back from the wall multiple times by waist-deep snow, illness, and avalanches.

All the while, I was getting to know Ernie, a practical joker but also a very good climber and a loyal friend. He'd slip vodka into my water bottle as a prank and watch as I took a massive burning swig to fend off dehydration. Then he'd laugh as I spat it out on the glacier. He didn't go into great detail about his daughters, but I sensed pain, that his passion for the mountains had caused damage to his home life. I didn't pry any further. He said it was always important to enjoy the climb, hardships and all. He was happiest when dangling from a rope and looking down on the world. He wasn't a wealthy man, didn't have state-of-the-art gear, and chose his expeditions based less on the mountains he wanted to climb than on the ones he could afford to climb. He'd invested a lot of money in this expedition and in the next one on K2. He really wanted to succeed on both of them, but he too was alarmed by how disorganized this expedition had become.

"You and me, we stick together, Gabriel," he said. "We are safe together. We do our thing here and go for K2."

He trusted me with his life. And I trusted him with mine. We'd only climbed together for a short while, but in that time we'd already talked about joining up on future expeditions.

By our seventh day on the mountain, a thick, impenetrable fog had settled down upon the glacier, forcing Ernie and me back to base camp. The next day, the winds picked up and everyone on the mountain sensed the same thing: a midsummer snowstorm was moving in. All through the night, the mountain roared with avalanches, burying the fixed lines, demolishing Camp 1 along with our efforts to secure a route to Camp 2. My sense of insecurity was heightened by the weather. I wrote for hours in that little pink notebook, telling Alex how much she meant to me and trying to address any lingering questions that might cause her pain if I were to die or disappear out here. Then I closed her notebook, pulled out my journal, and began preparing a list of "red flags" that might kill me on this mountain. They were mostly man-made. I stopped at seventeen.

The next morning, I trudged through the freshly fallen snow on the meadow, sipping tea and making friends with the other climbers. Among the memorable people I met that day was Peter Sperka, a fifty-seven-year-old Slovakian who'd recently arrived with three Ukrainians. Sperka was an imposing figure, tall and strong, with a weathered face and a calm yet knowing demeanour. You could tell just by looking at him that he was a man of accomplishment. He was one of the few men on the mountain older than me. I only shared a few words with him, but I understood quickly why the other Eastern Europeans at base camp held him in such high regard. He had been climbing and guiding for decades, had made his name as a mountain rescuer, and had already summitted five of the eight-thousanders.

There were about forty other climbers wandering around base camp that day, including a group of four from China, several Nepalese Sherpa, and a handful of local cooks, including our own. By nightfall, all but three climbers had come down from the mountain, seeking refuge in the meadow to minimize their exposure to a potential avalanche. The snow was still falling by the time I crawled into my tent for the night. I slept poorly, hearing the crack and roar of ice breaking away and rushing down the mountainside. I forced myself to wake up at regular intervals to beat the snow from my tent to keep from suffocating in my sleep.

Ernie and I got up at six a.m. to push for Camp 1. It was warm as we climbed; the sun was melting the previous day's snow. Ernie moved fast, carrying only his sleeping bag, while I moved slowly with over twenty kilos of gear on my back. Ernie was up to his old tricks with the vodka. I could hear him laughing as we made our way over the glacier. Then I noticed he was starting to slow down. He'd been developing a stomach ache as he climbed. I told him I'd go on up ahead and have soup ready by the time he arrived.

It was eight thirty a.m. when I reached Camp 1. There were hardly any traces of human settlement. The entire camp and all its tents except for mine had been wiped out by an avalanche during the night. It was a good thing nobody had slept up there.

I pulled out my stove and a small pot and began boiling soup for Ernie. Then I dug out a shovel near the cliff where my tent was and started excavating the camp. Ernie joined me. For eight hours we dug, and at the end of the day, a trio of Ukrainian climbers arrived just in time to see us finish our labours. By suppertime, we were exhausted and dehydrated. Sitting in my tent, I began heating a package of lasagna. Then Ernie shouted from outside: "AVALANCHE!"

I leaped through the canvas door, pressed my back against the nearby cliff wall, and watched as snow wiped out every tent but mine again.

The Ukrainians looked at me and shook their heads with a mixture of amazement and frustration.

"Lucky you," one of them said.

I nodded. I finished my lasagna, made them some soup, then grabbed my shovel and started helping them dig out their tents again. It was well past dark when I crawled back into my sleeping bag, turned on my headlamp, and began writing again to Alexandra. Five hours later, I put down my pen and tried to go to sleep.

That's when the vision set in.

CHAPTER 21

THE VISION IN THE NIGHT

I closed my eyes, and inside my head, a stranger waited for me. It felt as though I could see him but he couldn't see me. It was as if I were invisible. He was in a suit. He walked right past me, like I wasn't even there. He moved slowly toward a girl. I didn't recognize him, but I knew who she was: Alexandra. The man spoke, but all I heard was mumbling. She covered her face as he handed her something. Then I opened my eyes and I was alone again.

It was cold and I was sweating. I tried to make sense of what I'd just seen in my head. What was it? A dream? I never dreamed.

I lay in my tent, a distracted man on a frozen mountain-side, surrounded by death. I could feel it out there, along the unbeaten path between the snow-covered cliffs hanging over-head, the ones bearing the names of the men who'd died there. Men like me, driven by ambition and an urge to leave the safety of our homes and abandon our families. The urge to test our minds, punish our bodies, and risk our lives on the mountain.

I closed my eyes again. I wanted to sleep but I couldn't quite get there. The stranger and the girl were waiting inside my head. The scene was the same as it had been before. The man walked by, mumbled to the girl, she covered her face, and he handed her something.

I didn't like what I was seeing. But I didn't understand it either.

I turned on my headlamp. It was just me and the darkness and the distant sound of ice cracking. Sheets of lined paper, torn from the pink notebook, rested by the satellite phone at my side. They were filled with words for Alexandra. Precious words. Explanations for why I did what I did, went where I went, and risked what I risked when I knew that it hurt her.

I rolled over in my sleeping bag and began reviewing the list of the seventeen things that might kill me in the morning: "Not enough radios. Too many people on this mountain. No leadership! NO PLAN!"

A slow-moving breeze ruffled the yellow canvas of my tent, but it couldn't lull me to sleep as it usually did. Even now, I knew I wasn't really safe. At any moment, a slab of ice could crack, triggering an avalanche like the one that had rushed past my tent just a few hours earlier. I always said the mountains had their own way of speaking. Had this one been speaking to me? Had I not been listening?

I lay awake, welcoming my insomnia. But it wasn't the inherent danger of sleeping on a snowy incline 750 metres above base camp that kept me awake; it was the fear of what waited for me when I closed my eyes: the stranger in my head, my daughter before him, that thing in his hand. What was he handing her? It looked pink.

It was her inheritance. It was the notebook.

I opened my eyes, turned on my headlamp, and bolted upright. I was breathing heavily. My mind raced along with my pulse. My stomach was churning. I was pretty sure I'd just seen my death.

I took a deep breath and reminded myself that I was safe in my tent. I reached for the phone and dialed Annie.

"Hello?"

"Something's not right."

"What's wrong?"

"I need to get off this mountain."

"What do you mean?"

It wasn't the first time I'd called Annie and told her I was ready to come home. I had a habit of leaning on her in my darkest hours. I'd call her from the mountainside whenever I was dehydrated, sick, and miserable. I knew it was twisted. But I also knew I could always count on her to talk me into staying, no matter how much she wanted me to come home.

"Have you been drinking enough water?" she asked.

Water—the basic necessity of life, especially on the mountain. I sometimes didn't drink enough and I'd end up feeling terrible as a result.

"I haven't had enough, no."

"So drink some water, get some sleep, and you'll feel better in the morning."

"No," I said. "It's different this time. I really need to get off this mountain."

I don't know what she said after that; I wasn't able to concentrate on anything other than the words I kept repeating to her.

"I need to get off this mountain," I said again.

By three a.m., I was fully clothed and sitting cross-legged in my tent. I had packed up my bag in the dark, dreading the dawn and the moment I would unzip the canvas, look across the two feet of snow that separated my tent from Ernie's, and say, "I'm going back down."

* * *

The first sounds of morning came around five a.m. as a group of Ukrainians readied their gear and prepared for a day's push to Camp 2. We knew the statistics. For every five climbers who reached the summit of this mountain, one wouldn't survive. But neither they nor I yet realized, at this particular moment, that the probability of death on this climb had increased significantly in the night.

I unzipped my tent and looked outside. The sun was just beginning to light up the valley below. I fired up my stove and began melting snow for my morning cappuccino. There was a rustle from inside Ernie's tent. He poked his head outside. He looked terrible. I poured him the first cup from my brew and handed it to him.

"How do you feel?" I asked.

He groaned, then pointed to his stomach. "Not good," he said. "I must have eaten something rotten." He asked me if I was still planning to go up to the top of the Kinshofer Wall today. It had been our plan to take it easy this morning and then push off after breakfast.

I shook my head. "No, Ernie," I said. "I'm going back down."

He nodded. "I'll come with you," he said. "I need to recover before we come back up."

I paused and stared at him as he sipped his coffee.

"No, you don't understand," I said. "I'm going all the way down. Back to Montreal. I'm going home."

He took the coffee away from his lips and went silent. He seemed to be digesting the repercussions of what I'd just said. I knew what it meant and so did he. It meant he'd have to climb this mountain by himself. And it meant he'd be the third man, climbing behind Marty and Denali Schmidt when he got to K2. Without me, he'd be forced to climb solo or not at all. There wasn't much chance for him to get his money back now. I was letting him down, but I knew I had to get the hell off the mountain.

"There are too many red flags here, Ernie. I have to see my family again. I'm not ready to stay on this mountain."

He nodded into his coffee.

"We can leave here together if you want," I said.

He thought about that for a moment and what it would mean.

Then he said something I'll never forget: "I wish I could be like you, Gabriel. Make the choice you are making. But I can't go. Not yet."

I put more snow in the pot on top of my stove and began making porridge.

"It will take me two trips to get my stuff down from here," I said. "I'll go to base camp today, then come back up tomorrow and go back down with the rest of my gear."

"No, no," he said. "I'll help. Give me your boots; I'm just going down with my sleeping bag. This way, you don't have to come back up."

It was a kind gesture.

"I have some pills you can take for your stomach," I said. "But it means you'll have to stay at base camp while they do their thing."

"Thanks," he said as I handed him the pills. "I'll start these when we get down."

I loaded my gear onto my back while Ernie grabbed my boots. Then we headed down, talking about life and goals and the future. Somewhere out over the Diama Glacier, Ernie told me that he'd probably just go straight home after this climb.

"I'm sorry, Ernie," I said.

"Don't be!" he replied, brushing my apologies out of the air with a wave of his hand. "Next year. We'll climb K2 next year."

His new goal was to climb Nanga without supplemental oxygen and use that feat to attract sponsors for a follow-up attempt on K2 the next summer. It was late morning when we reached base camp. Our chef was just beginning the preparations for lunch. There were strangers on the meadow who hadn't been there before. Four men in traditional Pakistani clothing were just wandering around. I thought nothing of them and went straight to our base camp manager, a local hire named Faqir, whom I'd come to know over the previous ten days on the mountainside. I didn't even drop my bag at my tent. I was still driven to get out of here as quickly as possible. I handed Faqir my satellite phone and said, "Make all the calls you need. I just want off this mountain as soon as possible."

He cringed in disbelief. "This could be difficult," he said.

"Please just do what you can," I said.

It could take as many as two days to arrange transport to

pick me up by the bridge down in the valley. Faqir disappeared into his tent and began making phone calls, while I wandered back to mine and began preparing the rest of my gear for departure. Those strangers I'd noticed earlier seemed to be circulating the tents now. They made their way slowly toward mine. But I thought little of it. My mind was getting foggy and I began thinking only of coffee. I was on my way back to the dining tent when one of the strangers came up to me. He said he was a teacher at the University of Lahore. He said he'd come up here to talk to the climbers. I remember thinking at the time how odd it seemed that someone would come all the way up here just for that. We were at 4,100 metres. It was a cold and remote place. There was nothing else here except us and the mountain. He asked me my name and where I was from. Then he asked me my faith and my views on Islam. I told him I was Canadian. I didn't tell him that I had been raised Catholic by my mother, or that halfway around the world, a candle was probably burning to protect me, or that there was rice in a bag by my feet. I stepped away and headed into the dining tent.

Ernie was there, and Faqir.

I sat down, had coffee, a plate of french fries, and a bowl of soup. Faqir gave me back my satellite phone. "I fixed everything," he said. "If you're ready for a twenty-four-hour journey back to Islamabad, non-stop."

"Excellent," I said, relieved. "What time do I leave?"

"Five a.m.," Faqir said. "A red Jeep will be waiting at the Hilalay Bridge in the afternoon. It should take you eight hours to get down to the bridge."

I thanked Faqir, then I looked at Ernie. It was all very real then. I felt guilty to be getting out of there. He was my partner and leaving him there didn't feel so different from abandoning him up higher on the mountain.

"I've never done this before," I said, wanting to assure him that I wasn't some flake. I was being honest. I'd never just walked off a mountain before. Even at the base of Ojos del Salado in Argentina, when I'd gone to bed believing I was dead, I'd woken up and given the mountain a legitimate try before abandoning the climb. It was really sinking in at that moment that our expedition was over.

"Are we okay?" I asked.

He put up his hands to stop me from saying more.

"I understand," he said. "Go to your family."

After lunch, I finished packing my gear and gave my fuel and food away to some of the other climbers. The strangers from the morning were still wandering around camp. I watched them from a distance. As the sun began to set, they kneeled toward Mecca to pray, while I posed for a photograph on the meadow, the Diamir Face behind me. It looked deceivingly warm and inviting, its white canvas lit up with an orange glow against the darkening sky.

There was nothing left for me to pack except the old Buddhist prayer flags. They were still attached to a branch I'd planted next to my tent. I decided I'd pack them in the morning, on my way out of camp. I stood there admiring the full moon in the sky. It cast a silver frost on the mountain and added to the peacefulness of the meadow. Then Ernie came over to say one last goodbye.

"How are you feeling?" I asked.

He'd missed dinner.

"Still sick," he said. He thanked me again for the pills and pulled out a small bottle of vodka.

"We drink to friendship and the future," he said, then handed me the bottle.

I took a swig and handed it back to him. He took a swig for himself, wiped his mouth, and offered up a hug. Then we said our goodbyes and crawled into our tents.

CHAPTER 22

THE ESCAPE

I barely slept during my last night at base camp. The vision had gone, but I was afraid I'd sleep through the dawn and miss my chance to get off the mountain. It was still dark when I crawled out of my tent. Nina, the Serbian woman who'd introduced me to Ernie, was awake by the time I'd finished gathering my gear. I loaded my pack onto my shoulders and handed the barrel with the rest of my belongings to the porter who'd accompany me down the mountain. I walked over to Nina. She was sipping her morning coffee and readying for a two-day push up to Camp 2. I told her to take care of herself up there. My parting words were alarmingly prophetic.

"Something bad is going to happen on this mountain," I said. "Please be careful."

And then I was gone. I'd opted for the earliest possible start on the eight-hour trek down the path to the road below. I moved as fast as I could without even realizing it. My porter and I, with all my gear strapped to our backs, stopped only to catch our breath and drink water. The temperature rose quickly as we descended into the valley until it was forty degrees.

I believed that in departing base camp, I had skirted danger. There was nothing the mountain could do to me anymore. But still, I wanted to put as much distance between us as possible. I was oblivious to the fact that the real danger wasn't the mountain at all. Up in the meadow, those strangers from the day before had woken up, noticed I was missing, and begun asking the other climbers, "What happened to the Canadian?"

We darted downward through the valley, over streams and moraines, passing little one-room stone-walled huts, flockless goat herders, and small family orchards until suddenly the earth turned grey and dusty, and I realized we were about to reach the desolate, rugged-cut road two and a half hours ahead of schedule. I figured I'd be stranded down by the road for hours before my ride would actually arrive, conditioned to believe that when someone says a Jeep will pick you up at a decrepit old bridge on a dirt road in the middle of nowhere at one thirty p.m., it probably means they won't actually get there until suppertime. I slowed my pace and started scoping out places where I might sit in the shade, concealed from the road but still able to see it. On some level, I was aware that not everyone who used the road would welcome the sight of a Western climber sitting idly by, waiting for a ride. I crested one more slope and caught sight of the bridge. And there was my ride, a battered old red Jeep, ready and waiting, its driver resting with his feet hanging out the door. I hurried to it, paid my porter, threw my bag on the floor behind the driver's seat, and climbed into the back. We began the three-hour drive at a donkey's pace over the winding, rugged dirt road until we reached the town of Chilas. There, I jumped in another beat-up old car, accompanied by a police escort, and began the thirteen-hour drive back to Islamabad and onwards to the airport to catch a midnight plane out of Pakistan.

The plane ride was long but peaceful. I don't know how long it took. I didn't really care. I still felt guilty about leaving Ernie, but there was no way I could have stayed. Not with the things that I'd seen in my head in the night.

The plane touched down with a jolt and began taxiing toward the gate. I turned on my cellphone. I'd been wanting to text Annie and Alexandra all through the flight. Now I was waiting for my phone to find the network. I was still inside the cabin, standing in the aisle, when it finally buzzed. The first text was from Elia.

"Are you all right?" it read. He'd copied a web link into the text. It was from the *Washington Post*. I opened the link and started shaking as soon as I read the headline:

"Taliban Kills Foreign Climbers in Pakistan."

* * *

At ten thirty p.m. on June 22, 2013, around the same time that I was in an Islamabad taxi making my way to the airport, fifteen men armed with knives and guns and dressed as local paramilitary officers, some of them teenagers, arrived in the meadow. Ernie was still there, recovering from his stomach ache, waiting for the antibiotics I'd given him to finish doing their thing. He and nine other foreign climbers were nestled in their tents. Peter

Sperka, the fifty-seven-year-old Slovakian, had just accompanied one of his countrymen back down to base camp, seeking refuge from illness at Camp 1. Three Ukrainians, four Chinese, one Sherpa, and all the Pakistani cooks and porters had retired for the night when the gun barrels poked through the doors of their tents.

There wasn't any time to run once the shouting began.

"Taliban! Al-Qaeda! Surrender!"

One by one, the climbers were dragged out of their tents and onto the frost-covered grass. Some of them were naked; others were wearing only their underwear. One of the Chinese gripped a coat in front of his bare waist to protect his dignity. They were each beaten and robbed, and their satellite phones were smashed or shot to pieces. Faqir and all but two of the local hires were bound together, placed in a nearby tent, and told not to move no matter what they heard. Two of the Pakistanis were not so lucky. One of them, a cook from the Shia faith, and the other, a climber named Sher Khan, were placed in the grass with the foreign climbers. Khan begged for mercy, telling the gunmen that he was not Shia, even though he was. They unbound him from the other foreigners and told him not to watch but kept him close enough to hear every horrible thing that was about to happen.

No one knows exactly what happened to Ernie. It is believed that he tried to talk with the gunmen. He was separated from the other captives. Shouts of terror mixed with sobs as the climbers tried to reason with their captors. Ernie was heard to say, "I'm not American." They broke his nose and shot him twice in the chest in front of the others.

Frightened and cold, the climbers were instructed to kneel in the grass and turn their heads away from the guns. Then they were shot, their bodies dropping one by one in the meadow while the sound of gunfire echoed off the Diamir Face and dissipated into the night.

Then one of the gunmen spoke. He said, "Today, these people are revenge for Osama bin Laden." And shortly after he did that, another gunman stood over each of the climbers' bodies and fired one more shot into their heads.

Only one of the foreigners at base camp that night managed to escape the firing squad. He was a Chinese climber named Zhang Jingchuan. I'd seen him but had not properly met him before my departure. Dragged out of his tent in his underwear, he did exactly as he was told and knelt in the grass alongside the others. He was still kneeling there as the bodies began to fall. When the first bullet meant for his head missed its mark, he bolted up from his knees and started to run, zigzagging across the meadow in the dark, sprinting for his life as shots rang out around him. Soon he reached a nearby trench and dived out of sight. He hid in that trench for half an hour and waited as the Taliban ransacked the camp. When he began to freeze, he forced himself to sneak back to his tent to grab clothes, crampons, and an ice axe. Then he snuck back out into the dark, seeking refuge higher up on the mountain, scrambling over the glacier in the moonlight, where he hid until morning.

It was after midnight before the gunmen finally turned off their headlamps, walked out of base camp, and disappeared into the night.

It took a while for the Sunni porters and cooks who'd been spared to recover from the shock and rise to their feet. Their communication devices demolished, they had no way of reaching out to anyone—neither the climbers above nor the police, who were more than a two-day hike away in the valley. The Taliban hadn't been gone for very long when a trail of light began snaking down from the glacier. It was a team of Sherpa coming back to the meadow, completely oblivious to the carnage. One of the local porters who'd been confined to a tent while the massacre occurred ran to meet them before they reached camp. The porter grabbed their radio and called up to Nina and the rest of the climbers sleeping above the Kinshofer Wall. He told them of the attack. It was too late for anyone to do anything other than place an emergency call to the Pakistani police. It would be daylight before the first police helicopter arrived.

By then, Nina and the others could view the horror that dawn revealed down in the meadow. From their cliff-top perch, they could see that the grass was stained red. It wasn't easy to build up the courage required to descend, but they had no choice. None of them were yet acclimatized to stay up on the mountain. And so they started their descent, with a clear view of what awaited them below.

Ten bodies lying prone in a line. One resting off to the side.

Chapter 23

THE THIRD MAN FACTOR AND THE DAMAGE DONE

I'd seen a lot of terrible things over the years on the mountainside, but I hadn't become numb to the tragedy that plagued my sport. The attack at Nanga Parbat threw everything I believed into question. I'd preached for years that only the mountain could decide who would succeed on its slopes. The massacre in the meadow had challenged that.

I returned to Montreal to an empty house. Annie and the girls hadn't been expecting me home and were away on vacation at Mont Tremblant. I sat alone at our dining room table, reading reports about the terror I'd escaped. My phone and email were inundated with requests for interviews from journalists around the world. The Pakistani authorities were also trying to reach me. They were at a loss in their investigation. They'd arrested Faqir and the other local Pakistanis who'd survived the attack, and would hold them in custody for forty days.

The Pakistani Taliban took responsibility for the massacre immediately. They said it was retribution for an American drone attack that had occurred three weeks earlier. The drone attack had killed the second-in-command of the Taliban, who'd been sleeping among innocent civilians in a hideaway in a small hillside town near the Pakistan-Afghan border.

Back in Montreal, I kept my door locked and the blinds closed, and I screened all my phone calls. The media was after me. I sent out a quick statement and asked that I be left alone. I had my own questions about what the hell had led me to walk off the mountain and wasn't yet ready to try to explain the nature of an inexplicable vision to journalists.

I learned the particulars of the massacre in the meadow from Nina and a few of the other climbers who were fortunate enough to have been out of reach of the Taliban attack. We were all understandably scared, especially after some of the survivors began receiving emails from the Taliban, who'd retrieved their ID from the records at base camp. It only took one threatening text, email, or phone call in the night to lead any of us to fear that, even though we'd survived the attack, we still weren't safe. I felt anxious on the streets of Montreal, as if I were about to be shot in the back at any minute.

I wasn't yet ready to talk about any of it with anyone, but I knew I needed to email Marty Schmidt and explain why neither Ernie nor I would be joining him on K2. Marty was on Broad Peak with his son and had heard of the massacre. He'd been trying to reach me ever since. I let him know I was okay but that Ernie was gone. I didn't know what more to say. I still felt I should apologize for backing out of the climb on K2. I finished my message to Marty with an apology. Then a rush of anxiety crept up from my stomach and seemed to sit on my heart, and suddenly I was gasping for breath. I was becoming sick with anxiety and remorse. My conscience was telling me that I'd done something wrong by getting off that mountain. And yet it felt disingenuous to suggest that I was sorry for having made it home. Had I not backed out, I'd have been in one of the pine coffins sitting under armed guard on an Islamabad airstrip.

It was all very paralyzing.

I'd already missed a few nights' sleep by the time Annie and the girls arrived home. I tried to tell Annie all that had happened—about Ernie, the attack, the vision, everything. She didn't want to listen to any of it. Every element of the story terrified her. She wasn't sure that we should talk about it anymore with anyone. She was frightened. So was I. She'd always said I was playing Russian roulette with my life in the mountains, but now it seemed I'd brought the revolver home.

"I don't know what's to be gained from talking about any of this," she said. "You weren't there. You got out. You need to deal with this and move on."

I understood what she was saying and why. But I couldn't move on. I was stuck. And not talking about it just made it worse. I felt like I was pretending that nothing had happened. But it *had* happened. I knew it had happened. And I couldn't stop obsessing about it. I tried to act normal during movies, dinners, and conversations, but a part of my mind was still in that meadow.

Annie had grown increasingly uneasy with the incessant nature of my climbs. She'd gone from waiting for me at the base of the Khumbu Icefall to greeting me at home when I returned from my expeditions. I didn't blame her one bit for how she felt about it. I'd never done anything to deserve a hero's welcome and I had never wanted one either. All I had ever asked was that she trust me to be as safe as possible once I was on the mountain. In return, I'd do everything within my control to mitigate the risks associated with every climb. That was our deal. I knew she'd never forgive me if I killed or injured myself doing something stupid on a climb. But it was the things I couldn't control that had always scared her. She'd known from the get-go that the one defining feature about my chosen pastime and profession was that it could very easily kill me.

But now things felt different. The men who died in the meadow hadn't been killed by the mountain and they hadn't been killed by their own stupidity. They'd been targeted because they were unarmed foreigners in the middle of a hostile part of the world. It was a barbarous act that cast my views of karma and risk into disarray.

It seemed the rules by which I'd led my life no longer applied. That the spiritual connection I'd picked up from the Sherpa and implemented on the mountainside was all just a bunch of superstitious bullshit. That maybe it wasn't the mountain that decided who would summit after all. For a while, I wondered if I'd ever feel safe on the mountain again. I wasn't entirely sure I'd ever feel safe again anywhere. What kind of world did we live in where armed strangers would trek two days to reach a campsite to drag eleven unsuspecting, unarmed, innocent men from their beds and shoot them?

It didn't take long before the media stopped calling to talk about what had happened. Soon, everyone else seemed to have moved on. But I was still reeling from something I hadn't even witnessed. I knew, deep down, that it was irrational for me to think that the Taliban would strike out at me now that I was home in Montreal. But I couldn't shake that fear. It took a long while for me to realize that I couldn't overcome the fear by myself.

Fear haunted me most during the quiet times when I lay in bed. Annie would be sleeping and the house would be creaking, the wind brushing through the trees, the rain pattering against the window. I felt in tune with all of it, and none of it. I'd close my eyes and I'd feel as though I was back in the meadow, standing alone outside my tent, watching as Ernie fell to the grass, and then the others, lying there, with shadows hovering over them. Every morning, I'd get out of bed, groggy and confused. I'd make Annie her breakfast smoothie and prep her lunch. The morning ritual had always been my way of reminding her that I loved her and of thanking her for putting up with my exploits on the mountain. But she could tell I wasn't well. She knew my mind and body weren't in the same place.

"It's like I'm living with a zombie," she said.

I blamed my lethargy on lack of sleep. Insomnia is a terrible thing. I'd suffered it enough on the mountainside to know how it could change your mood. I didn't bother to tell her about all the shit that was swirling around in my head every time I closed my eyes.

Then I'd smile and we'd hug, and she'd head off to work and I'd be alone again. I'd turn on my computer and start rereading reports and emails about the attack. I felt morbid and sick for doing so. But I couldn't stop. The days passed and I contemplated unpacking my gear. I'd just sort of dumped it in the storage closet when I'd come home. I went downstairs, hung my crampons in their usual spot, and put my ice axes back on their hooks. I did the same with my helmet, harness, jumar, and ropes. It felt good to organize my gear. Then I picked up my moon boots—the ones Ernie had loaded onto his back and carried down over the Diama Glacier on the morning I told him I was leaving.

I felt sick to my stomach. His simple gesture had saved my life. And mine had sealed his fate.

Annie could tell that something was off when she came home to dishes in the sink. I never left dishes in the sink. I was obsessively clean. She gently asked me how my day had been. I told her I was struggling with the sickening belief that Ernie had saved my life and that, moments later, I'd killed him. She stopped me there. She didn't want to talk about the massacre at all. "You weren't there," she reminded me. "You need to appreciate this fact and get on with your life." To her, this seemed as good a time as any for me to give up on the climbs. To get a new job and start working toward retirement. She didn't quite understand exactly what I was saying. Then she recommended we take a vacation. Go somewhere to clear my mind. So later that week, we jumped in Annie's car and drove to Lac-Mégantic to visit my mother and unwind in a little bed and breakfast down by the lake.

We met my mother in the old town, not far from the church where I'd been baptized. I didn't have to tell her about the attack; she'd already heard about it. She'd been praying for me the entire time I was out there. She'd never stopped praying. We stuck around the town for a few days. It felt good

318

to unwind near the streets of my birth, to see my grandfather's old pharmacy, to sip wine by the lake, and admire the old town. By the time we returned to Montreal I was able to close my eyes without automatically finding myself standing in the meadow.

We'd only been back a day or two when I turned on the news to learn that Lac-Mégantic—my hometown, the place we'd just visited—had exploded in the night. An unattended freight train filled with crude oil had derailed, caught fire, and eviscerated the city centre. Forty-seven people were missing. The television was showing footage taken from a helicopter of the town still on fire. I could make out the steeple of the church where my mother prayed. I got on the phone immediately but couldn't reach her. It seemed like forever before she called to say that she was okay. The house she shared with my uncle (her little brother) hadn't been hit by the explosion, but she'd been evacuated nonetheless.

Everywhere I turned there seemed to be tragedy. Three weeks later, I opened up one of my favourite climbing websites and punched in Marty and Denali Schmidt's names. I wanted to follow their progress on K2. Instead, I found their obituaries. The duo had been swept off the mountain by an avalanche that hit their camp. The authorities said it was unlikely that anyone would find their bodies.

I closed my laptop and put my head in my hands.

I was still reeling from the news, thinking of Marty's wife and daughter and all they'd just lost, when it dawned on me that I was supposed to have been with them on that climb.

Suddenly it felt like maybe it wasn't just the Taliban that was chasing me. Maybe it was death itself. I went to bed that night feeling like I'd become a danger to everyone. I wondered if maybe the people I loved would be safer if I simply disappeared—if I just packed all my belongings into my car and drove away to a place where only death could find me.

* * *

For a long time, it felt like the adventure was over, like maybe everything I'd done wasn't worth anything anyway. So I climbed mountains—who cared?

It didn't help when an Austrian millionaire completed the dream that had driven me for nearly ten years: to be the first man to climb the Seven Second Summits. I felt like a failure again. There was nothing left for me to accomplish on the mountains. The things I wanted to accomplish wouldn't matter to anyone but me anyway.

All the while, I was troubled by what might have been the most upsetting question of all: the source of the vision that had saved my life. I didn't talk much about it because I worried it would make me sound crazy. But it had felt so real. I'd always been open about my superstitions and spiritual beliefs on the mountain, but I still self-identified as agnostic. I didn't have strong beliefs in any religion, but I didn't discredit them either. Now I was struggling with the very nature of what had saved me. I didn't know whether the man I'd seen handing my daughter her inheritance was some sort of guardian angel or just a figment of my imagination. He could have been Claude, Babu, Sean, Frank—any one of them. He had no face and no discernible features other than the book in his hand. I was less comfortable thinking of him as an angel than as a hallucination brought on by fear, exhaustion, and lack of oxygen. Still, I had questions—primarily, why had he not appeared in Ernie's head as well?

I wasn't the only person ever to have been visited by such a stranger in the night. There were many other explorers, mountain climbers, aviators, sailors, and soldiers who'd narrowly survived harrowing ordeals only to return home and explain how they'd been led out of danger by a vision or a voice. It's referred to as the "Third Man factor," an inexplicable phenomenon in which an unseen or unidentifiable presence encourages those on the edge of death to make one final effort to survive. Ernest Shackleton had experienced it, as had Charles Lindbergh, Reinhold Messner, Peter Hillary, and a number of other people who credited a mysterious premonition or being for helping them survive in extreme environments. I still wasn't sure what to make of any of it. I was more troubled by the knowledge that despite having gotten myself out of danger, I hadn't managed to save anybody else.

I knew I had to get back on the stage to make some money and inspire people. But I was afraid to talk about what had happened at Nanga. I felt sick at the thought of it. Like I'd be somehow profiting from the deaths of my friends. I just couldn't do it. It just didn't feel right to talk about my adventures any more than it did to talk about the things going on inside my head.

I didn't realize how lost I actually was until one midsummer afternoon while out with a couple of friends, including a doctor who'd trekked with me to Everest in 2006. I don't know what I said that caused him concern, but at some point over lunch,

I slipped one too many hints to the group that I was feeling a mixture of guilt and grief over what had happened to Ernie.

The doctor took me aside after lunch and asked me if I'd spoken to anyone about the massacre.

"I wasn't even there when it happened," I said. "I didn't see anything. I'm not really talking about it with anyone."

"You have to be careful with survivor's guilt and trauma," he said. "It can really change you. You have to do something about it now. It's like a whirlpool. It will keep taking you down."

I nodded and wondered if maybe it already had. In the middle of lunch, while everyone else had been talking, I was just sitting there, staring at their mouths and replaying in my head how Ernie had saved my life and how moments later I'd killed him.

* * *

I could feel myself drifting toward my usual autumnal funk when I reached out to Sylvain Guimond, the psychologist who'd coached me back to health in the days after the incident with Frank. In many ways, Sylvain felt less like my psychologist and more like my friend. I began the conversation hoping that he would understand my fears. That he'd tell me he'd lived with the same feelings after being diverted away from the World Trade Center on the morning of 9/11. That I wasn't going crazy and everything I was saying seemed rational.

Instead, he told me, "You're like a soldier who has just come back from war."

His words caught me off guard. I'd never wanted to be a soldier. I hated the idea of going off to war and being anything like my father. My father was a fucked-up man. I was normal. It was important that I maintain my normal.

Sylvain explained to me how the depth of my survivor's guilt was causing me to relive an unseen trauma over and over inside my head. It was quite common among people who had narrowly escaped certain death, and was frequently diagnosed in airline passengers who had missed a doomed flight. It is, in essence, a mental condition that occurs when a person believes they've done wrong by surviving a traumatic event when others have not. It's a condition that was first diagnosed en masse among survivors of the Holocaust. Anxiety, depression, withdrawal, insomnia, nightmares—these are all symptoms.

I'd gone to Sylvain hoping for a quick and easy cure. Instead, I'd come back with the understanding that it was going to be a long time before I recovered. It took several hours of talking with Sylvain over several months before I felt comfortable enough to get back on the public stage. Addressing a group in Sherbrooke five months after the attack, I paid tribute to the men who'd died at Nanga and reiterated my message that you could not live your life in fear.

My return to the public stage helped me understand that I had to climb again. If I stopped, I would be forced to rebuild myself from scratch. The economics just wouldn't work. I'd risk losing my sponsors, my livelihood, the treks, my clients—everything. I couldn't afford to give up. But it went way beyond economics.

The toughest thing for any athlete to accept is the end of their career—especially when it's taken from them before they're ready. I knew there were only so many more years that I could keep heading out on expeditions. I was a grandfather now, but I wasn't prepared to let the Taliban be the ones to dictate whether I'd ever climb again. By January 2014, I felt empowered enough to begin planning my return to the mountains. I sat at my table with a map of the Himalaya in front of me, preparing notes about Manaslu, an 8,156-metre peak in northern Nepal that the Sherpa call the "Mountain of the Spirit." I whipped myself into shape both physically and mentally.

But when the day came for me to buy an airline ticket and begin the final preparations for my next great adventure, I froze and backed out of the climb. I still wasn't strong enough emotionally.

* * *

Soon, it was June 22 again. A year had passed since the night of the killings. I tried not to think about it, but it was impossible. Despite all the progress I'd made over the previous year, the massacre was still altering my view of life and freedom. I reached out to Sylvain again. He told me to come and meet him in the city, and we'd go for a walk.

He'd spent months working me through my survivor's guilt and PTSD, recalibrating my understanding of risk and explaining that it was ultimately just me and the mountains that had the final say in whether I was done with climbing. He hadn't exactly pushed me to get back out to the Himalaya, but he'd helped me understand that I needed to confront the demons in my head if I was to have any chance of reclaiming my former sense of self.

As we paced up and down the sidewalk of one of Montreal's busiest streets, Sylvain listened while I tried to explain all that was still going on inside my head.

"I've lost sight of who I am," I said. "Of what I'm capable of. It's like I'm afraid to dream."

It wasn't often that Sylvain just nodded and listened, but there was a heaviness to what I was saying, and he took his time to answer. When he did respond, he didn't dance around. He just came at me with a question that would stump most people, but to which I'd always had a very simple answer.

"Let me ask you," he said. "What's your purpose in life?"

"That's the problem," I said. "I don't know anymore."

"Well, can you retire and just be a family man now?"

"I'm trying to be."

"So then why can't you just stop climbing?"

There was no point in going any further down this road, so I cut him off with full disclosure. "Do you want to find me hanging in a closet? I just can't stop. I can't. I can't go back to what I was before I became a climber."

I'd never vocalized my need to climb so forcefully to anyone. I'd never let on that I climbed, at least partially, because I feared that if I didn't, I'd revert back to the lost and lonely man I was before I wandered up to the top of a Colombian volcano.

I had no idea what he'd say next. I'd just revealed a deep-seated fear that I'd never really talked about to anyone. Not even to Annie.

That simple revelation gave Sylvain the tools he needed to help me understand what it was I was trying to say, what it was I was actually dealing with.

Suddenly, Sylvain was telling me the story of a famous doctor named Viktor Frankl. Frankl was an Austrian psychiatrist who'd been imprisoned at Auschwitz during the Holocaust. While in that concentration camp, Frankl had devised a theory that he later wrote about in a book called *Man's Search for Meaning*. "What Frankl found," Sylvain explained, "is that there is an actual power to positive thinking. Your view of the future affects your longevity. Those who give up hope are generally the first to die."

"So what are you saying?" I asked.

"You're willing to die in order to pursue your passion, right?"

"Yes."

"And now you say that if you don't pursue your passion, then we might find you hanging in a closet. So if you're not willing to die for something, then you're not willing to live."

It sounded suicidal the way he said it. I'd never believed myself to be actually suicidal in my entire life. And yet I felt that if I weren't to continue on as Gabriel Filippi the climber, then I would be killing my soul anyway.

"So what do I do?" I asked.

"You have to figure that out yourself," he said.

CHAPTER 24

THE CLIMB TO END ALL CLIMBS

"How long are we going to keep doing this?" Annie asked when I told her I was heading back to Everest. She wasn't happy. "You're completely addicted."

"I'm not addicted," I replied.

"You say for you the mountain is like oxygen. That sounds a lot like an addiction, Gabriel."

We'd been through this so many times, both of us drawing invisible lines as we debated the definitions of *passion* and *obsession*.

"So how are we supposed to explain this to your grand-daughter if you don't come home?"

"I'm not going back in order to die."

I needed to renew my faith in the mountain as the arbiter of who summits and who does not.

"If I don't go back to the mountains, I'll have dishonoured the dead," I said. "I can't give in to the feelings of terror." Terror was the motive for their murders. If I'd allowed myself to live the rest of my life in fear, then their deaths would have served the Taliban's purpose.

We were at an impasse, but there was no way to stop me from going back now.

I felt invigorated just thinking of venturing up the same winding trail that I'd taken time and again, all in an effort to move beyond the trauma of the massacre and re-engage with my passion. And yet returning to Everest felt like the toughest, most consequential decision of my life. I was more aware than ever of the emotional toll the climbs had taken on my family. And it seemed I was being reminded of it by almost everyone I knew.

They were all asking the same question: "After all these years, have you really learned nothing? You're just going to keep playing Russian roulette until you find the bullet?" They said I was addicted and maybe they were right. But the only thing I felt addicted to was the therapeutic sense of belonging. And I was pretty sure I belonged on that mountain. There was nothing I could have said to anyone to make them understand that I no longer had anything to prove. That I was more convinced that I'd die if I didn't climb than if I did.

I packed my bags and departed for Kathmandu and then onwards into the Himalaya, en route once more to Everest. I led a team of trekkers up from Lukla, trying, as best as I could, to impart my knowledge of the region and passion for the mountain to them while also navigating our way through a throng of climbers. A stray dog had attached itself to my shadow way down in the valley and followed my every step into base camp, even going so far as to build itself a little bed in the snow outside my tent. I'd taken my usual moments of solitude, away from my trekkers, to pay respect at Babu's chorten before moving onto Sean's. It was easier to talk to them now than it had been in the past. I no longer cared whether it looked awkward to the trekkers and client climbers passing by.

I spoke to Sean the longest. There was so much to say.

"I'm a grandfather now, Sean. If you can imagine that." I laughed, thinking back to some of our very first conversations, at my tent back in the spring of 2000, when he'd been studying the psyche of the climbers. "You'd have your work cut out with me now." I told him about the vision in the night that had saved my life and about the massacre. I mentioned Ernie by name. I don't know why, but I thought they might run into each other wherever they were. "If you see him, tell him a good joke. He likes jokes."

Then I reconnected with my trekkers and, together, we continued on to base camp.

The spring had been unseasonably cold in the Khumbu Valley, and the rocky moraine leading into base camp was covered by a few centimetres of powder. But the snow and the cold had done nothing to keep the pilgrims away. The crowd forming at the base of the mountain was actually the largest ever: 350 climbers and roughly as many Sherpa and guides—the inevitable effect of the previous year's tragedy, when sixteen Sherpa perished after an ice serac gave out and crushed them in the icefall. The accident prematurely shut down that whole season and not a single climber made it to the summit.

I showed my trekkers around the Khumbu Glacier, spent a night with them camped out in the snow under the stars, then sent them back down to Lukla while I stayed behind to prepare for the climb ahead.

I had no intention of getting trapped with the horde as it moved its way up the mountain. I was here as the personal guide for a friend and doctor named Sylvie. We'd arrived with our eyes set not on Everest, but on Lhotse instead. To get there, we'd have to work our way through the icefall and the Western Cwm just like everybody else, before veering east at the South Col and travelling on our own.

I pitched my tent in the same place as always, right in Babu's favourite spot. It felt comfortable, as if I were home, even if I didn't recognize any of my neighbours. There were so many unfamiliar faces at camp. So many cameras. So many reporters. So many clients. Elia was there, as was Russell Brice, Namgyal, and some of the other Sherpa I'd come to consider my brothers on the mountainside. But there were hundreds of others there too. Men and women I'd never seen before, all of them hoping to get to the top of the world. For a week, I wandered the glacier, seeking out the few friends I could spot in the crowd, and waiting for the opportune moment when I could lead Sylvie through the icefall and upwards, away from the mass pilgrimage at the top of the Lhotse Face. We were still at base camp when the earthquake hit, shifting the earth in Kathmandu by an estimated three metres and sending tremors rippling through the countryside, toppling temples and buildings, dislodging a serac from the side of Lingtren, and sending a wall of snow straight into base camp.

* * *

The earth shakes and I hear the distant roar of an avalanche coming near. It sounds like a freight train rolling fast toward my tent. I know immediately that I'm not safe inside my canvased dome, that it will be wiped away by the snow or ripped from its moorings and tossed into the air. The wind is deafening and getting louder as I get to my feet and break outside into the open. Everest Base Camp sprawls out before me; people are scrambling in every direction, unsure what to do. The dog that has been following me around day and night, eating my food, and sleeping by my tent is already gone, and I don't know where. A dark cloud of flying rocks and sheets of ice gather at my back, and I begin to run, straight for the icefall. I'm only a few steps from my tent when I spot some client climbers trying to film the cloud on their cellphones.

"RUN!" I scream.

There's no time to say anything more. I hunch my back as I run, trying to keep my head low as chunks of ice and rock strafe past me like bullets. I'm not far removed from my tent when I lose a shoe. I'm running awkwardly now, increasingly aware that I'm not moving fast enough to escape the cloud of snow wrapping itself around me. Then I spot a boulder at least five times the size of my body and begin sprinting for it, just as a gust of wind hits me in the back and lifts me from the ground. For a moment, it feels like I'm flying. Then I catch up to the boulder and force myself into the eddy behind it. I crouch in the fetal position and shut my eyes while rocks and ice smash against my newfound shield. I try to scream but I can't even breathe. A jet of air rushes into my mouth and nostrils as I struggle to inhale. The freight train is running over me now. I'm suffocating. It feels like forever, though it's only forty seconds. I can feel the snow accumulating on my face and body. I remain as still as can be. Then the roar begins to pass me by. Soon it's just a distant rumble, and then it's gone and everything is quiet.

I cough snow, ice, and dirt from my mouth and keep on coughing until finally I can breathe. I open my eyes, brush the snow from my face and body and check myself for blood. There is none. I rise to my feet and take a desperate look around. I can't see a thing. I can't hear anything either. And in that moment, it seems I'm completely alone.

The blinding whiteness begins to thin and I get my first glimpse of the extent of the destruction. I'm standing in the aftermath of the deadliest disaster in the mountain's history. I'm unaware that down in the villages and streets below, more than eight thousand people have just been killed. Right here at base camp, ninety bodies lie twisted and broken, eighteen of them beyond repair.

I begin running again, moving as fast as I can toward my tent, to the first aid kit I keep in a pocket next to my bed. On the way, I come upon my shoe; it's full of snow. I pick it up and shake it out. I have no sooner got my foot in my shoe than I hear the first people screaming. They aren't crying for help; they are screaming incoherently from every direction. I continue to my tent, grab my kit, and spot Sylvie in the distance. She's on her feet, looking startled but moving back to her tent as well. I yell out to her, asking her if she's okay. She says she's unhurt and that she's gathering her medical gear. I throw my kit under my arm and head back out into the mess. The white cloud continues to clear as I run, revealing an apocalyptic scene of shattered tents, destroyed bodies, and blood-soaked snow.

At the moment, I think only of Elia. I begin running toward his camp, fearing that he might not be as lucky as me. But I take only a few strides in Elia's direction when I find myself turning instead toward what seems the nearest voice calling for help. It's a woman's voice screaming loudly from somewhere out in the snow. I'm still running toward that voice when I start to notice broken tents filled with broken bodies wrapped around boulders. In every direction, I can see snow marked by the blood of the injured. I come upon a Sherpa lying on his back in the snow, breathing heavily and clutching at the ground with his hands. A demolished tent lies beside him, as does a bloodied rock that has flown through the air and taken off the left side of his face. His skull is open, his socket crushed, and his left eye completely exposed. He spots me with his one good eye, and in it I get a glimpse of pure shock, desperation, and momentary hope that my arrival might save his life.

I crouch in the snow by his side, place his hand in mine, and try to speak to him. He doesn't reply, and I get the horrible feeling that there's nothing that I or anyone else can do to help him. I focus on his one good eye. He looks at me, and even though there are no words coming out of his mouth, his eye is begging me to save him. A soft and weakened gurgling noise emanates from his throat. He's still breathing, and I tell him to hold on, that help is coming. But when I look around, there's no one else in sight. He stops gurgling and I see his eye starting to lose its focus. I worry he's about to die in my hands. I've seen a lot of crazy things in my life, but nothing has prepared me for this moment. I don't know what to do, so I continue trying to talk to him. "Keep your eyes open," I say. "Talk to me. Your family is waiting for you. Stay with me. Stay with me." I don't know how many times I repeat that line before I pull my focus away from his eye and look up. I want to yell but I know there's no point. I look around at his clothing to see if I know him. I can't tell by his face if I've climbed with this man, sipped tea by his side, or shared a laugh with him in one of the dining tents here at base camp. His face is so badly damaged that I doubt his family would recognize him.

I'm by his side for two, maybe three, minutes when the little sound from his throat stops. He's no longer breathing. I squeeze his hand, tell him again to stay with me. It's no use. I feel for his pulse and it's gone. I stare at his body for a few moments. My eyes well up and there's nothing I can do to stop the tears. I brush them from my face and begin acting on impulse. I grab the sleeping bag lying in the bloodied snow next to his body. I unzip the bag and place it over him to preserve his dignity.

There's no time for prayer or reflection. I hear more screams coming from other parts of the camp, and I feel I should be running again. I head south, making for the nearest, loudest cries for help.

I overhear on the crackle of a passing radio that Elia's camp has survived the earthquake. I'm relieved, but only for a moment. I look around me and notice I'm standing in the smashed remnants of the Adventure Consultants' camp. It's a mess of ruined bodies and red-splattered snow. There's a tent, belonging to a married couple I've climbed with before, collapsed and destroyed under the weight of a boulder. I search around it for the bodies of my friends. They aren't here and I begin to fear they may be somewhere up the mountain.

A dozen or so people are scattered about. Some are dead while others are halfway there. Barely five minutes have passed since the earthquake. I see uninjured climbers trying to stop the blood pumping out of a man's twisted body. I see another man lying alone. I don't know the injury he's suffered, but I can see that he's too far gone to warrant anyone's attention. In this particular place at this particular moment, the injured outnumber the uninjured, and decisions are being made about who can be saved and who will be left to die. I crouch by the man's side and grab his hand, just as I did the Sherpa's a few minutes earlier. Again I focus on his face. Shock has set in and I'm no longer sure that I'm functioning. I look into his eyes. His head is as bloodied as his body, and I can tell he isn't going to make it. I know there's nothing I can do but be here with him when he dies. I tell myself that at least that's something. I don't think anyone wants to die alone. So I kneel in the snow and ask him to stay with me and talk about his family, while I cling to an irrational hope that if I can convince him to keep breathing, maybe, just maybe, he'll be okay once proper help arrives. I know, first-hand, how climbers can sometimes keep themselves alive by thinking about their families. I remind this man that he too has a family and that he should think of them now. I want him to live, and I tell him that his loved ones do too. He makes no noise as I speak to him, doesn't even blink, and I wonder if he's already dead. I slip my finger onto his wrist and feel for his pulse. It beats faintly and sporadically against my finger for a minute, maybe more. And then it's gone.

I step back from his body, look at his face and then at my hands, which are covered in blood. I'm overcome by a sickening feeling that I'm useless. That I can't save anyone.

I stumble through the carnage, distraught and covered in blood, in search of Sylvie. I find her at her tent. She's kitted out and ready to go.

"It's a mess, a big mess!" I shout. "It can't be like this all day. Can it?"

Sylvie can tell just by looking at me that I'm feeling lost. Helpless even. I'm not broken, but I need guidance. "I'm ready," she says. "Can you take me to where you just came from?"

I nod.

Then together we head back out into the disaster, and soon I am kneeling by Sylvie's side, acting like some kind of medic on a battlefield. I follow Sylvie's command to put pressure on wounds. A Serbian doctor passes by. I look at him and don't understand why he isn't helping anyone. He is packing up his bags and getting ready to leave. "Are you going to help?"

He shakes his head and replies, "There's nothing I can do."

"Are you kidding me?" I shout at him. "You can save people!"

He doesn't respond.

I want to grab him by the jacket and shake him or smash him. I don't know what's wrong with him until a half-hour later, when I spot him wandering aimlessly through camp. I wonder if he's broken.

All through the afternoon and into the night, I work under Sylvie's direction, ferrying the injured on makeshift stretchers made out of ladders into a triage of hospital tents. We place the dead in sleeping bags and put them under a tarp that we designate as the morgue.

It's nightfall. I start for my tent, my mind filled with the faces of the dead. As I stare up at Everest through the icefall, the stars in the sky remind me that there are two hundred or so climbers marooned up above. I find myself questioning what any of us are actually doing here. On a day like today, when the earth moves, and the plate beneath India wedges itself a little bit deeper under the plate beneath China, Everest grows. It's a deep realization that right now, the peak of the world may well be one step closer to the stars above. I pull my attention down to earth and look at the destruction that surrounds my tent. There is absolutely no damage to my campsite. And that's when I cry. I ask what I've done to deserve this.

A dog barks, and suddenly nothing else matters. I fix my eyes on the shadowy figure standing in the snow outside my tent. Another bark and I approach with my hands out. Someway, somehow, this dog has survived where sixteen men and two women have perished. I pat his fur, then look into his face. He strikes me as oblivious to the horrors of the day. Then I crawl back into my tent, place my head on the pillow, and think not of the dog, but of the corpses lying under a tarp in the makeshift morgue. It will be dawn before the choppers arrive to take the first few survivors down into the valley below. I kick my shoes off but keep them near as I crawl into my sleeping bag. The earth is restless. I close my eyes. The faces of the dead reappear inside my head. I already know I won't be getting any sleep tonight. I turn my headlamp back on, reach for the Ziploc bag of sacred rice in the top of my knapsack, clutch it in my hand, and lie awake in the cold and the dark.

CHAPTER 25

KARMIC POTENTIAL

The needle came out and the nurse said, "That should do it."

"No more tests?" I asked.

"This will be the last one. It's been six months now, so we should know after this if you're infected."

I rolled down the sleeve of my shirt and hopped off the examination table. It was a beautiful November day and I was glad to be alive—even if, right then, I might have been sicker than I'd ever been.

The nurse looked up from the bagged vial of my blood. "How are you handling the stress? Any anxiety issues?"

"Just a bit of trouble sleeping sometimes, but mostly normal, except for this," I said, looking at my blood. "If I have it, I have it. No sense obsessing."

She says I'm handling the stress better than she'd expected.

I certainly didn't feel sick. Not mentally or physically, anyway. I knew that emotionally, I'd been traumatized, but I felt like I was coping.

I jumped in my car and took the scenic route home from the clinic. Six months had come and gone since the earth shook and an avalanche struck and all those people died. Six months since I felt two men's pulses fade away against my finger. Since I washed the blood of the dead from my hands right before Sylvie took me aside and told me that one of the injured men, whose life we'd been unable to save, was HIV positive. "We know that one of the dead up here was infected," she said. "You'd better get checked out as soon as you get home."

Eric, my doctor friend who'd trekked with me to Everest on more than one occasion, had been at the airport to greet me when my plane touched down from Kathmandu. He'd picked me up and ushered me past the waiting media so I wouldn't have to give an impromptu press conference right by the arrivals gate. We'd stopped for a beer on the way home that day. He listened as I cleared my mind of all the scenes of pain and suffering I carried with me.

"I'm feeling mixed up inside," I told him. "Their faces. They were all smashed."

"Just keep talking about it," he said. "Don't keep it in."

He knew I'd seen enough to be permanently scarred by it all. And no doubt I was. But he helped me to realize scars aren't injuries that need to be concealed. They're lasting proof that you *can* heal.

Annie greeted me as soon as I opened the door. She'd expected me to come back from the avalanche more messed up than I'd been when I returned from Nanga. And I was messed up—for sure I was messed up—but the trauma of it all felt different.

* * *

"How are you holding up?"

It was the one question everyone who knew me wanted to ask as soon as they saw me. This time it was Sylvain, my therapist and friend, talking to me over lunch.

"I have good days and bad," I said, knowing full well he'd never let me leave it at that. He had a way of making me talk through the things inside my head.

I told him about the HIV scare and that sometimes, when I looked in the mirror after a shave, I felt I really had to make sure that I wasn't bleeding. I didn't want my blood to hurt somebody. I'd survived the last twenty years with a karmic view of the world—not the capitalist "you reap what you sow" sort of view, but more in line with the Tibetan Buddhist understanding of karma as a force that connects all things in life to one another. It was why I always did my little ritual with the tobacco and the mountain before every climb. I wanted to believe that the karmic potential of contracting HIV while assisting others was low, but I still couldn't shake the feeling that maybe death was still following me. I knew it was a narrow-minded view. But I still felt sometimes like I was a cursed man. Like maybe I'd brought the revolver home again.

"It's all part of the post-traumatic stress," Sylvain said.

"I know that. But it still creeps up on me in the night or in the day, and when it does, a wave of images and sounds rushes over me. And then I can't stop feeling sorry for myself. Like I must be the unluckiest man in the world. Even though, deep down, I know it's the opposite."

"Do you feel guilty that you survived?" he asked.

I thought about his question for a moment. He was on to something. I didn't feel guilty. Not like last time. Not at all.

"No," I said. "But I don't understand why."

He explained: "You've gained perspective here because this time you were able to help others. The avalanche was an act of God. Not human madness. You got to see human kindness post-avalanche, and that has helped you maintain your perspective."

I hadn't thought of it like that before.

"But what about the HIV?" I asked.

"You have no control over that now. If you could go back, would you do anything differently?"

I'd asked myself that question several times since leaving the mountain. My conclusion was always the same. "Had I known then what I know now—that I could die from trying to help others survive—it wouldn't have changed a thing."

* * *

Everyone, at some point in their life, has to decide how they'll live while waiting for news they can't change. You either move forward or you get stuck. There's nothing you can do to change the outcome, so why let it beat you down?

I've read a lot about PTSD in the last two years. I wanted to understand the nature of my own struggles. In so doing, I've learned a lot about the way others struggle, including my father. I understand now that emotions like terror, sadness, regret, and guilt are ingrained in the mind after a traumatic experience. These emotions are hard-wired into our brains and manifest themselves in anything from an anxiety attack to blind rage. The symptoms of PTSD are often hard to diagnose because they're not always easily described by patients, especially those who've been led to believe that PTSD is an illness that only affects those who are weak of mind. I've been extremely fortunate the last two years to have had good friends in the medical profession to help me through what I'm dealing with. Were it not for Sylvain especially, I might never have climbed again after my failure to remove Frank from the mountainside back in 2010. Sylvain helped me to accept that failure. He showed me that life isn't about turning an A into an A+. It's not about your next great accomplishment. It's about getting into the hearts and minds of those who see us, and impacting their lives. Had I not learned that lesson, I would have never left Nanga Parbat. I would have died there in that meadow while searching for my A+ on K2.

I don't pretend to be over and done with the post-traumatic stress of it all. But I'm trying to deal with the two main residual symptoms: fear and guilt. Fear can be unlearned if you're willing to face it. I figured that one out the moment I jumped headfirst into the Gulf of Mexico and stopped thinking about my father. Guilt is different. Guilt can only be addressed by discussion. I know I've been particularly fortunate to have survived where others have not. It's not my fault any more than it is my doing. What's important is that I not lose sight of how little I actually had to do with any of their deaths.

It's impossible for me to understand why others died and I lived. All I can say is that I know now that human beings respond to every individual danger in one of three ways: we either fight, take flight, or freeze. We never know exactly how we're going to respond until our lives are truly in jeopardy. You might think you know how you'd react if an armed man dragged you from your tent and told you to kneel in the meadow as he cocked his gun, but you don't know any more than I do. Likewise, an avalanche turns your campsite into a disaster zone, but you survive. Do you run away from the chaos or do you run straight into the destruction? Or do you freeze, broken by what you've just seen? You don't know until you're there. And when you're there, you might not have much say in what you do. This is how we deal with trauma in the moment.

It's in the days that follow, when the danger's gone, that even those of us who chose fight or flight often find ourselves frozen. Our minds are trapped in time, facing the memory of that danger over and over again and no longer sure which way to react. And so our minds begin to spin through the shadows of memory, reliving deep-seated fear until it changes our nature. You don't necessarily realize how much you've changed until suddenly you've hit your son so hard that he's falling down a flight of stairs, or you're sitting at home with the blinds closed in the middle of the day, unsure if a stranger's out there meaning to do you harm.

* * *

"We read about you in the newspaper and were hoping you'd come and speak to our soldiers." The email arrived in my inbox from out of nowhere. It was written on behalf of the commanding officer of the 5 Canadian Mechanized Brigade

Group, a Quebec-based battle group of close to five thousand servicemen and -women.

The military was hoping I would go to the regimental headquarters in Valcartier, Quebec, and speak at the tail end of an outdoor winter-endurance challenge meant to help soldiers focus on teamwork as well as stay tough and ready for action. I hadn't been to the regiment's base since I was sixteen years old—when, as an army cadet, I'd gone there to learn how to drive.

I'd been thinking a lot about my dad in the few months since the avalanche. I'd been talking about him more and more with my mother and my siblings, questioning my view of why he was as he was and did what he did. He'd been dead for twenty-three years, but I thought I finally understood him. He was on my mind as I stood outside the gate to the base, waiting for a soldier to pick me up in a truck and take me to a field where five hundred of his colleagues stood at attention, listening to their colonel.

"Have you been here before?" the soldier in the driver's seat asked as we rolled through the snow, passing armoured vehicles and the barracks as we made for the parade ground.

"A long time ago," I said.

"Do you have much experience speaking with soldiers?"

"Only when I call my brothers. Two of them are in the French military. My father was a French soldier too. He fought in Algeria."

The driver didn't ask many more questions, and I assumed that meant he knew what that war had been like.

Soon, I was standing next to the colonel, dressed in the same North Face jacket I usually wear on the mountains, listening as he congratulated his men on a job well done in their recent games. "I'm proud of each of you," he said. Then he said a few words about the importance of mental health. He wanted to make sure each of his soldiers knew that they weren't alone on the battlefield and they weren't alone at home. I hadn't put much thought into what I would say to these guys, until he passed me the microphone.

In falling snow, I looked out at a crowd of men, dressed in their camouflage gear, standing at ease, and staring up at me. They were all so young. Half of them had already been to war. They knew what it was to feel targeted and to run through a battlefield while people died all around them. Some of them had lost friends in Afghanistan. Others had killed.

I didn't know what to say first, so I opened with a joke. I told them I was here to recruit members for my next expedition to the top of the world. That got a few laughs. Then I thanked them for giving me the privilege to meet them. "I think you guys deserve more recognition than you get," I said. "I don't pretend to know what it's like to be in your shoes. Your colonel talked a moment ago about the importance of mental health, and, well, I can tell you first-hand how important it is to take care of yourself. Especially after you've been through something seriously traumatic. A friend of mine was killed by the Taliban, along with ten other climbers, on a mountain in Pakistan. I was supposed to be there, but I got out, and I struggled with feelings of guilt for more than a year."

I had every man's attention. Every one of them was staring at me, wanting to know more. So I went a bit deeper: "I couldn't sleep. I couldn't be around people anymore. I couldn't be myself. It was bad.

"I'm not ashamed to say that I had to go to counselling in order to get better. It was the best thing I ever did for myself. It gave me my life back. It helped me to get to a point where I could dream again and live my life and be happy with who I was and what I was doing.

"If you're feeling lost, detached from where you are or what you're doing, if you feel like you're still stuck on the battlefield, seek help."

I hadn't really expected applause. I didn't even realize they were allowed to raise their arms when they were standing at ease. But pretty soon, they were all clapping as if what I'd said had really resonated. I've given a lot of talks in my life, but this one stood out as rawer than most.

Afterwards, I was standing off to the side, waiting for my drive back to the front gate, when a young soldier came up to me. He shook my hand and thanked me for sharing what little of my story I had told. "I've been having some issues," he said. He seemed like he was about to open up, but then he stopped. Some of his fellow soldiers had gathered around to speak with me, and suddenly this boy no longer felt comfortable sharing anything. His face was empty, his shoulders hunched. He didn't look like a soldier anymore. He looked broken.

"Were you in Afghanistan?" I asked.

He nodded.

I could tell by the way he was responding that he hadn't really talked to anybody. He was keeping everything inside. He looked at his colleagues through the corner of his eye, then back at me, and said, "Thank you again."

Then he turned around and walked away.

Epilogue

It has been 230 years since a goat herder and a physician from Savoy scaled Mont Blanc and ushered in the era of modern alpinism. Nearly a century has passed since the first climbers set out into the Himalaya, supported by local porters and Sherpa on quests to be the first to summit the world's highest mountains. For more than fifty years, men and women from around the world have found gratification walking in the footsteps of Maurice Herzog, Hermann Buhl, Achille Compagnoni, and others who pushed themselves in leather boots and woollen underwear to do what any right-minded human would deem insane. And though the commercialization of Everest and the world's other great peaks has led some to believe that there's little left on this Earth for anyone to actually explore, I prefer to think that the words of Herzog remain as inspirational today as they were when he dictated them from a hospital bed in Paris a year after he climbed Annapurna and became the first man to reach the summit of an eight-thousander. He was still recovering from gangrene and multiple amputations when he looked to the writer by his side and gave some perspective to his most harrowing accomplishment.

349

"Annapurna, to which we had gone empty-handed," he said, "was a treasure on which we should live the rest of our days. With this realization, we turn the page: a new life begins.

"There are other Annapurnas in the lives of men."

I have spent long hours these past few months at home and in my tent, a map of the Himalaya sprawled out before me, 104 unclimbed peaks having just been opened to climbers by the Nepalese government in the hope of attracting more and more tourism to their damaged country.

I have notes about two such peaks that the Sherpa have just named after Sir Edmund Hillary and Tenzing Norgay. At 7,681 metres and 7,916 metres respectively, they represent two of the highest unclimbed peaks on the planet. But it's not their elevation that attracts me to them so much as it is the words imparted to me by Sir Edmund Hillary, who explained that of all his accomplishments in the mountains, it was what he did in the valleys below—helping to build schools and hospitals for the Sherpa people—that he ultimately believed was the most important contribution of his life.

And so I make my final preparations for an autumnal ascent up two mountains whose summits have never before been reached. It won't be long until I'll grab the sacred rice Babu once gave me, the photos of my family, and the pink notebook for Alexandra. I'll put them in my bag and then watch as Annie drives away from the airport once more. Then I'll board a plane with Elia and together we'll head out to the Himalaya. We're not setting out with any illusions of beating everyone else to the summits. No, that's not the goal. We're setting out to climb with a Sherpa friend, a man we've come to know and respect, to break trail together and scale rocks all the way to the edge of the Death Zone. Then we'll stand back and watch from a close distance as he takes his last few steps to the summit of both peaks.

It's impossible to frequent the Khumbu without developing a great respect and admiration for the Sherpa. And it's arrogant to imagine that I, or any Western climber, could actually reach the summit of the world's highest mountains without their support. They are, without a doubt, the most noble and giving people I have ever met. They are never ones to complain about anything and yet are so often treated like servants by their Western employers. I wonder how many Western climbers ever understood how different Tenzing's motivations were for getting to the top of Everest than those of the Westerners he helped. "I climbed Everest so that you wouldn't have to," the great Sherpa once told his second-born son, Jamling, when he asked permission to join an Indian expedition to the mountain. "You can't see the entire world from the top of Everest, Jamling. The view from there only reminds you how big the world is and how much more there is to see and learn."

* * *

It's Tuesday, May 10, 2016: I wake at Everest Base Camp once more to the sound of boots crunching in the snow beyond my tent. It's just before dawn as a hundred or so climbers prepare for another push into the icefall. They're loud in the night, propelled by an ambitious mixture of energy and fear. I crawl out of my sleeping bag and begin packing up my gear. When day breaks, I say goodbye to base camp for one more year and make my way into the valley below to meet up with Pasang-Kaji (P.K.) Sherpa, my friend and companion, with whom I will soon cut a new trail toward Tenzing and Hillary Peaks. The afternoon snow falls hard as we trek west from the Khumbu Valley, over the Cho La pass to the hamlet of Gokyo, a spattering of Sherpa huts and lodges nestled on the shores of a glacial lake. Night has fallen by the time we arrive. We drop our packs on our cots and warm our hands by a stove that's heated by the combustible power of dried yak dung.

The air is cold and damp, but we don't care. I look to P.K. as we sip our tea by the fire. How privileged I am to even know him. He's among the finest climbers in Nepal, and therefore the world. An industrious entrepreneur who, like so many Sherpa before him, has made most of his living by helping people like me reach our goals in the Death Zone. We speak of his wife and children back in Kathmandu, of the restaurant and sporting equipment store he runs when he's not climbing into the thin air above, and I wonder if, for him, our pending journey carries the same romance as it does for me.

"Tomorrow, we go to where the trail ends," I say.

He nods. "We head north. Follow the Gyazumba Glacier on our right until we're forced to cross it. We'll have a good view of our mountains from there."

We're still three months removed from setting up what will be our base camp for our attempt on those two new peaks. We're not yet sure if we'll climb Tenzing Peak first or focus east toward Hillary Peak.

It's just after dawn again when P.K. and I depart our lodge. We head out over the beaten trail of snow-covered rock and sand. The sun peeks in and out of the clouds, as do the towering peaks that surround us. We know our two mountains are located somewhere to the west of Everest and to the east of Cho Oyu, the sixth-highest mountain in the world. We've eyed them on Google Earth, but there's only so much you can learn from an image taken from outer space. So we trek over the rugged moraine on a mission of reconnaissance, hoping to map out our route to the summits of both. It's mid-morning by the time we reach the end of the trail and get our first glimpse of the peaks on the horizon.

We look out in awe as the clouds break before us and reveal the summit of Tenzing. We can only see the top thousand metres of the mountain, but already I'm pointing my finger toward a narrow line of white wedged between two giant walls of rock beneath the eastern summit ridge.

"I see a couloir beneath the ridge on the left," I say. "I think that's our best approach."

P.K. agrees, but we don't know what's below it. There could be a serac or a massive cliff making the couloir impossible to reach. We won't know until we get close enough to properly survey this mountain, and to do that, we'll need to find our way across the two glaciers that lie between us and the base. The first glacier filters into a narrow pass a few hundred metres before us, but it's covered in a thick layer of gravel that hides its potential dangers. I can see the second glacier in the distance. It looks like a field of popcorn, which means it's riddled with crevasses.

"This is going to be tougher than I imagined," I say.

P.K. nods. "I don't even know how we're going to reach base camp."

"Well, we've got a few months to figure it out," I say, my mind racing through all the preparations that still need to be made before we come back here and set out across these glaciers.

"I think it'll be a three-day hike from here to the base," P.K. says.

I do the math in my head. That'll mean three days to the nearest village and the nearest helipad if we get in trouble.

"We'll have to bring absolutely everything we need over these glaciers to set up our camp," P.K. says. "We're going to need yaks."

I shake my head as I look out over the glaciers. "No yak is going to cross over that."

"A helicopter then?"

"No," I say. "I think we're going to have to carry it in the old-fashioned way."

Together, we steal one last look at the mountain as the clouds close in like drapes on either side of the summit. Soon, even the glaciers are shielded from view and there's nothing left for us to look at.

P.K. turns back for the trail. It's almost noon and he needs to get back to his job on Everest. For a moment, I just stand there, watching the clouds roll over the glaciers, listening to the breeze in silent wonder. Then I turn back and follow his lead until the trail splits. He carries on north, back to base camp, while I head south and begin the long journey home.

Author's Note

A lot of people have told me over the years that the adventures of my life could fill a book and maybe appeal to a few readers. I've read a lot of adventure books in my day, and though I've certainly taken a lot of inspiration from them, I've always been most interested in stories that explore the honest depths of the human soul. We all have our vulnerabilities, whether we choose to mask them from the world or not. They dictate who we are and what we do. I was always uneasy with the thought of opening myself up and revealing my entire story. I've never gone on stage and spoken about my relationship with my father or tried to dissect how that relationship drove me in the years after his death. Nor have I ever really revealed how much my climbs have impacted the lives of those who love me. And I haven't talked about my own struggle to differentiate between passion and obsession.

It wasn't until I left Everest in the days after the earthquake in Nepal, and saw the extent of the destruction in Kathmandu and beyond, that I found myself scribbling more and more into that pink notebook for Alexandra. I decided then that it was time to try to make as much sense of my little life as possible. This book was never meant to be an act of catharsis, nor a glorification of my feats, nor a defence of my own decisions on climbs. It is meant to be just a simple, honest account of my trajectory through the last fifty-five years.

I was midway through the writing of this book when my phone buzzed with a message from Eric: "Your test results are in. You're all clear."

It was a message I'd waited a long time to receive. I'd been living under the assumption that I had HIV while I went through all the tests, unsure exactly how a diagnosis would impact my life. I'd been determined to not allow the virus to change who I was, but it was impossible not to be affected by the stress of it all. I'd been dreaming up my next great adventure for more than a year, but I'd been unable to set any plans in motion for fear that a diagnosis would ground me.

I'm often asked if there is any historical significance to my accomplishments on the mountain. And to some extent, I understand why. The commercialization of Everest and other peaks has, in many ways, lowered our respect for the mountains and diluted our universal appreciation for human accomplishment. I'm reminded of that whenever I read an editorial in a newspaper or see a talking head on television saying that the peak of Everest should be cordoned off from humankind, that the age of exploration is over and those who still count themselves as explorers are just vain little people caught in an unending quest for glory.

I admit there are times when this mindset makes me question the merits of why I do what I do. But then I look at a map of all the places I still want to go, and I realize it doesn't really matter where others have been. We're all navigating through our own uncharted territory.

People ask if, after twenty years in the mountains, I've learned anything more about myself and our world. I sum up my current state by telling them that I've become somewhat of a fatalist, believing that we are all meant to die on a certain day in a certain place, and that it's up to us to do the best we can with our lives until we find ourselves standing in our final place in our final time. This view has helped me to continue on with my life.

All climbers are junkies in one way or another. In my early years, it wasn't the adrenalin rush that kept me coming back, but rather the sense of accomplishment. I discovered climbing at a time when I had little else going for me. I owe my livelihood and my life to the mountains. And maybe that's why I find myself now on the verge of another great adventure.

I've already been back to Everest once since the avalanche, not as a climber, but as an expedition leader, ferrying trekkers and climbers up through the Khumbu Valley, passing the chortens of old friends, and pitching my tent near to the very spot where two men died in my hands—all in an effort to introduce others to the mother goddess and help them live their dreams and explore their passion. I'll never climb a mountain just for the challenge again. No, I'll do it because there's still a need inside. And because there's still a lot of uncharted ground out there for me to explore.

Acknowledgements

There are seven women in my life who deserve more thanks than I can ever give. To Annie, my love—every day, I feel privileged just to be with you. You've taught me more about myself than anyone else I've ever known. You ground me and protect me even when I'm halfway around the globe. Alexandra, my daughter—you amaze me with your parenting skills. I watch you with your own daughter and it makes me realize how important it is to be there for your children. Together with Kim, Kelsey, and Amy, you make up the most endearing quartet in my life. My mother, Claire, is the strongest yet gentlest woman I've ever known. And my granddaughter, Rosie—in your young eyes, I see an adventurer's spirit. I can't wait to see where your life takes you, and I thank you for reminding me that I'm a grandfather and I have to come home.

I would also like to thank my friend Brett Popplewell. In embarking on this adventure with me, he climbed a mountain higher than Everest. Without him, this book would never have happened. From the start, I stepped back and gave him carte blanche to interview all those around me. I wanted this book to reflect the fullness of my reality, with no exaggerations or glorifications, just the naked truth. There's no one else I could ever have trusted to open me up so completely for the benefit of you, the reader. He helped me dig deeper into my memories than I thought myself able to, and he helped me find the reasons why I do the things I do. He spent days and nights reading through twenty years' worth of illegible journals and listened to hours' worth of inaudible mini-cassette recordings. He viewed past interviews, read countless mountaineering books, and watched documentaries about the individual mountains that have made up my many adventures.

Thank you also to my agent, Rick Broadhead, who read an early draft and believed in the potential of this book. I remember his first words: "Gabriel, I'm mesmerized by your adventures." This from a guy who represents an astronaut! Thank you for your trust, your valuable advice, and your excellent work getting our proposal into the right people's hands. And thank you to my other agent, Ron Eckel (Cooke International), who ensured this book found a home with a French publisher as well.

Thank you to Kate Cassaday and the team at HarperCollins Canada. Kate, from our first call, your enthusiasm for this book was contagious. I got the sense that you wanted nothing more than to deliver this project to the world even as you prepared to deliver your own baby. It is an honour and a privilege to be able to call myself a HarperCollins author.

Thank you also to the team of Guy Saint-Jean Éditeur in Montreal. The translation of this book into French meant a great deal to me, and I knew it was in good hands when the director general, Jean Paré, informed me that after thirty years in publishing, this was only the second book he'd signed without having read the manuscript. My faith in you was reconfirmed when I visited your office in Montreal and met your team of adventurers and outdoor maniacs.

Thank you to my brother Jacques, who convinced me to tell my story and introduced me to the world of publishing. Without you, I'd still be on Google, trying to figure this whole industry out.

Thank you to my great friend Elia Saikaly, whom I also consider a brother. Together we have won, lost, laughed and cried, fallen and gotten back up. We've abandoned climbs but we've never abandoned each other or our innovative projects. *Au futur!*

Thank you to my friends Dr. Eric Contant and Dr. Sylvain Guimond. You have literally picked me up in the most difficult moments of my life. Is that not the definition of true friendship? Your expertise has helped me climb out of the darkest valleys and reach new heights.

Thank you to Jacques Olek, who shared with me his passion for the world's eight-thousanders. Before I'd really climbed anything, you threw me a phrase that inspired me, and which, twenty years later, still resonates: *"Tu as déjà la passion et le physique; je n'ai pas de doute, tu vas réussir."*

Thank you to Patrice Beaudet, guru and guide on my earliest climbs. It was a privilege to learn from one of the greatest climbers in Quebec. And my thanks go to all my other climbing partners and those who trusted me to accompany them on the adventures of their lifetimes.

Thank you to my friend Dr. Guy Thibault, who gave me the

know-how to target my training and become a more complete athlete than I ever thought I could be.

I owe more thanks than I could ever write to the many Sherpa of Nepal who have taught me important lessons about compassion, self-help, and personal discovery. I am indebted especially to the late Babu Chiri Sherpa and to his trusted friend and colleague who has become *my* trusted friend and colleague, Babu Sherpa.

Thank you to David Larose and his staff at Orizon, who believed that the many stories that make up this book could profoundly help others when told on the public stage.

Thank you to everyone else in my life who helped teach me to appreciate every moment and not take anything for granted. And thank you to the mountains for all that they have taught me about myself and my place in this world. The friendships I have made while on the mountains have been a source of great happiness.

Thank you to my sponsors, especially The North Face, without whose generous support my expeditions would not be possible. My relationship with The North Face began thanks to the help of my friend Gino Timbro. I am beyond proud to be associated with you. Thank you also to the entire TNF management team, who make their athletes feel like part of a family and a team. And to Jano Arabaghian for believing in my most recent unclimbed project. Thank you to Charles Spina for your endless support of all my endeavours—the best is yet to come, buddy! And to Adidas Eyewear (Manuel Magini and his team) and my friends at SmartWool.

I'd like to end this with a tribute to all the friends I've made and lost on the mountainside: Babu Chiri Sherpa, Sean Egan,

ACKNOWLEDGEMENTS

Ernie Marksaitis, Christine Boskoff, Frank Ziebarth, Nima Sherpa, Wangchu Sherpa, Ngima Sherpa, Jangbu Sherpa, Sona Sherpa, Ihor Sverhun, Dmytro Koniayev, Anton Dobeš, Peter Šperka, Chunfeng Yeng, Jianfeng Rao, Honglu Chen, Ali Hussain, and Michael Heck. This book is very much for you.

—Gabriel Filippi

I'd like to reiterate Gabriel's thanks to HarperCollins Canada for their unreserved enthusiasm for *The Escapist* from the start, and for recognizing that this book was always about so much more than just the climb and that it needed to be shared across Canada. My thanks to Kate Cassaday for her editorial guidance on this book and for working on it right up to the day she went into labour. Thanks also to Brad Wilson and Adrienne Kerr, who picked up the torch and helped guide us to the finish line. And to Stacey Cameron for carefully proofing these pages, and Natalie Meditsky for keeping us on schedule. Thank you also to Rick Broadhead for believing so strongly in this story and in my ability to write it.

This book evolved out of a *Sportsnet* magazine article written during the winter of 2014. The idea for the article had come from the magazine's photo editor, Myles McCutcheon, who'd heard of the attack on Nanga Parbat in the summer of 2013. Without Myles informing me of Gabriel's story, or my editor Craig Battle's dutiful work in helping me craft that initial article, this book might never have come to be. Thank you to both of you and to the rest of the *Sportsnet* team.

Thank you to Gabriel's family and friends who gave their time, energy, and memories to help fill in the gaps in Gabriel's life. Their participation was integral to the process. And to my own family and friends for their support. But especially to my wife, Corina, who lent countless hours to transcribing interviews, allowed portions of our house to be taken over by maps of distant mountains, and literally joined us on the final chapter of *The Escapist* by travelling with us all the way to Everest Base Camp.

I would also like to acknowledge the work of those who have taken readers to the great peaks of the world in previous books and whose writings were essential to my own understanding of the mountains and the people who flock to them. Those books include, but are not limited to, *Into Thin Air* by Jon Krakauer; *Touching the Void* by Joe Simpson; *Where the Mountain Casts Its Shadow* by Maria Coffey; *The Third Man Factor* by John Geiger; *Annapurna* by Maurice Herzog; *Seven Summits* by Dick Bass, Frank Wells, and Rick Ridgeway; *No Shortcuts to the Top* by Ed Viesturs and David Roberts; *Into the Silence* by Wade Davis; *Seven Years in Tibet* by Heinrich Harrer; and *Touching My Father's Soul* by Jamling Norgay.

Finally, thank you, Gabriel, for your trust and continued friendship. In pursuit of reporting your story, I often asked you not of what happened but of how you felt when it happened. You were always candid and honest, even when the answers were difficult to share. To you, I am indebted. It was a privilege to chronicle your memoirs.

—Brett Popplewell